# HOW TO
# Make Your Band Sound Great

Bobby Owsinski

Hal Leonard Books
An Imprint of Hal Leonard Corporation
New York

Copyright © 2009 by Bobby Owsinski

All rights reserved. No part of this book may be reproduced in any form, without written permission, except by a newspaper or magazine reviewer who wishes to quote brief passages in connection with a review.

Published in 2009 by Hal Leonard Books
An Imprint of Hal Leonard Corporation
7777 West Bluemound Road
Milwaukee, WI 53213

Trade Book Division Editorial Offices
19 West 21st Street, New York, NY 10010

Cover photo: the Glorious Unseen (www.thegloriousunseen.com)
Photographer: John Williams (www.soundartmanagement.com), 615-429-2800

Printed in the United States of America

Book design by Stephen Ramirez

Library of Congress Cataloging-in-Publication Data is available upon request.

ISBN 978-1-4234-4190-8

www.halleonard.com

# ACKNOWLEDGMENTS

Thanks to all the people that I've played with over the years, especially Vince Kalochie, Jimmy Siemanis, Charlie Kirschner, and Kim Burns, who helped give me my first modest brush with fame. Thanks to Eddie Frank for being an early mentor when there was no one else around. Thanks to LA Jones, Joe Houston, Greg Senich, Ed Costick, Larry Kanezo, Mike Forbes, Jackie Modesto, Ronnie Ciago, and Michael Wright. I learned something about music from all of you. Thanks to Jim Strohecker, who gave me my first lesson in dynamics. Thanks to Mick Taylor and Gerry Groom. I only wish I could have been at my best when we played together. Also, thanks to Frank Fitzpatrick, Peter Thorn, Brian Ray, Chris Boardman, and Brian and Ron MacLeod for the interviews and insight. A special thanks to Paul Ill, who has been a great friend and exceptional musical collaborator along the way, and to Mike Lawson for his publishing help and advice.

# CONTENTS

Foreword . . . . . . . . . . . . . . . . . . . . . . . . . . . . . . . . . . . . . . . . . . . . . . . . . xi
Introduction . . . . . . . . . . . . . . . . . . . . . . . . . . . . . . . . . . . . . . . . . . . . xiii

**Part One    Your Instrument and Playing** . . . . . . . . . . . . . . . . . . . . . . . 1

**Chapter 1    How Do I Make Myself Sound Great?** . . . . . . . . . . . . . . . 3
Influence vs. Imitation . . . . . . . . . . . . . . . . . . . . . . . . . . . . . . . . . . . 3
Know Your Limitations—Play What You Play Well . . . . . . . . . . . . 6
Use Great-Sounding Gear That Fits . . . . . . . . . . . . . . . . . . . . . . . . . 7
Play in Tune . . . . . . . . . . . . . . . . . . . . . . . . . . . . . . . . . . . . . . . . . . 10
Play in Time . . . . . . . . . . . . . . . . . . . . . . . . . . . . . . . . . . . . . . . . . . 12

**Chapter 2    The Guitar Player** . . . . . . . . . . . . . . . . . . . . . . . . . . . . . . 15
Two Defining Moments for a Guitar Player . . . . . . . . . . . . . . . . . 15
That's What Tone Controls Are For . . . . . . . . . . . . . . . . . . . . . . . 18
Clash of the Guitar Players . . . . . . . . . . . . . . . . . . . . . . . . . . . . . . 19
Laying In with the Rhythm Section . . . . . . . . . . . . . . . . . . . . . . . 21
What Your Audience Hears . . . . . . . . . . . . . . . . . . . . . . . . . . . . . 22
The Recording Guitar Player . . . . . . . . . . . . . . . . . . . . . . . . . . . . 23
The Guitar Player's Utility Kit . . . . . . . . . . . . . . . . . . . . . . . . . . . 25

### Chapter 3  Bass .................................................. 27
  The Defining Moment of a Bass Player ............................. 27
  What You Hear Onstage ............................................ 29
  Your Sound—That's What Tone Controls Are For ..................... 29
  The Recording Bass Player ........................................ 30
  The Bass Player's Utility Kit .................................... 33

### Chapter 4  Drums ................................................. 35
  Simple Is Best ................................................... 35
  The Concepts of Feel and Internal Time ........................... 36
  Rushed or Lazy Fills ............................................. 38
  Are You Playing Too Loud? ........................................ 38
  What Makes a Drum Kit Sound Great? ............................... 39
  Drum Construction ................................................ 39
  Tuning the Drums ................................................. 41
  The Recording Drummer ............................................ 47
  The Drummer's Utility Kit ........................................ 49

### Chapter 5  Keyboards ............................................. 51
  Defining Moments for a Keyboard Player ........................... 51
  The Classic Patches .............................................. 52
  The Keyboard Player Onstage ...................................... 54
  The Recording Keyboard Player .................................... 56
  The Keyboard Player's Utility Kit ................................ 59

### Chapter 6  Vocals ................................................ 61
  The Three Ps—Pitch, Pocket, Passion .............................. 61
  Change the Key ................................................... 64
  Take Care of Yourself ............................................ 64
  Take Some Voice Lessons .......................................... 66
  Mic Technique .................................................... 67
  Harmony Vocals Take More Time .................................... 68
  Phrasing Is Everything ........................................... 68
  The Recording Vocalist ........................................... 70

### Chapter 7  Percussion, Horns, DJs, and Others .................... 73
  For Percussionists ............................................... 73
  For Horn Players ................................................. 75
  The Horn Player's Utility Kit .................................... 76
  For DJs .......................................................... 77
  For Other Instruments ............................................ 77

# Part Two  How Do I Make My Band Sound Great? . . . . . . . . . . . . . . . . . . . . . . . . . . . 79

## Chapter 8  The Keys to Greatness . . . . . . . . . . . . . . . . . . . . . . . . . . . . . . . . . . . . . . . . . . . 81
Dynamics. . . . . . . . . . . . . . . . . . . . . . . . . . . . . . . . . . . . . . . . . . . . . . . . . . . . . . . . . . . . . 81
Play Together—Listen to Each Other . . . . . . . . . . . . . . . . . . . . . . . . . . . . . . . . . . . . 84
Timing Is Everything . . . . . . . . . . . . . . . . . . . . . . . . . . . . . . . . . . . . . . . . . . . . . . . . . . 86
Turnarounds. . . . . . . . . . . . . . . . . . . . . . . . . . . . . . . . . . . . . . . . . . . . . . . . . . . . . . . . . . 89
Tempo. . . . . . . . . . . . . . . . . . . . . . . . . . . . . . . . . . . . . . . . . . . . . . . . . . . . . . . . . . . . . . . 90
Play Big, Not Loud . . . . . . . . . . . . . . . . . . . . . . . . . . . . . . . . . . . . . . . . . . . . . . . . . . . . 92
You Don't Have to Sound Just Like the Record. . . . . . . . . . . . . . . . . . . . . . . . . . . . 93
Play In Tune . . . . . . . . . . . . . . . . . . . . . . . . . . . . . . . . . . . . . . . . . . . . . . . . . . . . . . . . . . 93

## Chapter 9  It's All in the Song . . . . . . . . . . . . . . . . . . . . . . . . . . . . . . . . . . . . . . . . . . . . . . . 95
The Arrangement Is the Key. . . . . . . . . . . . . . . . . . . . . . . . . . . . . . . . . . . . . . . . . . . . 95
Cover Song Arrangements. . . . . . . . . . . . . . . . . . . . . . . . . . . . . . . . . . . . . . . . . . . . . . 97
Original Song Arrangements . . . . . . . . . . . . . . . . . . . . . . . . . . . . . . . . . . . . . . . . . . . 97
Rules for Arrangements . . . . . . . . . . . . . . . . . . . . . . . . . . . . . . . . . . . . . . . . . . . . . . . 101
Let's Discuss Your Songs . . . . . . . . . . . . . . . . . . . . . . . . . . . . . . . . . . . . . . . . . . . . . . 102
Dynamics on Records. . . . . . . . . . . . . . . . . . . . . . . . . . . . . . . . . . . . . . . . . . . . . . . . . 105
They're Not "Originals" . . . . . . . . . . . . . . . . . . . . . . . . . . . . . . . . . . . . . . . . . . . . . . . 107

## Chapter 10  Rehearse Wisely—Plan Ahead . . . . . . . . . . . . . . . . . . . . . . . . . . . . . . . . . . 109
Have an Agenda . . . . . . . . . . . . . . . . . . . . . . . . . . . . . . . . . . . . . . . . . . . . . . . . . . . . . 109
You Gotta Hear Yourself . . . . . . . . . . . . . . . . . . . . . . . . . . . . . . . . . . . . . . . . . . . . . . 111
A Few Rehearsal Tips . . . . . . . . . . . . . . . . . . . . . . . . . . . . . . . . . . . . . . . . . . . . . . . . . 112
Production Rehearsals . . . . . . . . . . . . . . . . . . . . . . . . . . . . . . . . . . . . . . . . . . . . . . . . 114
The Dress Rehearsal . . . . . . . . . . . . . . . . . . . . . . . . . . . . . . . . . . . . . . . . . . . . . . . . . . 114

## Chapter 11  You Need the Stage Time . . . . . . . . . . . . . . . . . . . . . . . . . . . . . . . . . . . . . . 115
All Gigs Are Welcome. . . . . . . . . . . . . . . . . . . . . . . . . . . . . . . . . . . . . . . . . . . . . . . . . 115
How Not to Get Gigs . . . . . . . . . . . . . . . . . . . . . . . . . . . . . . . . . . . . . . . . . . . . . . . . . 116
How Loud Should We Play? . . . . . . . . . . . . . . . . . . . . . . . . . . . . . . . . . . . . . . . . . . . 131
Volume Wars . . . . . . . . . . . . . . . . . . . . . . . . . . . . . . . . . . . . . . . . . . . . . . . . . . . . . . . . 133

## Chapter 12  Record Yourself . . . . . . . . . . . . . . . . . . . . . . . . . . . . . . . . . . . . . . . . . . . . . . . 135
Recording Rehearsals. . . . . . . . . . . . . . . . . . . . . . . . . . . . . . . . . . . . . . . . . . . . . . . . . 135
Recording Your Gigs. . . . . . . . . . . . . . . . . . . . . . . . . . . . . . . . . . . . . . . . . . . . . . . . . . 137
Now for Some Serious Recording . . . . . . . . . . . . . . . . . . . . . . . . . . . . . . . . . . . . . . 143
There's No Such Thing as a Demo . . . . . . . . . . . . . . . . . . . . . . . . . . . . . . . . . . . . . . 144
The Way to Make Your Recordings Sound Great. . . . . . . . . . . . . . . . . . . . . . . . . 145
Pros Are Pros for a Reason . . . . . . . . . . . . . . . . . . . . . . . . . . . . . . . . . . . . . . . . . . . . 146

    It's a Different Mindset . . . . . . . . . . . . . . . . . . . . . . . . . . . . . . . . . . . . . . . . . . . . . . . . . . . . . . . . . . . . . . . 147
    Different Gear for Different Jobs . . . . . . . . . . . . . . . . . . . . . . . . . . . . . . . . . . . . . . . . . . . . . . . . . . . 149
    Tips for a Great Recording. . . . . . . . . . . . . . . . . . . . . . . . . . . . . . . . . . . . . . . . . . . . . . . . . . . . . . . . . 149

**Chapter 13    The PA**. . . . . . . . . . . . . . . . . . . . . . . . . . . . . . . . . . . . . . . . . . . . . . . . . . . . . . . . . . . . . . . . . . . . . 153
    Voices Come First . . . . . . . . . . . . . . . . . . . . . . . . . . . . . . . . . . . . . . . . . . . . . . . . . . . . . . . . . . . . . . . . . 153
    The Graphic EQ Is Not a Tone Control. . . . . . . . . . . . . . . . . . . . . . . . . . . . . . . . . . . . . . . . . . . . . 154
    Let's Hear Those Vocals . . . . . . . . . . . . . . . . . . . . . . . . . . . . . . . . . . . . . . . . . . . . . . . . . . . . . . . . . . . 157
    Monitors . . . . . . . . . . . . . . . . . . . . . . . . . . . . . . . . . . . . . . . . . . . . . . . . . . . . . . . . . . . . . . . . . . . . . . . . . 157
    What's in Your Mix? . . . . . . . . . . . . . . . . . . . . . . . . . . . . . . . . . . . . . . . . . . . . . . . . . . . . . . . . . . . . . . 164

**Chapter 14    Be a Professional**. . . . . . . . . . . . . . . . . . . . . . . . . . . . . . . . . . . . . . . . . . . . . . . . . . . . . . . . . 165
    What Is a Professional? . . . . . . . . . . . . . . . . . . . . . . . . . . . . . . . . . . . . . . . . . . . . . . . . . . . . . . . . . . . 165
    The Importance of Diplomacy . . . . . . . . . . . . . . . . . . . . . . . . . . . . . . . . . . . . . . . . . . . . . . . . . . . . 168
    Steps in Resolving a Conflict . . . . . . . . . . . . . . . . . . . . . . . . . . . . . . . . . . . . . . . . . . . . . . . . . . . . . . 169
    How to Keep a Band Together . . . . . . . . . . . . . . . . . . . . . . . . . . . . . . . . . . . . . . . . . . . . . . . . . . . . 170
    There's Always Somebody Else . . . . . . . . . . . . . . . . . . . . . . . . . . . . . . . . . . . . . . . . . . . . . . . . . . . . 171
    Who's the Leader? . . . . . . . . . . . . . . . . . . . . . . . . . . . . . . . . . . . . . . . . . . . . . . . . . . . . . . . . . . . . . . . . 172

**Chapter 15    Your Show**. . . . . . . . . . . . . . . . . . . . . . . . . . . . . . . . . . . . . . . . . . . . . . . . . . . . . . . . . . . . . . . 175
    It's More Than a Collection of Songs . . . . . . . . . . . . . . . . . . . . . . . . . . . . . . . . . . . . . . . . . . . . . . 175
    The Big Ending . . . . . . . . . . . . . . . . . . . . . . . . . . . . . . . . . . . . . . . . . . . . . . . . . . . . . . . . . . . . . . . . . . 177
    Playing with Backing Tracks . . . . . . . . . . . . . . . . . . . . . . . . . . . . . . . . . . . . . . . . . . . . . . . . . . . . . . 178
    Sound . . . . . . . . . . . . . . . . . . . . . . . . . . . . . . . . . . . . . . . . . . . . . . . . . . . . . . . . . . . . . . . . . . . . . . . . . . . 179
    Stage Lighting . . . . . . . . . . . . . . . . . . . . . . . . . . . . . . . . . . . . . . . . . . . . . . . . . . . . . . . . . . . . . . . . . . . 179
    The Stage Plot . . . . . . . . . . . . . . . . . . . . . . . . . . . . . . . . . . . . . . . . . . . . . . . . . . . . . . . . . . . . . . . . . . . 186

**Chapter 16    The Importance of Video** . . . . . . . . . . . . . . . . . . . . . . . . . . . . . . . . . . . . . . . . . . . . . . . . 189
    Video as a Learning Tool. . . . . . . . . . . . . . . . . . . . . . . . . . . . . . . . . . . . . . . . . . . . . . . . . . . . . . . . . . 189
    Making a Great Live Video . . . . . . . . . . . . . . . . . . . . . . . . . . . . . . . . . . . . . . . . . . . . . . . . . . . . . . . 190
    If You're Making a Music Video . . . . . . . . . . . . . . . . . . . . . . . . . . . . . . . . . . . . . . . . . . . . . . . . . . 192
    Some Special DVDs to Check Out. . . . . . . . . . . . . . . . . . . . . . . . . . . . . . . . . . . . . . . . . . . . . . . . . 194
    The EPK . . . . . . . . . . . . . . . . . . . . . . . . . . . . . . . . . . . . . . . . . . . . . . . . . . . . . . . . . . . . . . . . . . . . . . . . 196

**Chapter 17    To Summarize**. . . . . . . . . . . . . . . . . . . . . . . . . . . . . . . . . . . . . . . . . . . . . . . . . . . . . . . . . . . . 197

**Part Three    The Interviews** . . . . . . . . . . . . . . . . . . . . . . . . . . . . . . . . . . . . . . . . . . . . . . . . . . . . . . . . 201

**Chapter 18    The Interviews**. . . . . . . . . . . . . . . . . . . . . . . . . . . . . . . . . . . . . . . . . . . . . . . . . . . . . . . . . 203
    Chris Boardman . . . . . . . . . . . . . . . . . . . . . . . . . . . . . . . . . . . . . . . . . . . . . . . . . . . . . . . . . . . . . . . . . 203
    Frank Fitzpatrick . . . . . . . . . . . . . . . . . . . . . . . . . . . . . . . . . . . . . . . . . . . . . . . . . . . . . . . . . . . . . . . . 209

Paul Ill. . . . . . . . . . . . . . . . . . . . . . . . . . . . . . . . . . . . . . . . . . . . . . . . . . 213
Brian MacLeod . . . . . . . . . . . . . . . . . . . . . . . . . . . . . . . . . . . . . . . . . 221
Pete Thorn . . . . . . . . . . . . . . . . . . . . . . . . . . . . . . . . . . . . . . . . . . . . 232
Brian Ray. . . . . . . . . . . . . . . . . . . . . . . . . . . . . . . . . . . . . . . . . . . . . 236

Glossary. . . . . . . . . . . . . . . . . . . . . . . . . . . . . . . . . . . . . . . . . . . . . . 243
Index. . . . . . . . . . . . . . . . . . . . . . . . . . . . . . . . . . . . . . . . . . . . . . . . 249

# FOREWORD

This book and DVD have a lot of great suggestions that will really help you and your band play and sound a lot better, and even rise to the level of greatness, if you're willing to put in the time. But before reading or watching, there are a few big questions you must ask yourself that will really help you focus on what your ultimate musical goals are, and therefore just what you have to learn in order to get there.

> What exactly is my idea (or my band's idea) of success?
> Is it really important that a lot of people really like what my band is playing?
> How big an audience do we ultimately want to reach?
> Will we be happy just playing in clubs or do we want to go further by creating our own music?
> How important is it for us to do things our way?
> Is our way of doing things the only way that we feel we can achieve success?

> Let me help you answer those questions with another one:

> Is making music, writing songs, or playing in a band an art or a craft?

> To help answer that question directly (which will lead to answering the questions above), here's a little rule that I've always lived by:

> Art is something you do for yourself.
> A craft is something you do for everyone else.

Playing music constantly requires walking the tightrope between art and craft. Fall too much toward the art side and you can wind up an acquired musical taste with a tiny energetic following like Zeitgeist, Scissor Shock, The Residents, John Cage, or Philip Glass, but with the inability to grow your audience much beyond that. Step too much to the craft side and you might gain a large audience at the expense of credibility like so many pop idols. (Britney Spears, The Backstreet Boys, and N'Sync all come to mind.)

While you should be so lucky to have even a portion of the success of any of the artists mentioned above, you still have to determine how important it is for you to do things entirely your way in order to express yourself. If you think that you'll compromise your art by taking advice, then you'll still find a lot of things in this book very useful (even the artiest of art bands still have to play well together). If developing as wide an audience as possible is important to you, then a lot more of the tricks and tips in the book will resonate with you and your band.

The suggestions in this book and DVD are the result of many years of personal and collective experience, and they'll really make your band sound great if you put the time in. But like most other aspects of life, every situation is different and there are exceptions to every rule. Try everything and keep what works for you.

# INTRODUCTION

I remember when I was a kid of about fifteen, playing in my first real band that actually got gigs. Just like every kid in every band there ever was, we just wanted to play as much as we could, preferably in front of people. And we knew that the only way to get more gigs was to get better as a band. But how?

We'd go and watch other bands and try to dissect what made them better than us. Was it because the individual musicians were technically better? Usually that was the case, but not always. Sometimes musicians on our skill level just played together in a way that made the sum much greater than the parts. (These were usually the most popular bands, by the way.)

When I asked these more-popular bands why they sounded so good, no one could ever tell me ("I dunno, it just works" was the usual answer), which was really frustrating. Only once did I get a real piece of advice that actually worked ("It's the dynamics, stupid," which is covered in Chapter 8). Then if I'd go to a concert to see and hear a band with a hit record, they were on a whole other level completely. How did they get to sound this way? "They're playing simple parts that even I can play, but, boy, does it sound better!" was my usual thought.

Having played in bad bands and having played in great bands; having had a few record deals; toured with some greats; and made records, commercials, movies, and television shows through the years, I can tell you that I do know why bands play well together. As a producer, I've had to take bands that have never made a record and mold them into something that could pass for major-label ready. I've had to take A-list session musicians and get what they played to work too (even great musicians can sound bad together).

Getting your fellow musicians to play together well is an art form in itself. And it's a skill that's distinct from just learning to play an instrument. It usually takes years and years of experience to unveil the mysteries of why a guitar, bass, keyboard, vocalist, and drummer (and any additional instruments) really gel, and even then it's only after lots of studio experience that these secrets are revealed. And make no mistake, the studio experience is important because that's where everything is under a microscope so you can really hear what works and what doesn't. This book and DVD cut to the chase on multiple levels to relate these secrets that are the benefit of my years of experience working live and in the studio with bands of all types as a player, engineer, and producer.

"Why don't we sound like X (you pick the artist)?" and "why does X sound so good?" are age-old questions that everyone in a band has at some time. This book and DVD will answer those questions and help any band (as well as its individual members) realize its full potential faster than they ever thought possible.

Along the way, we're going to hear from players who started out just like you, reached the top, and will give you some tips to help you excel on your individual instruments.

These guys are not what you'd call superstars or virtuosos. They didn't catch a break early in their careers and start out at or near the top. They are just like you in that they started in a garage band and worked for years and years in clubs. Each has gradually worked his way up the musical food chain, graduating from clubs to the road and to tours and sessions. They are really great players, but they've dedicated themselves to a life-long pursuit of getting better and honing their craft. They've all been where you are now, so they can relate to you (and hopefully you to them), and I'm sure you'll find their tips extremely helpful.

I'll also be giving you examples of songs that you've probably heard before in order to illustrate a musical point. To be honest, I struggled with how timely these songs should be. Should they be recent hits? Should they be songs that everyone has been exposed to? What musical genre should they be from? I finally settled on using the most widely known, widely played by a band, widely played on the radio, widely sold and widely downloaded songs across multiple musical genres. These are songs that some might call "classic" and some might just call old (not all of them are, though), but if you're in a band, then I'm pretty sure you've heard them before. You don't have to like these examples, just learn from them.

Like my other books, this one is laid out in three parts. Part One is aimed at your individual playing in the context of your band, Part Two is aimed at your band itself, and Part Three is the full text of the interviews conducted for these books. These interviews are always popular and a fun read in that they give you some real insight into the person behind the quotes that you'll see elsewhere in the book, and they contain a lot of really useful info as well. Let's take a look at some of the musicians interviewed.

## CHRIS BOARDMAN

Chris went from playing keyboards in clubs in Utah to playing in the road band for Seals and Crofts and becoming musical director for Tom Jones. After a lot of hard work, he's gone on to become an extremely successful film composer and orchestrator with over 120 films to his credit and a winner of multiple Emmys.

## FRANK FITZPATRICK

Being in the middle of the Detroit music scene as he grew up helped shape the background that eventually made guitarist Frank Fitzpatrick one of Hollywood's most sought-after producers and composers. Frank has written and produced songs for gold and platinum artists including Jill Scott, Fat Joe, Dave Hollister, K-Ci & JoJo, Brownstone, Lina, Carl Anderson, Ice Cube, Akil (of Jurassic 5), Jazz (of Dru Hill), and The London Symphony. He also wrote the opening song for the *High School Musical* tour, and the *Angeli* theme for the Victoria's Secret advertising campaign. Frank also has contributed to the soundtracks for over two-dozen feature films (including *Scary Movie 3, Queen of the Damned, Friday,* and *In Too Deep*) and scores and themes for several television shows, including the renowned *Larry Sanders Show*.

## PAUL ILL

A little bit of disclosure here: Paul is one of my oldest and dearest friends, and we've played in many bands together through the years. In every band, he was always the best musician with the most musical ideas, attributes that have taken him far in the industry jungle known as Hollywood. Paul has since become one of the most in-demand bass players in Los Angeles, doing sessions for such diverse artists as Courtney Love, James Blunt, Tina Turner, Bill Ward (of Black Sabbath), Christina Aguilera, Pink, Alicia Keys, and Daniel Powter.

## BRIAN MACLEOD

Brian has been one of the most sought-after session drummers in L.A. for quite some time now and with good reason. He has the ability to make tracks feel not just pretty good, but awesomely great. He has plenty of chops, but listen to the groove in Sheryl Crow's breakthrough hit "All I Want to Do" and you'll hear what Brian really is known for. (He was a member of and played on Crow's *Tuesday Night Music Club*.) And if you're a fan of the television shows *The Office* or *Dirty Sexy Money*, that's him playing on the theme song. Add credits like Christina Aguilera, Madonna, Chris Isaac, John Hiatt, Tears for Fears, Jewel, and many more, and you get an idea of just why the Brian MacLeod touch is so valuable.

## BRIAN RAY

At a time of life when many professional musicians are a bit jaded or burned out, Brian Ray still has the same sense of fun and enthusiasm as a 15-year-old in his first garage band. Never mind that he may be at what many might consider a musical pinnacle by being in Paul McCartney's touring band, or that he's had a career studded with great gigs and hit writing (like a number-one hit in three formats for Smokey Robinson), Brian's still the same down-to-earth guy that you'd expect to find at the local Tuesday night jam.

## PETER THORN

Another highly sought-after player, Pete has a wide variety of studio credits (Alicia Keys, Courtney Love) and is currently on the road with Chris Cornell. Pete is a shining example of a professional musician—he's got excellent chops, excellent sounds (he sings great as well) yet is easy-going, humble, and approachable.

If you bought this book, I know that you really love music and love your band and will do anything to make it sound the best it can. Hopefully this book will provide a shortcut to reaching your goal.

# Part One

## Your Instrument and Playing

# CHAPTER 1

# How Do I Make Myself Sound Great?

In this section we're going to look at how you play your instrument in the context of a band. It doesn't matter what instrument; we're going to provide you with some general tricks that will help you play better with others, teach you how to learn and rehearse, and get your gear in shape.

Be aware that we're not talking about your technical skill in playing your instrument per se. We won't teach you new riffs, or how to increase your speed, or learn new songs. The technique part is up to you, and there are plenty of teachers, books, DVDs, and methods out there that you can use for this.

But, hopefully, you'll see that there's a lot more to playing than technique, and this is what actually takes you to the next level both individually and when you play with others.

## INFLUENCE VS. IMITATION

Let's discuss your influences first. Every musician naturally gravitates to another musician and tries to emulate his or her style. Let's face it; that's how you really learn to play, and in the very common case of someone who's never taken a lesson (or who never is going to take a lesson, for that matter), it's the only way. Your influence could be a teacher, a local musician mentor, or most likely, a recording artist (or two or ten). Doesn't matter, influences are important.

## How to Get the Most Out of Your Influences

There are actually three levels on which someone influences you. First, you like their music. No, you *love* their music. It speaks to you on a primal level. You enjoy the experience of listening. You identify with the music and want to play it and emulate it.

Second is general technique, which means the general things that you like about the artist's performance: the tone of his voice, the licks that she sings or plays, the way he does his drum fills. You identify and want to cop those traits as closely as you can. So you learn his signature licks, get the same growl or vibrato that she has in her voice, or put that double kick-drum signature that he does in just the right place in the song.

Last, and maybe most important (and frequently overlooked), is nuance. After you've learned the lick, it's time to learn how to really play it. That means the bends, ghost notes, phrasing, and breaths—all those little things that are essential to really copping the same feel as your hero.

I'll give you an example. One of my greatest influences (the same as about a million other guitar players) is Eric Clapton. As soon as I heard "Badge" and "Sunshine of Your Love," I copped those solos as close to note-for-note as I could. But even though I had the notes right, something was still missing. I still didn't sound like Eric (not that anyone can, but still, it was not as close as I wanted).

Many years later I felt a newfound need to shed again, so I broke out those same solos and listened a lot more carefully. This time I learned the little bends he does at the end of a phrase, the way he slides into a note, and the way he hammers a ghost note in a phrase. I listened closer to his tone and found out that the maple neck of Blackie (his famous Strat) was integral to playing a certain way—his way. I discovered how his amps (a Marshall JTM-45 combo in the Bluesbreakers, a Marshall 100-watt "plexi" Super Lead during Cream, a Fender tweed Champ during the "Layla" sessions, for instance) made such a difference in the sustain that he got and in how he played everything.

Eventually I got to the point where my playing sounded a lot closer to Clapton's style than I ever thought I could get. I'm still not him (never can be), but now I'm much closer. And in the process I learned a whole lot that became useful in other areas of my playing.

## Imitation

While having outside influences is a necessary part of learning to play, so is imitation—to a point. Imitating your influence is simply trying to be exactly like him or her, which could mean not only playing, but also using the same gear, and even dressing to try to look like him. Most of these are important (except for maybe the dressing), as that's part of learning, but you should be aware of the limitations this puts upon you.

First of all, if you identify too much with an artist you may try to go beyond your current limits of technique, which is great during practice or rehearsal but could be disastrous on a gig. (Who wants to hear someone play a bunch of clams in the name of imitating an artist?) There comes a point where imitation can be downright stifling to your growth as a musician or vocalist. Ultimately what makes you interesting is the collection of influences that you fuse into something new—the thing that only you have. Unless you're planning on playing in a tribute band all your life (not that there's anything wrong with that), sounding exactly like Mick Jagger, or Billy Corgan, or Amy Winehouse, or Zach de la Rocha, or Jack White will actually stop your career growth in its tracks. They're already out there doing their thing with celebrity and fame. You can't get there by being an imitation—you've got to be you!

## Just Because X Does It

Regardless of where you are in your own personal evolution as a player, you can't be so tied to your influences that it stops you from sounding or playing your best. Just because X (fill in your favorite artist) uses an X pedal, it doesn't automatically mean that you should as well. Maybe his pedal has been modified; maybe it's the total combination of his rig (which you really can't be sure about unless you've seen it yourself—the Internet and magazine articles don't always get it right, and artists can be very deceiving in the information they give out); maybe it's his playing style or touch that makes this pedal work. It doesn't automatically mean that if you buy one and use it in your rig, it will work the same way for you. If it does, then good for you, but you have to have a discerning ear that tells you that you're going in the right or wrong direction. If it makes you sound worse, don't use it! If you connect it and the result is magic, then who cares what your influence uses!

Just because your influence X is using a 24-inch kick drum, it doesn't mean that it'll work for you in the context of the music you're playing. If it does, then good for you, but if it makes you sound worse, you've got to be honest with yourself and go with something that works right now. The 24-inch kick will give you a big, woofy sound, while the sound that you might really need is smaller and punchier.

Just because Slash (for instance) uses a Les Paul, it doesn't mean that you should too. Maybe your hands are too small for the neck, or the axe is too heavy for your body, or you don't have the right amp to get the sound you're looking for. You've got to be honest with yourself and get a guitar that works within the context of the music you're playing and the other musicians you're playing with (a lot more on this in upcoming chapters). As you'll read many times throughout the book, you've got to tailor your gear to the gig that you're playing.

Just because X plays her signature fast triplet fill in the intro of a song, it doesn't mean you have to; if you can't play it to the point where it sounds great, don't play it on a gig until it does!

Finally, the most egregious of all (if you're playing in a club band): Just because the song you're trying to play is in G on the record, it doesn't mean you have to do it in that key if you can't sing all the notes! This is perhaps the most constantly violated rule by most garage and club bands. You have to change the key to fit the vocals—pros do it all the time—because if the vocal sucks, your audience will think you and your song sucks. Granted, a song written in E on the guitar might only sound great with E-chord guitar voicings, but that's also why you see pros change guitars so often (or use a capo) onstage. An alternate tuning (like down to E♭ or D for example) puts the song in the natural range of the vocalist.

All of these examples (and I can give you plenty more) are to illustrate that sometimes trying to imitate your favorite artist or influence too closely can really be detrimental to you and your band sounding its best. *Your goal is to sound great all the time, which means playing within your present limitations.* Only play songs or use gear that make you sound your best at all times!

> Your goal is to sound great all the time, which means playing within your present limitations.

## KNOW YOUR LIMITATIONS—PLAY WHAT YOU PLAY WELL

Believe it or not, this is what all the big-time recording artists do. You never hear them playing or singing something that doesn't totally work. This is due to either an innate sense the artist has about the music or to some direction from a producer or other band members. The idea here is to keep an open mind. You want people to like what you do. They'll like you so much better if you play or sing something that's simple but totally works rather than attempting something difficult that you can't pull off. That's one of the big differences between being a pro or an amateur.

That's not to say that you shouldn't continue to practice a difficult riff. Keep trying during your personal practice time and band rehearsals until you can play it perfectly every time; then pull it out on a gig.

## USE GREAT-SOUNDING GEAR THAT FITS

This is one of the toughest things for just about every band and every player to learn. As I said before, just because X (your favorite player) uses a certain guitar or amp or bass or pedal or keyboard or snare drum or vocal mic, it doesn't necessarily mean that you should too. It might not fit with your style or the style of the band, and you have to be open to that possibility. On the other hand, there's a reason why the pros use what they use, and you have to be open to that too.

Ever wonder why a vintage Les Paul or Strat or Marshall Plexi or 1959 Fender Bassman or '60s Ludwig drum kit or Hammond B3 are so coveted that they've all been reissued in versions that are as close to the original as possible? It's because they sound so good, and using one of these items can instantly make you a better-sounding player. That's why you see some of the same gear from concert to concert, video to video. Pro players learn what makes them sound their best. Certain instruments, amps, effects, and accessory brands and models are just "tried and true" (when properly maintained, of course).

That's not to say that inexpensive gear isn't worth having. Musical gear in any price range is far better than it's ever been. In fact, since about 1985, it's been really difficult to buy something that doesn't perform at a reasonably high level of quality. Automated manufacturing has driven the price down and raised the quality in a way we never could have imagined in the '50s, '60s, and '70s. That being said, the homogenization of manufacturing has also taken what might be called the "character" out of most of today's low-cost instruments, because they're all pretty much the same.

One of the reasons vintage gear is such a draw is that it's all a little different. Much of it was hand-made and the tolerances were much broader than they are now. As a result, sometimes a drift in tolerance because of human error (an instrument constructed on Monday morning or on Friday before quitting time for example) resulted in magic that's still difficult to duplicate.

So what are some tried and true things that usually work? Here's a quick and very incomplete list of instruments, amps, and accessories that are prized for their sound (and the older they get, for their collectibility, too). I'm not recommending that you run out and buy any of these, but it's worth knowing exactly why something is so sought after. If you get a chance to try one of these for just a couple of minutes, then you'll have a good idea about why they're so special.

## Guitars

Fender Telecaster (the '52 reissue is a good example of the Tele at its best)
Fender Telecaster Deluxe or Custom (with humbucking pickups)
Fender Stratocaster (the most widely played guitar in the world—the models from 1957–60 are the most desirable)
Gibson Les Paul Standard (the most expensive vintage instrument on the market today, and some say the best guitar ever made)
Gibson Les Paul "Goldtop" (the original Les Paul with single-coil pickups instead of humbuckers
Gibson Les Paul Junior (an entry-level Les Paul used by Billy Joe Armstrong and Leslie West)
Gibson Firebird (as used by Johnny Winter)
Gibson Les Paul Special (with smaller humbuckers—extensively used by Pete Townshend during the '70s)
Gretsch 6120 (this hollow-body Chet Atkins-style guitar was used on a variety of huge hits, including The Who's "Won't Get Fooled Again")
Gretsch Silver Jet
Rickenbacker 360 (the guitar responsible for the British Sound)
Rickenbacker 360-12 (a 12-string version of the 360)
Gibson ES-335 (the "dot neck" versions that use simple dots for position markers are the most desirable)
Epiphone Casino (as used by John Lennon)
Martin D-28 (an acoustic standard)
Gibson J-45 (also an acoustic standard)
Guild F412 (the only acoustic built from the ground up as a 12-string)
Coral/Dano Electric Sitar

## Guitar Amplifiers

1959 Fender Bassman (some think this is the best guitar amp ever made!)
Any tweed-covered Fender
Any brown-covered Fender
Any blackface Fender (has a black control panel, hence the name)
Deluxe Reverb (a circuit design different from most Fenders makes it sound different when overdriven)
Marshall Plexi (has a control panel made out of Plexiglas, hence the name)
Marshall JMP head with model 1960 cabinet
Marshall 1968 Super Lead head
Marshall JTM-45 combo
Mesa Boogie Mark II
Hiwatt Custom 100
Vox AC30 Top Boost (has extra factory-installed circuitry that gives it more overdrive)
Roland Jazz Chorus 120

## Basses

'60s, '70s, even '80s Fender Jazz Bass
'60s, '70s, even '80s Precision Bass
MusicMan Sting Ray
Rickenbacker 4001
Danelectro Longhorn
Hofner Beatle bass
Gibson EB-2 or 3

## Bass Amps

Ampeg B15A (the standard for the studio)
Ampeg SVT (the standard for touring)
Acoustic 360 (the sound of the '70s)

## Pedals

Fuzz Face (the original Arbiter version)
Electro-Harmonix Big Muff Pi
Ibanez Tube Screamer (the older TS-808 and TS9s are the most desirable for their sound)
Pro Co Rat
Octavia (by Roger Mayer)
MXR Dyna Comp
Mu-Tron III (by Musitronics)

Boss CE-1 Chorus Ensemble
MXR Phase 90
Uni-Vibe (the original Univox model)
Vox V847 Wah (the original, and some say still the best)
Cry Baby Wah
Electro-Harmonix Deluxe Memory Man
Digitech Whammy Pitch Effect
Maestro Tube Echoplex
Roland RE-101 Space Echo

### Keyboards

Hammond B3 (or A3 or C3—same electronics, different cabinet) with either a Leslie 122, 145, or 147 (basically the same except for cabinet size or connecting cable)
Wurlitzer Model 120 or 200 electric piano
Fender Rhodes Stage 88 or Suitcase 73 electric piano
Hohner D6 Clavinet
Minimoog

### Drums

'50s/'60s Gretsch "Round Badge" kit (the logo is a round badge)
'60s Ludwig "Keystone Badge" kit
'70s Gretsch "Stop Sign Badge" kit
Ludwig Supra-Phonic 6-1/2-inch snare drum
'70s Ludwig Black Beauty snare drum
Ludwig Acrolite snare drum
Noble & Cooley 5-1/2-inch maple snare drum

## PLAY IN TUNE

Excluding drummers and keyboard players for a minute, one of the most serious offenses (and the easiest to control these days) is playing in tune. Young string musicians (horn players, too) tend to overlook this critical aspect of playing partially because they're unsure of exactly how precise they should be, or their ear is undeveloped. Before cheap electronic tuners, *everybody* was a little out of tune. If you don't believe me, just listen to a few records from back in the '50s and '60s.

By the '70s most recording musicians had discovered the Conn Strobotuner (see Fig. 1.1), an electronic tuning device developed primarily for tuning pianos. This was an expensive ($350 in 1970's money) way to get in tune, but it made all the difference in the world. This fueled the demand for an inexpensive version, which resulted in the models you can purchase today for as little as ten bucks (see Fig. 1.2). Since they cost so little and do so much (much more than their predecessors), there's no excuse for any musician not to own at least one tuner and know how to use it.

*Fig. 1.1. A Conn Strobotuner.*

*Fig. 1.2. An inexpensive tuner/ metronome.*

Being in tune at just one position on your instrument isn't enough. It's absolutely imperative that your instrument be properly intonated. This means that the instrument plays in tune in any octave up and down its playable register (up and down the neck for guitar and bass players). While setting the intonation is a skill that's useful to learn at some point in your career, it's best to leave this to a professional in the beginning. If you don't know what you're doing then you could make things a lot worse or even damage your instrument.

Intonation on guitars and basses can be tricky at best. Just like a piano, they're never completely in tunc at all points up and down the neck. A new system developed by session guitar player Buzz Feiten (called the Feiten Tuning System) actually solves this problem, but requires a qualified pro to install it and reset both the bridge and nut. The bottom line is that the closer to being perfectly in tune you are, the better you and your band will sound!

Playing in tune applies to drummers as well. Properly maintained and tuned drums with fresh heads make both you and your band sound much better. We'll discuss this more in the chapter dedicated to drums, Chapter 4.

## PLAY IN TIME

Playing in time is somewhat of a cliché, but it's one of the things that make a huge difference in your individual performance. Simply put, this means playing with the pulse of the song. If you practice to a metronome, click, or loops, it means you're playing on the downbeat. If you're playing with a band, you start on the 1 of the song and you're always playing with the snare on the 2 and 4 (assuming that you're in 4/4 time).

You should be conscious of tempo, attacks and releases, and turnarounds (which we'll discuss in detail in Chapter 8). A steady tempo is essential for every instrument and can make a huge difference in a player's ultimate skill level. Even if you have great chops, they don't mean anything unless you can perform them with a steady tempo. Tempo can be best practiced by playing to either a metronome or loops. Once again, metronomes are built into just about every tuner these days, as well as every DAW (digital audio workstation) and personal digital recorder, so there's no excuse for not practicing with one.

Attacks and releases are one of the most overlooked, yet most important, elements in playing. Attacks and releases usually refer to how you approach a phrase that you're either playing or singing. The attack part is usually easy as it's the beginning of the phrase. A release is how you end the phrase and is just as important as how you start it (listen to vocals at the very end the theme song of the television show *American Dad* for a good example). Your attacks and releases are essential parts of making your playing or singing tight and precise.

Another often overlooked part of playing that needs attention is the turnaround between sections. This is the part of a song between the verse and chorus, chorus and verse, verse and outro, chorus and bridge, and so on. (listen to the bar just before each chorus of Lynyrd Skynyrd's "Sweet Home Alabama" for a great example). This section requires a lot of focus because it's usually played a little differently from the rest of the song. For the drummer, it's usually a tom or snare roll into the next section of the song. Take care not to rush or slow down the tempo in the section. For all other players (singers usually don't have to worry about this), you should pay attention to exactly what you're playing during the turnaround since unless it's a build in volume, most of the other players usually just randomly play something over the roll. If you're covering a song from a recording, listen carefully to exactly what's going on in the turnaround. You'll find it's a precise line that you have to play in order to keep your playing tight.

You'll find a lot more about playing in time, attacks and releases, and turnarounds in the context of band playing in Chapter 8, and for each instrument in the next few chapters.

# CHAPTER 2

# The Guitar Player

There's so much to being a guitar player that's easy. There's a vast variety of gear to choose from, a host of excellent players in every genre to learn from, and plenty of ways to get you to a place where you can make music quickly and easily. That being said, playing guitar well takes a lot of thought and effort that goes way beyond technique. It requires some dedication to not only do it well, but also do it in a way that makes the rest of your band sound better as a result.

Here are all the things to either think about or work on to take your individual playing to the next level and, as a result, bring your band there, too.

## TWO DEFINING MOMENTS FOR A GUITAR PLAYER

There are two defining moments that can change an electric guitar player from an amateur into a professional. What I'm going to tell you might be hard to take, because it might go against your idea of what sounds good and is fun to play, but believe me when I tell you that it will help you in the long run.

**Defining Moment 1**: The day you hear that your sound can be bigger without pedals or anything else between your guitar and amp.

Yes, it's true. That's the way it usually works. Most of those guitar sounds that you've been hearing on recordings (especially on classic '60s and '70s recordings) have been made by a guitar plugged straight into an amp with no pedals (or one at most) in between. What gives it that big sound is the type of amp (like the vintage ones discussed in Chapter 1) and the fact that it's turned up pretty high, if not to max!

Let me tell you about when this moment happened to me. I was jamming in a garage with slide guitarist extraordinaire Gerry Groom and a bass player and drummer. Gerry was a protégé of Duane Allman (of the famous Allman Brothers Band) and was so close to Duane that he willed Gerry his beloved Les Paul when he died. The guy really had some amazing chops and a lot of experience and was once dubbed by Jimi Hendrix' former manager as "the next great American guitar player." I was no pup either, as I had been playing about 15 years at the time and had a couple of major label record deals (back when they actually meant something) under my belt.

Gerry plugged his 1960 Les Paul Black Beauty into his 1964 Fender black-faced Super Reverb, and the sound was glorious—lots of sustain with some really good-sounding overdrive. I plugged my 1981 Strat into a small rack (which was popular to have at the time) of distortion devices, chorus units, EQs and noise gates, which then went into a fabulous 1977 Marshall JMP 100-watt half-stack. While Gerry's guitar sang with richness and as much sustain as he wanted, mine sounded thin and buzzy, although just as loud. After about a half-hour of jamming Gerry looked at me and said, "Why do you even use that crap (meaning my rack gear)? You'd sound a lot better without it." I loved my pedals and rack gear and the way it made me sound while I played by myself, but I had to admit that his rig sounded better than mine by a mile. He had the sound I kept trying to get by using all the pedals and rack gear, but he got it by using none of it!

I unplugged everything and when straight into the amp, turned it up and . . . wow! It really did sound better once I tweaked the amp's controls a bit. I was a little shocked by how high I had to turn the amp up to get the sound, but it really was the sound I had heard on countless records and had been trying to achieve. It was that simple.

But it did take a new technique to learn how to control the amp. I couldn't just jump on a pedal to get enough volume to go from rhythm to lead any more, I had to do it with the volume control on the guitar. And much to my amazement, it was easy! *You turn down the volume control and the sound cleans up; you automatically get some highs in your sound, giving you some nice rhythm definition.*

No longer were my rhythm parts heavy handed and too full. Now they were always just right. This was my moment of clarity.

Granted, it really depends on the amp. Most amps (like the ones described in Chapter 1) will work well, but a few won't. That's one of the reasons that guitar players much prefer tube over solid-state amps. Tube amps have the right sound when you turn them up, while solid-state amps, for the most part, just don't. Likewise, if the amp has too much power, you just might never be able to turn it up where you need to in order to get the right sound, especially if you play in small venues. That's why a 50-watt amp is a lot more versatile than a 100, because you just can't drive a 100 to where it needs to go without your audience wearing hearing protectors like you see on an airport flight line.

Now I'm not saying throw away all your distortion and overdrive pedals (because they certainly have their place), but get the sound from the amp first, then add your pedals. If you can't make the guitar sound great plugged directly into the amp, consider an amp that will get you where you want to go.

> **Defining Moment 2:** When you learn to play clean without the help of distortion or sustain.

This might sound like the same thing as Defining Moment 1, but it's not. Playing with distortion is fun, but the sustain gives you a false sense of security. The problem is that it can also cover up a lot of mistakes and technique problems that you might have. Distortion and artificial sustain can give you a false sense of your ability, and the way to get around that is to learn to play completely clean. Yes, you might not like what you hear at first, but with some practice you'll find that it'll make you a much better player, because now you can hear all the nuances—the ones you're doing well and the ones you need work on—that you just can't hear through the distortion. Remember back in Chapter 1 when we talked about your influences and how important the nuances in the playing were? This is the way you learn and refine them in your playing. If you can sound great clean, you'll sound even better dirty!

## Less Is More

Expanding on the above, playing with fewer effects and less distortion helps your band in another big way—it's a lot easier for you to fit into the mix. The more effects (reverb, delay, chorus, flange, vibrato, and so on) and distortion you use, the harder it is for the audience to discern exactly what you're playing. This means that the sound of the band turns into a mushy din instead of an exciting mix of instruments greater than its parts.

I'm not saying to stop using your pedals. I'm saying that you should use them with discretion. You don't need to use them on every song, and you usually need a lot fewer of them than you think.

When you're playing live, if you think of your set as a record or CD (meaning a group of songs released at the same time that are designed to fit together), you'll notice that the guitar sounds change a lot from song to song. In the studio, this means using different guitars, different amps, different effects—all in the name of keeping the sound fresh. While it's impractical to do this to that extreme when playing live, you can still do some subtle things toward this end like using different pickup combinations, using different effects in different songs, or using different amp settings if your amp will allow you to do it. But once again, the word is discretion. A little goes a long way!

## THAT'S WHAT TONE CONTROLS ARE FOR

Most players seem to have either questions or a misunderstanding on why and how to use their tone controls, so don't feel bad if you do too.

First of all, you want to adjust the tone controls so that all the notes of your instrument speak evenly. That is, no note (or group of notes) is way louder or softer than any other.

On a guitar this might sound something like the low end is really too boomy when you play a Les Paul or something with humbucking pickups through your amp setup, but it's nice and even with a Strat or something that has single coil pickups. Or the other way around where the Paul sounds balanced while the Strat sounds light on the low end. In this case, adjusting either the bass or mid controls on the amp will make sure that all notes are equal in level.

Another situation might be where the midrange is so bright and strident that it tears your head off, but it's close to the sound you like. In this case, it's great to have the flexibility of a parametric tone control if available. Sweep the frequency until you find the band of frequencies that's too loud, narrow the bandwidth until just that frequency is affected, and then lower it. Your tone will remain pretty much the same but the offending frequency will be lowered so it's balanced with the rest. This is also a big thing with basses, where one note on the neck is so much louder than everything else.

But where these controls really shine is in the context of the band (either live or in the studio). You want to be sure that every instrument is distinctly heard and the only way to do that is to be sure that each one has its own frequency space. It's especially important with two guitar players with similar instruments and amps (something like two Les Pauls and two Marshalls would be the worst-case scenario). Then you have to shape your sounds so that one guitar occupies a higher frequency register and the other is in a lower register.

This might mean that the lead guitar has more high-end while the rhythm guitar is fatter sounding. Or both guitars might have different midrange peaks.

Plus, the guitars have to sit in a different frequency space than the bass and drums (and keys, percussion, and horns, if you have them) so you alter your tone controls to make this happen.

This all takes a while to dial in, so don't get discouraged if it doesn't happen right away. Listen closely to some big-selling CD/MP3s; you'll get the idea when you hear how everything is layered.

## CLASH OF THE GUITAR PLAYERS

Most bands have more than one guitar player, so it's important to learn how to refine your sound so that your band sounds big and fat instead of loud and thin. As I said above, the tone controls on your amp is the first place to start to carve your sound so that it's not covered up by the other guitar (or other band instruments for that matter), and doesn't cover anyone up either.

But with two guitar players in the band you have to take things to the next level. You have to make sure that the songs are arranged so the guitars stay out of each other's way. If you listen closely to just about any recording by a popular artist you'll see that this is just what's happened in the studio already. If you can hear within the song (which isn't always easy with certain types of music or with data-compressed MP3s), this is what you'll hear.

**Each guitar is playing something completely different.** One guitar might be playing full chords while the other is playing a line. Going back to early Motown for an example (they always used three guitar players on each record), listen to the Supremes' "You Keep Me Hangin' On." One guitar plays the lead line, the second guitar plays the chords, and the third guitar enters on the B section. Another example is Eric Clapton's (actually Derek and the Dominos') "Layla" with the first guitar playing the opening bar, the second guitar playing the chords going down, and the lead guitar playing the signature line. Yet another example would be Lynyrd Skynyrd's "Sweet Home Alabama" with the first guitar playing the signature intro line, the second guitar playing the lead line, and the third guitar playing a line against the first when the band comes in. Skynyrd is a great example of interplay between three guitars, and just about anything by them is worth studying.

**Each guitar is playing in a different register or voicing.** If one guitar is playing an A chord on the second fret, the second guitar is playing it on the fifth fret. If one guitar is playing a line on the fifth and sixth strings, the second guitar is playing the same thing only up an octave on the first and second string. For a good example of this, listen to Lenny Kravitz's "Are You Goin' My Way" with the signature line being played in the open E position with the other guitar one octave higher on the 12th.

**Each guitar is playing a different rhythm.** If one guitar is playing long sustained chords (called "power chords" or, in the studio, "footballs" because they're whole notes that look like footballs when transcribed), the second one is playing a faster rhythm like quarter or eighth notes. You'll find this a lot in hard rock and metal music, although two guitars can just be playing different lines where the two rhythms seamlessly integrate as in the Eagles' "Hotel California," or the verse of "Sweet Home Alabama."

If you playing in a cover band, you've got to start listening extra closely into the arrangement to hear these different lines, rhythms, and voicings. This is where a high-quality playback system and a CD really come in handy, because sometimes you just can't hear the detail on an MP3 or AAC (iTunes) file.

If you and your band are writing your own songs you must employ these techniques so that the guitars will lay in better with the track and better support the vocals and rhythm section. It'll make the song a lot more interesting to boot.

# LAYING IN WITH THE RHYTHM SECTION

Regardless of whether you play all the solos in the band or none at all, more times than not you'll be playing some chordal rhythmic part, and this requires you to lock in with the rhythm section. In the studio, you can always edit the part in your DAW to make it lay in better with the bass and drums, but you can't do that in live performance. Even if you could edit your part live, you wouldn't want to. Playing rhythm so that you lock in with the rhythm section is an essential part of your guitar-playing technique and a super-essential part of getting your band to sound great, so let's take a look at just how to do this.

Locking into the rhythm section means that you're playing in rhythm with the drummer, in particular. It doesn't mean you're playing exactly the same rhythm as he's playing, but it means that you're exactly with him on every quarter note (the 1 - 2 - 3 - 4 of the beat) of the part that you're playing. Metallica does this a lot in their music, with *Master of Puppets* being a good example.

The easiest way to lock in with the drummer is to actually watch him as much as you can. Whenever he hits the snare drum, you have to be exactly with him as closely as possible. Even a small amount before or after is too much. It has to be exactly on!

After you play with the same drummer for a while and you get to know one another, you naturally lock into each other's rhythms, so watching all the time is no longer necessary, but it's still important to watch when you're learning a new song or during recording, since it's the absolute easiest way to lock in as closely as possible.

*Set up so that you can see all of the drummer's appendages, so that you watch his feet and hands as well as listen. It's a visual idiom sometimes. Watch his body. Watch his face. When he grimaces, maybe you can lean into a note with your body. It's choreography almost, but it makes a difference.* —Paul Ill

So that takes care of beats 2 and 4. How about the 1 and 3 with the kick drum? The kick drum usually isn't that easy to hear whether you're playing live on stage, in rehearsal, or while recording. A trick that experienced studio players use is to put your foot against the kick drum so you feel the vibration and play to that. This usually isn't practical on stage, but if you're on with the 2 and 4, the 1 and 3 come naturally.

# WHAT YOUR AUDIENCE HEARS

It's important to take into consideration what your audience hears, and that's not always an easy thing to do. In order for you to get your sound, it might require levels that will blow the drinks off the table. Or it might require you to turn the treble up so high that it sounds like an ice pick in the ear in the third row or table. And anyone who's played a club with a soundman or has a big enough PA rig that they need a soundman, knows that they're usually after you to turn down your stage volume so they have more control of the mix. But there are easy fixes for all of the above if you're willing to find them.

Assuming that you've already adjusted your tone controls as above to no avail, one solution is to turn your amp or speaker cabinet away from the audience. By turning it into a wall you not only give the audience a break, but you also can still actually hear it pretty well from the reflections, as long as the wall isn't too soft.

If your position on stage is at one of the corners, you can turn the amp or speaker cabinet so that it faces across the stage. This has the added advantage of helping the rest of the band hear you.

Another way is to just raise the amp up, making it closer to your ears. Put it on a chair or road-case. Angle it up so that it's pointing at your head instead of at your legs and straight at the audience. There are a lot of amp stands that can help you with this, such as the Standback (Fig. 2.1). You'll find that when you hear yourself better, you'll need a whole lot less volume to get the sound you like.

*Fig. 2.1. Angled amp using the Standback amp stand.*

Any of these methods will work, but you have to go out in the audience yourself to find out what it really sounds like. It's time for that extra-long guitar cable or wireless unit. Your audience and your soundman will thank you.

## THE RECORDING GUITAR PLAYER

The approach and mindset for a recording session is somewhat different from a live performance. While many of the following rules apply to a gig as well as a session, there's a slightly different emphasis on preparation. Everything below applies to every recording session, with the possible exception of recording in your own studio.

**Arrive early.** This goes without saying, but I'll say it again to reinforce it. You should always arrive at least a half-hour before the downbeat of the session. This means that if your session starts at 7:00 p.m., you need to be there at 6:30 to be ready for 7:00. You can't expect to get there at 6:55 and for everything to be cool. If the session starts at 7:00 p.m., find out if that means load-in time or actual downbeat time. No one likes to be kept waiting.

**Make sure your guitar is in tune.** This means that you should have the intonation professionally checked so that you can play in tune anywhere on the neck. The one thing that brings down a session faster than anything is a guitar player who either can't get in tune or stay in tune.

**New strings help the sound.** Unless you're one of those players who actually likes the sound of old strings, change your strings right before you get to the session (or if you get there early enough to have time). Not only will they stay in tune longer, but they'll sound a lot livelier as well.

**Bring all your guitars and amps to the session.** A recording is made interesting by multiple layers of different-sounding instruments. You'll never know when something that you haven't used in years will be just the right sound for the song. Bring every amp that you can, regardless of how small they are (some of the best recording amps are the smallest). Bring every effect and guitar. The exception here is if the studio is so small that you can't fit everything or the producer or engineer specifically tells you what to bring or what not to bring.

**Bring extra strings, picks, tubes, cables, and batteries.** Just like onstage, this is the professional thing to do. You have to have backups in case you break a string, lose your pick, or your battery dies. Even if you think you have everything in your case or gig box, double check to make sure. It's easy to forget the last time you broke an E string and never replaced the replacement.

**Know your parts before you arrive.** This is a little deceiving in that it's altogether possible that your parts will change once you start recording. Until you actually hear the playback, you really don't know how a part fits with all the others. Still, you want to have a starting point, so it's best to be well rehearsed before the session's downbeat.

**Have your amp tuned up.** While you might be able to get away with it on stage, you'll never be able to successfully record with an amp that is either buzzing, farting, or randomly spitting and quitting. If it's good enough to play through, then it's good enough to have in good working order. If not, the tracks you put down will only have to be redone later. Plus, you do want it to sound the best it can, don't you?

**Make sure your cables are working.** I know that it's easy to keep playing with a guitar cable that cuts out or makes noise occasionally. We all do it, but anything less than a perfect cable is a definite no-no for recording. Having to redo the perfect take because your cable cut out is bound to upset not only you but everyone else in the studio as well. Cables are cheap. Buy a new one if you have any doubts about the one you're using. By the way, if you're used to going wireless onstage, you'll probably find that your guitar sounds a little better with a cable in the studio. Also, unless you have a real expensive wireless setup, it's susceptible to outside interference from police and fire-station radios operating at or near the same frequency. Be prepared to use a cable to make sure that doesn't happen to you.

**Make any charts, notes, or cheat sheets beforehand.** Once again this comes under the heading of being prepared. You don't want to be wasting anyone's time for something that so easily could have been done beforehand.

**Turn your cell phone off!** The session should be your main priority with as few distractions as possible. One of the easiest ways to achieve this is to turn your cell phone off. If you leave it on, not only do you risk ruining a good take if the ringer goes off, but talking on the phone is the best way to stop the momentum of a session in its tracks. Don't even bother to put it on vibrate since this will cause you to lose your focus just as easily as when the ringer is on. Turn it off; leave it outside the studio so you won't be tempted to use it.

## THE GUITAR PLAYER'S UTILITY KIT

As Murphy's Law states, "If something can go wrong, it will go wrong!" so you have to be prepared for any eventuality during a gig or recording. Things break, but a pro is always ready. The following list of items prepares you for just about anything. Each item should be considered just as essential to playing a gig as your guitar and amp.

- 2 spare power tubes (if you use a tube amplifier)
- 2 spare 12AX7 preamp tubes (if you use a tube amplifier)
- Package of fuses
- 2 spare sets of strings
- Spare E strings
- String winder
- Wire snips
- Needlenose pliers
- Phillips screwdriver
- Flat head screwdriver
- A set of Allen wrenches
- A light source (like a flashlight or a clip-on book light)
- Gaffer's or duct tape
- Super glue
- At least two extra 10-foot instrument cables (1/4" to 1/4")
- An extra 5-foot instrument cable
- RCA to RCA cable
- Various cable adapters like 1/4" to RCA, RCA to 1/4", 1/4" to XLR
- Cable tester
- An extra AC cable
- An AC extension cable
- Lots of picks
- Spare guitar strap

Spare tuner (digital)
Slide
Capo
Spare microphone (if you sing)
Spare microphone cable
Spare mic stand adapter
Spare 9V batteries (if you use pedals or have a preamp built into your guitar)
Spare AA batteries
Spare universal 9V wall wart
A small notepad
A pen
A magic marker
Band-aids
Throat lozenges
Aspirin or Advil
A towel
Earplugs

# CHAPTER 3

# Bass

As with the other chapters, we're going to look at bass from the perspective of the audience and the bass player, and from a stage and studio perspective as well.

It used to be that the job of bass guitar was given to the weakest guitar player because he had to play only four strings—and only one of those four at a time. While that may still be the case in your first band, being a bass player today means you have to be a specialist just as skilled as (maybe even more than) any of the other players in the band.

The bass player must have real chops, but not the kind that means playing a lot of notes really fast. The bass player must handle the low end of the music and anchor the rhythm section. The bass player has to be the ultimate team player, doing his or her best to blend in, first with the drummer and then with the rest of the band. This means not only playing whatever the music requires, but also locking in with the drummer.

## THE DEFINING MOMENT OF A BASS PLAYER

As with guitar players, there are two defining moments in a bass player's career that turn him into a professional. What I'm going to tell you might be hard to take because it might go against your idea of fun, but an understanding of the defining moments will help you in the long run.

**Defining Moment 1:** When you understand how to lock in with a drummer.

The bass player's job is as a support player, but the support really can only come from locking in with the drummer. The day that a bass player feels what it's really like to lock with a drummer is the day he jumps to the next level. The day a bass player learns to listen to the drummer more than to himself is the day he leaves the amateur ranks behind.

*I think that a defining moment for most bass players comes when they really hit a groove with a drummer and they go, "This is what's been lacking." Not that they've been playing with marginal drummers up until then; they just haven't found that magical mesh.*—Paul Ill

"Laying in" with a drummer requires a bit more than listening; it's watching the drummer as well. It's watching his arms and feet so that you can see where he physically puts the beat. It's putting your foot up against the bass drum to feel the drummer's pulse. It's all about locking in with your rhythm mate.

*It's a visual idiom sometimes. Watch his body. Watch his face. When he grimaces, maybe you can lean into a note with your body. It's choreography almost, but it makes a difference.*—Paul Ill

**Defining Moment 2:** When you understand what a bass really is supposed to sound like.

Besides anchoring the rhythm section, the bass anchors the low end of the band, so the sound is important. If the low end is thin, then the band doesn't seem as powerful. There's a reason why most bass players don't use any kind of pedals, or choose to use a Fender Precision bass or an Ampeg SVT or B-15. It's the sound! Even more so than a guitar, the bass can make such a huge contribution to the sound that when you finally hear a fine example of these instruments, your first reaction probably will be, "Oh, now I get it."

While every guitar manufacturer also makes basses, there are only a few models that you consistently see name players use: a Fender Precision or Jazz bass, for example, or a Rickenbacker 4001, or a Music Man StingRay. While you might see famous bassists play other models, you'll usually find that they use these for recording.

*I brought a P-bass (Fender Precision bass) with flatwounds and plugged into whatever was there and went, "Yeah, you don't really need anything else to sound good."*—Paul Ill

Amplifiers are another important aspect. There's a reason why you see Ampeg SVTs on stage after stage and hear Ampeg B-15s on record after record: it's the sound. While both of these amplifiers are expensive items (and the SVT is overkill in most applications because it's *extremely* powerful and heavy), it's worth doing everything you can to play through one for five minutes. Just having that point of reference will make a big difference in how you shape your sound from that point on.

## WHAT YOU HEAR ONSTAGE

The bass is one of the most difficult instruments to gauge the best volume for the room while onstage. Without getting into the physics of sound, this is because the low frequencies from the instrument take a lot of air space to develop, so what seems barely adequate to you and your band mates on stage might be blowing out everyone in the audience. Also, bass players tend to stand close to their amps on stage, so they never really get to hear exactly what they sound like.

Now is the time for either a long guitar cable or a wireless setup. Before you reach for any controls, get off the stage and walk around to hear just what the audience will hear. You may be very surprised at the sound.

Have to turn down because you're too loud in the audience but now you can't hear yourself onstage? Do what guitar players do; try to angle your speaker cabinet upward so that it's aiming at your ears. If that's impractical, now's the time to invest in some type of in-ear monitors to get a little more of your sound where it counts—in your own ears. Check out Chapter 13 to get some tips about your PA.

## YOUR SOUND—THAT'S WHAT TONE CONTROLS ARE FOR

Most players seem to have either questions or misunderstandings about why and how to use their tone controls, so don't feel bad if you do, too.

First of all, you want to adjust the tone controls so that all the notes of your bass speak evenly. That is, no note (or group of notes) is way louder or softer than any other. This is a common occurrence somewhere on the neck of just about every bass. Some of the loud or dead notes can be fixed with proper nut and bridge adjustment and intonation, and some problems can be fixed with tone controls. Either way, you still can expect that a note or two will be softer than the rest, and a couple might just roar. The idea is to limit these uneven spots if you can't totally fix the problem.

> *I never like to go to a gig with only a single bass, in case there's a technical difficulty with that instrument. Most of my instruments are vintage, so when the weather changes, my instruments can change noticeably fast. Usually what will happen is that the neck will shift and one string will have less volume than the other strings—markedly so, to where it takes you out of the moment.* —Paul Ill

Adjust the tone controls of your amp to get all the notes of the bass to sound about the same in level, and then adjust for general tone. You want to add more or less bottom (bass or low end) to complement the kick drum frequencies, which will make the low end of your band powerful. Then you want to adjust either the mid or high frequencies (depending on the bass, the amp, and the room you're playing in) so there's enough clarity that each bass note is well defined. If you're playing in a trio, you'll probably want more high end than bass players in other types of bands to sound as full as possible (it'll almost sound like another guitar). If you're playing in a metal band, you'll want more high end, because that's the sound of the genre.

## THE RECORDING BASS PLAYER

As you'll read throughout this book, the approach and mindset for a recording session is somewhat different from that of a live gig. While many of the following rules also apply to live performances, there's a slightly different emphasis on preparation. Everything below applies to every recording session, with the possible exception of recording in your own studio.

**Arrive early.** This goes without saying, but I'll say it again to reinforce it (you'll hear it a lot in this book). You should always arrive at least a half-hour before the downbeat of the session. This means that if your session starts at 7:00 p.m., you need to be there at 6:30 to be ready for 7:00. You can't expect to get there at 6:55 and for everything to be cool. If the session starts at 7:00, find out if that means load-in time or actual downbeat time. No one likes to be kept waiting.

**Make sure your bass is in tune.** This means that you should have the intonation professionally checked so that you play in tune anywhere on the neck. The tuning of the bass is really easy to overlook when you're tracking because sometimes the tuning isn't that obvious, but if it's out of tune and you didn't take the time to fix it, then it will bug the heck out of you every time you hear it played back. .

**New strings might help the sound.** There are two schools of thought on this one. Many players like the sound and feel of well-used strings, while others really want the life and brightness of new strings. Let the music be your guide for this. If you're playing the type of music that requires a bright midrange sound (like metal for instance), change your strings beforehand.

**Bring all your basses to the session.** All basses sound different (even two of the exact-same models, such as Fender Precision basses). You never know when something that you haven't used in years will be just the right sound for the song. Bring every bass you can, but if you have to limit the number due to space considerations, just bring the ones that are really different from each other like a Rickenbacker and a Fender, or a Fender Precision and a Jazz bass.

*If you're not sure what you're going to be doing or where the music is going to go, that one extra piece you bring can make the difference. I'll bring a P-bass and something that's going to sound markedly different. I'll also try to bring something in between like a Rick with flatwounds. You get a feel talking to the person for what you're getting into idiomatically. If they're doing an Americana kind of thing that's sort of like a Lucinda Williams or T-Bone Burnett kind of thing I might think, "That's more for my Kay than for the Hofner."*—Paul Ill

**Bring extra strings, picks, tubes, cables and batteries.** Just as you would onstage, this is the professional thing to do for a studio gig. You have to have backups in case you break a string or a battery dies. Even if you usually only play with your fingers, bring several kinds of picks, because using one could give you the perfect sound for the track. Even if you think you have everything in your case or gig box, double check to make sure. It's easy to forget the last time you broke a string and never replaced the spare.

*I also bring a vast selection of picks. I bring felt picks, soft picks, and picks of varying thicknesses to get a different tone. I'll demonstrate what each one sounds like at different pickup positions so they can see if it fits the song. On the Christina Aguilera record I did, one of the songs was a Hofner Beatle bass with a felt pick, which you'd never expect on a record like that.*—Paul Ill

**Know your parts before you arrive.** This is a little deceiving in that it's altogether possible that your parts will change once you start recording. Until you actually hear the playback, you really won't know how a part fits with all the others. Still, you want to have a starting point, so it's best to be well rehearsed before the session's downbeat.

**Have your amp tuned up.** While you might not be able to use the big rig that you're used to onstage (or maybe you just don't want to), bringing a smaller amp is never a bad idea for recording. Just make sure that it's in good working order with no buzzing, humming, farting, or other unwanted noises. You also might want to check with the studio first to see if they have a bass amp you can use (they usually do). Obviously this doesn't apply if you're not going to a professional studio, in which case you're best off to bring what you use onstage or what you know works and records well.

**Make sure your cables are working.** Using anything less than a perfect cable is a definite no-no for recording. Having to do the perfect take over because your cable cut out is the ultimate downer for a session. Cables are cheap. Buy a new one if you have any doubts about what you have. If you're used to going wireless onstage, you'll probably find that your bass sounds better with a cable in the studio. The wireless is also susceptible to outside interference, so be prepared to use a cable to get the best and cleanest sound possible.

*Make sure that your gear is comfortable to you. Make sure everything's working, the cables aren't crackling, your basses are in tune and intonated, your tuner is working, and your amp sounds good. Make sure that you can set everything up quickly and be zero hassle to anybody. You don't want to cause a problem for anybody, either technically or personally.* —Paul Ill

**Make any charts, notes, or cheat sheets beforehand.** Once again, this comes under the heading of being prepared. You don't want to waste anyone's time on something that could so easily have been done beforehand.

**Turn your cell phone off.** The session should be your main priority with as few distractions as possible. One of the easiest ways to achieve this is to turn off your cell phone. If you leave it on, not only do you risk ruining a good take if the ringer goes off, but talking on the phone is the best way to stop the momentum of a session in its tracks, and it's disrespectful to everyone else at the session as well. Don't even bother to put it on vibrate since this will cause you to lose your focus just as easily as when the ringer is on. Turn it off; leave it outside the studio so you won't be tempted to use it.

*Turn off your cell phone. Make it a point that everyone sees that you're turning off your phone or leaving it outside the studio so they all understand that you're not interested in phone calls while you're working. Make the session a priority. Don't bring reading material into the session with you. Don't be net surfing on your phone during a session.* —Paul Ill

## THE BASS PLAYER'S UTILITY KIT

As Murphy's Law states, if something can go wrong, it will go wrong, so you've got to be prepared for any eventuality during a gig. The following list of items prepares you for just about anything. Each item should be considered just as essential to playing a gig as your bass and amp.

- 2 spare power tubes (if you use a tube amplifier)
- 2 spare 12AX7 preamp tubes (if you use a tube amplifier)
- Package of fuses
- 2 spare sets of strings

String winder
Wire snips
Needle nose pliers
Phillips screwdriver
Flat head screwdriver
A set of Allen wrenches
A light source (like a flashlight or a clip-on book light from Radio Shack)
Duct tape
Super glue
At least two extra 10-foot instrument cables (1/4" to 1/4")
An extra 5-foot cable
RCA to RCA cables
Cable tester
Different kinds of picks (guitar picks of different thickness, felt)
Spare guitar strap
Spare tuner (digital)
Various cable adapters like 1/4" to RCA, RCA to 1/4", 1/4" to XLR
Spare microphone (if you sing)
Spare microphone cable
Spare mic stand adapter
Spare 9V batteries
Spare AA batteries
Spare universal 9V wall wart
A small notepad
A pen
A magic marker
Band-aids
Throat lozenges
Aspirin or Advil
A towel
Earplugs

# CHAPTER 4

# Drums

Drum-great Buddy Rich once said in a fit of egotism, "You can't have a great band without a great drummer." While he was no doubt referring to himself, truer words pertaining to bands have never been spoken. You *do* need a great drummer to really have a great band. But what does great really mean?

Contrary to what you might think, being a great drummer doesn't necessarily mean having great chops and the ability to play great polyrhythms. In fact, sometimes having too much technique can actually get in the way of your ability to drive a band.

In modern music, drums are the pulse of the song and the heartbeat of the band, and this is the drummer's major priority. Listen to just about any record and you'll hear that the drummer drives the band and complements the song the same as any other instrument.

## SIMPLE IS BEST

No matter what kind of music you play, the drummer's role is first and foremost as timekeeper. You may have the greatest collections of chops on the continent, but if you can't play in time, none of your skills matter. It's true that most musicians (especially drummers) want to get better technically and then show those skills off, but playing in time and on tempo is the first order of business when you sit on that drum throne. Drummers practice forever trying to be as good as Neil Peart, yet it's not about the technique, but the feel!

Nothing extra played, just hits in all the right places. Simplicity, yet perfection.

*A lot of drummers miss the boat because they're not concerned with playing time and playing simple basic beats and being able to clone that beat over and over again like a drum machine, but with soul. A lot of drummers are into the flash and are constantly looking for stuff to play. They put the kitchen sink into every tune. I heard a story once where Miles Davis told someone, "When you think you want to play something, don't." That story is kinda funny, but it's also true. Don't try to always be playing something. Lay back, play the groove, and wait for your spot. They won't be as often as you think. A lot of times drummers try to play too much, and I'm not talking stylistically, either. Whether you're a fusion drummer or a groove drummer, a lot of young drummers are looking to play too much, too often. If you have amazing chops, wait for that right moment to use them. It will mean a lot more.*—Bernie Dresel, L.A. session drummer formerly with The Brian Setzer Orchestra

*The first thing is to play good time. Secondly, you have to make it feel good. If you don't, you're going to get beat up from having to play it over and over again.*—Ricky Lawson, renowned L.A. session drummer, former musical director for Michael Jackson

## THE CONCEPTS OF FEEL AND INTERNAL TIME

So what does playing in time actually mean? We can break the concept down into feel and internal time. Feel means an intuitive ability to know where the beats are placed in a given type of music. This is something that can be learned to some degree, but for the most part you either have a great feel for a type of music or you don't. A drummer who has a great feel for one type of music might not have it for another. For instance, a drummer who has a great feel for a blues shuffle might not have it for bebop, while another drummer with a great feel for polyrhythmic progressive jazz might not have it for world music, and a drummer with a great R&B feel might have none for metal. If you don't have a great feel for a type of music, you either have to play and listen to it until you do, or play some other kind of music that you have a natural feel for. Either way, the music can only feel good to everyone else (your audience and the mates you play with) when it feels good to you first.

The concept of internal time is what affects a drummer's either sounding like he's moving furniture or making people want to get up to shake their booty. Even though you might be keeping a steady tempo, you can still have bad internal time. Internal time means how evenly you play individual drums. For instance, you may be steady with your kick drum on beats 1 and 3, but a little ahead or behind on beats 2 and 4, or always steady time-wise with your snare drum, but unsteady on your high hat. Now it's okay if you're *consistently* behind with your time, but *wavering* in time makes you lose the feel and groove. For instance, if your kick drum is always behind the beat by the same amount on beats 2 and 4, it might actually be the perfect feel for the music. It's when you waver, sometimes ahead, sometimes behind, always by a different amount, that everything falls apart (see Fig. 4.1).

*Fig. 4.1 Good and bad internal time.*

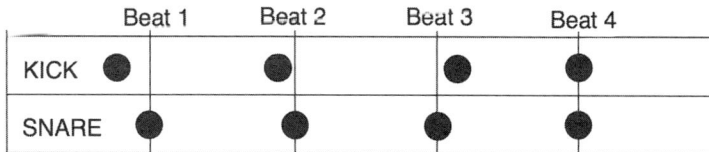

**BAD INTERNAL TIME** - Snare is on the beat. Kick is sometimes in front of the beat, sometimes behind.

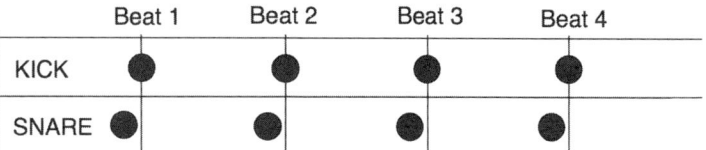

**GOOD INTERNAL TIME** - Kick is on the beat. Snare is behind the beat always by the same amount.

I was once in a band with the fabulous drummer, Bobby Caldwell (of Johnny Winter, Captain Beyond, and Armageddon ), who ironically didn't want to drum but wanted to be the front man. Although we had a really good drummer, Bobby would sit down to show him his concept of how to play a part, and the difference would be amazing. Although Bobby had rock 'n' roll chops equivalent to those of Buddy Rich, that's not what overwhelmed us. His groove was so wide that he instantly made everything and everybody sound a lot better. His sound was so *big* (yet not loud) that the band instantly went to a new level. When our main drummer sat back down, he could execute everything Bobby had just played, but it never felt or sounded the same. Bobby's concept of internal time was more acute for that type of music.

Although it seems that the best drummers are born with an innate sense of internal time, it can be learned. The problem is that it's relatively boring and not many drummers want to spend the time. You have to concentrate on playing as steadily as possible with each limb first, and then gradually add them together. You should constantly record yourself (with a click or loops, and without) to gauge how much you've improved. Most drummers aren't even aware of the concept of internal time, but if you concentrate on it, you'll certainly get better; it's the one thing that can give your skills the biggest jump in feel and groove.

## RUSHED OR LAZY FILLS

A problem that plagues many drummers—amateurs and pros alike—is rushed or lazy drum fills. This includes any fill that drifts out of time with the rest of the song and destroys the groove and feel. There's really no excuse for this breakdown, and it can be overcome with practicing to a click or loop and recording the results. The big trick is to be aware that you're doing it.

> *So work on your feel, your time, and your fills. A lot of drummers have great time except for when they do fills. I've heard from producers, "So and so has such a great feel but his fills are always out of time." Rushing the fill is a really common thing for a lot of drummers. The way to cure that is just practicing to a click track a lot.*—Brian MacLeod

## ARE YOU PLAYING TOO LOUD?

Sometimes it's not the guitar player who's playing too loud in the band, it's the drummer. This is usually the case with a drummer who's a heavy hitter and has a big loud drum kit but no concept of dynamics or how to lay in with the band. While it's true that the drummer drives the band, a drummer who only thrashes at his loudest volume level sounds again like he's moving furniture instead of playing music, and will usually cause the neighbors or audience to flash the "turn it down" signs.

While feel usually applies to where the beats are laid within the music, it also has to do with the volume level of the drums within the band. Being able to feel the right volume and intensity to drive the band is something that you can learn—it's called dynamics and is something that we'll cover in depth in Chapter 8. It's one of the basic keys to making your band sound great.

## WHAT MAKES A DRUM KIT SOUND GREAT?

Playing well is only half the equation; the other half is having a great-sounding drum kit. A great-sounding kit can instantly improve how you and your band are perceived, not only by your audience, but also by your peers.

So what does great sounding actually mean? While the definition of great varies from person to person on a general level, to a pro it usually means a kit that is well tuned and free of buzzes and sympathetic vibrations. For instance, when you hit a rack tom, the snare doesn't buzz and the other toms don't ring along with it. Or if you hit the snare, the toms don't ring along. So how do you achieve this drum nirvana? It's all in the tuning and the kit maintenance, which we'll check out in depth later in the chapter. But first, let's look at drum construction itself, since having a little background will help you understand what your drum kit is capable of.

## DRUM CONSTRUCTION

There are a number of parameters that determine what a drum will sound like. Let's take a look at them.

**Shell Size.** The larger the diameter, the lower the natural pitch, although you can obviously change this a bit by tuning the heads.

**Shell Depth.** Mostly responsible for how loud the drum will be, and, to some degree, the articulation of the sound.

**Shell Thickness.** Thinner shells are actually more resonant since they're easier to excite because they have a lower mass than a heavier, thicker shell. As a result, thicker shells have to rely much more on the head for the overall tone of the drum.

**Shell Material.** The material used to make the drum shell affects the tone of the drums more than any other component. Here are the most common drum shell materials:

**Maple** is the most prized construction material by drummers because it helps make the drums sound more even across the frequency spectrum.

**Mahogany** drums sound warmer than maple because they enhance the low end.

**Birch** is a very dense wood, which, thanks to its hardness, results in a brighter drum with a lot less low end than a maple drum.

**Poplar** is a fast-growing tree, which translates into cheaper wood and inexpensive drum kits. It has a sound very similar to birch, with a bright top end and less bottom.

**Basswood** is also a fast-growing tree, resulting in inexpensive kits, but exhibits an increased low end that's similar to mahogany.

**Luan** is an Asian tree that provides the least expensive wood available. It has a warmer sound with less top end, similar to mahogany.

**Shell interior** has a lot to do with the pitch of the drum. A smooth interior results in a more resonant drum, which means it's easier to tune and control.

**Bearing edges** means the cut at the edge of a drum shell where the hoops are attached. The way the bearing edge is cut affects not only the pitch of the drum, but also the tuning—the sharper the cut, the brighter the drum.

**Hoops.** The type of hoop and the number of lugs used to seat the drumheads also determines how the drum will sound. In general, the thicker the hoop, the easier the drum will be to tune. A drum with fewer lugs provides more complex overtones.

### The Snare
Since the snare is the most important drum in the kit, it's best to look at it on its own since there are so many other factors that influence the tone besides the parts we just discussed.

*Snare Construction*

There are a lot of other materials used for snare drums, but here are a couple of things to consider.

- ▶ Metal snare drums are generally very loud, resonant, and bright. Shell thickness makes a real difference, with 3mm and thicker creating more low end and midrange.
- ▶ Be conscious of how the stand can affect the sound. If it's wrapped too tightly around the drum, it will stop it from vibrating and cause the sound to be more muted with fewer overtones.

*The Snare Unit*

Another important aspect is the snare unit itself.

- ▶ The snare count, type of material, curl, and diameter all determine the volume of the snare as well as any sympathetic vibrations that may occur.
- ▶ Make sure that the snare unit is flat against the head and has no sharp or uneven protrusions.
- ▶ Less curl will mean less volume, while a wider snare unit will have more volume.
- ▶ Too much snare volume will mean that the snare is hard to control when other drums are hit.

## TUNING THE DRUMS

All drummers are taught the basics of drum tuning at some point in their education, but knowing how to do it and knowing what to listen for are two different things. The majority of drummers I've heard over the years don't know what a good-sounding drum kit sounds like. Here are some tips from the famous Drum Doctor to get you started.

### Tips from the Drum Doctor
If you're doing a recording session in Los Angeles and you want your drums to instantly sound great, then your first call is to the

Drum Doctors to either rent a fantastic-sounding kit or have your kit tuned. Ross Garfield is the Drum Doctor, and you've heard his drum sounds on platinum recordings from Alanis Morissette, the Black Crows, Bruce Springsteen, Rod Stewart, Metallica, Marilyn Manson, Dwight Yoakum, Jane's Addiction, Red Hot Chili Peppers, Foo Fighters, Lenny Kravitz, Michael Jackson, Rage Against the Machine, Sheryl Crow, Nirvana, and many more. Not many people know as much about drums and drum tuning as Ross. The following tips resulted from years of experience working closely with the likes of drum greats Jeff Porcaro, Jim Keltner, Charlie Watts, Terry Bozio, Jeff Hamilton, Steve Jordan, Charlie Drayton and Peter Erskine (to name just a few).

### *How Long Does It Take to Tune a Drum Kit?*

If I have to change all the heads and tune them up, it'll take about an hour (and that's even on a cheap starter set). I try to tune them to where I think they should be—a little on the high side for starters—then after we open up the mics and hear everything magnified, I'll modify the tuning more to the song.

### *Prepping the Drums for New Heads*

In order for drums to sound their best, the edges of the drum shell have to be cut properly, and this is something that no one ever checks, or even thinks of checking, until it's time to change the heads. When you take the heads off, all the edges of the shell should lie exactly flat against a flat surface. I'll put the shell on a piece of glass or granite and shine a light over the top of the shell, and then I'll get down to where the edge of the drum hits the granite. If I see a light at any point, then there's a low spot on the edge of the shell and the drum will be hard to tune and will probably have some funny overtones. So the first thing is to make sure that your drum shells are true. The next thing is for your shell edge to have a bevel to it, and not be flat on the bottom, because again, this affects the tuning and overtones.

If you have either of these problems with a drum, send it back to the manufacturer. Don't try to cut the edges of your drum shells yourself since it doesn't cost that much money for the manufacturer to do it, and it's really something that should be done by someone who knows exactly what they're doing. Once your drum shells are in good shape, then tuning is a lot easier.

### *New Heads*

The first thing I'll do is put a fresh set of top and bottom heads on. Nine times out of ten, I'll put white Remo Ambassadors on the tops, clear Remo Ambassadors on the bottoms, and a Remo clear Powerstroke 3 on the kick drum. I'll use a white Ambassador or a coated Black Dot Ambassador on the snare top and either a clear Diplomat or coated Ambassador on the bottom.

A lot of the decision on the type of head depends on how deep the drum is. If it's five inches or less, then I'll usually go with an Ambassador. If it's six-and-a-half inches or bigger, then I'll usually go with a Diplomat. Just this little bit of information really makes a difference in how the kit sounds.

A heavy hitter will get more low end out of a drum that's tuned higher just because of the way he hits, so, as a result, I usually tune a drum a little tighter if the drummer is a heavy hitter. I might move into different heads as well, like an Emperor or something thicker.

> *I move the combination of drum heads around to get different things. If I want a heavier sound, I'll use a thicker head. If I want it brighter with more attack, I'll use a thinner head. I usually don't go any thinner than an Ambassador and I usually don't go any thicker than an Emperor.*—Ricky Lawson, Los Angeles session drummer and former musical director for Michael Jackson and others

### The Tuning Technique

Most engineers (and even a lot of drummers) don't know the proper way to tune their drums, but it's really not that hard. For a proper tune job, you've got to keep all of the tension rods even so they have the same tension at each lug.

Hit the head an inch in front of the lug. If you do it enough times you'll hear which ones are higher and which are lower. What you want is for the pitch to sound the same at each lug. When the pitch (the tension) is the same at each lug, you should have a nice, even decay when you hit the drum in the center.

Tune the top and the bottom head to the same pitch at first; then take the bottom head down a third to a fifth below the top head.

> *What I try to do is to tune to where the drum sounds good. You can take a drum and tune it out of the range it likes to be in, so I try to find the sweet spot for that drum with the combination of heads I'm using. I like the top head a little bit tighter and then I use the bottom head just to bring in some tone.*—Ricky Lawson

*There are a lot of different theories about how a drum should sound, but the one that works best for me is when the top head is not exactly the same pitch as the bottom. I tune the top head about a minor third above the bottom head when just barely tapping it right on the edge near the lug.*—Bernie Dresel, Los Angeles session drummer, formerly of The Brian Setzer Orchestra

*I tap the side of the shell to see how it will sound in the room; then I tune it accordingly so that the drum is working at its maximum value in relation to the room. I do that everywhere I go whether it's a ballroom, or a wedding, or Studio D at Village Recorders, or Conway (famous Hollywood recording studios), or The House of Blues, or the Gibson Amphitheater. I always tune the drums for the room. My idea of a good-sounding drum is when you can just throw a mic in front of it and it works without any EQ or processing, which engineers love.*—Johnny "Vatos" Hernandez, Los Angeles session drummer, formerly of Oingo Boingo

### Tuning the Snare

The snare is probably the most important drum in the set; because you hear it almost every bar on beats 2 and 4, it's the voice of the song, and so it's important to get the snare tuned to where you want it first.

**Snare Drum Tuning Tips**

I like the ring of the drum to decay with the snares. If the snare drum has too much ring:

- ▶ Tune the heads lower.
- ▶ Use a heavier head like a Remo coated CS with the dot on the bottom or a coated Emperor.
- ▶ Use a full or partial muffling ring.
- ▶ Have the edges checked and/or re-cut to a flatter angle.

If the snare drum doesn't have enough ring:

- ▶ Tune the head higher.
- ▶ Use a thinner head like a coated Ambassador or Diplomat.
- ▶ Have the edges checked and/or re-cut to a sharper angle.

If the snares buzz when the tom-toms are hit:

- ▶ Check that the snares are straight. Replace as needed.

- ▶ Check that the snares are flat and centered on the drum.
- ▶ Loosen the bottom head.
- ▶ Retune the offending toms.
- ▶ Use an alternate snare drum.

*I don't think it's good to tune the snare drum on the snare stand. It's better on a table or floor so it's laying flat. Make sure you get the head on flat if you have to change one, then tighten each lug so that it's barely touching the rim, then just finger tighten the lugs (criss-crossing as you go) to be sure you don't over-tighten one. Then you can start using the drum key.* —Bernie Dresel

### Tuning the Kick Drum

If the kick drum isn't punchy and lacks power when played in the context of the music, you can try the following:

- ▶ Try increasing and decreasing the amount of muffling in the drum, or try a different blanket or pillow.
- ▶ Change to a heavier, uncoated head like a clear Emperor or PowerStroke 3.
- ▶ Change to a thinner front head or one with a larger cutout.
- ▶ Have the edges re-cut to create more attack.

### Tuning the Toms

The kick and snare are the two most important drums. I tune the toms around them to try to make sure that the rack toms aren't being set off by the snare.

I like the toms to have a nice, even decay. Usually, I'll tune the drums so that the smallest drums have the shortest decay with the decay getting longer as the drums get bigger.

I tend to tune each tom as far apart as the song will permit. It's easy to get the right spread between a 13- and a 16-inch tom, but it's more difficult to get it between a 12 and a 13. What I try to do is to tune the 12 up and the 13 down a little.

If one or more of the tom-toms are difficult to tune, don't blend together, or have an unwanted "growl," try the following:

- ▶ Check the top heads for dents and replace as necessary.
- ▶ Check the evenness of tension all around on the top and bottom heads.
- ▶ Tighten the bottom head.
- ▶ Have the bearing edges checked and re-cut as required.

If the floor tom has an undesirable "basketball-type" after-ring, try this:

- ▶ Loosen the bottom head.
- ▶ Check the top heads for dents and replace as necessary.
- ▶ Loosen the top head.
- ▶ Switch to a different type or weight top or bottom head like a clear Ambassador or Emperor.
- ▶ Have the bearing edges re-cut to emphasize the lower partials.

*I try to have my three toms (the 12-inch, 14-inch, and 16-inch) a fourth apart in pitch so there's not an octave between the highest tom and the lowest and they sound musical together. If you have a lot of toms, then maybe tuning them a major third apart could work, but with three toms I think a fourth is good because all three are tuned within the same octave. A fifth is too much because then they're not within the same octave.—Bernie Dresel*

## Cymbals

Be careful when you mix cymbal weights for recording. For example, if you're using thin Zildjian A Custom crashes, you don't want to mix in a medium Rock Crash because a thinner cymbal would probably disappear in the mix.

Thicker cymbals are made more with a live situation in mind. They're made to be loud and to cut through the band, but they can sound a little gong-like when recording. On the other hand, if you're playing all Rock Crashes and the engineer can deal with the level, that's not so bad either because the volume will be even.

If the cymbals are cracking or breaking with greater frequency, try the following:

- ▶ Always transport the cymbals in a top-quality, reinforced cymbal case or bag to avoid nicks that can become cracks.
- ▶ Use the proper cymbals felts, washers, and sleeves at all times.
- ▶ Avoid over-tightening the cymbal stand.
- ▶ Use larger or heavier cymbals that you won't have to over-play to hear.

You can find out more about the Drum Doctors at www.drumdoctors.com.

# THE RECORDING DRUMMER

If you've read the previous chapters, you know that the approach and mindset for a recording session is different from a live situation. While many of the following rules also apply to a live gig, there's a slightly different emphasis on preparation. Everything below applies to every recording session, with the possible exception of recording in your own studio.

**Arrive early.** This goes without saying, but I'll say it again to reinforce it. You should always arrive at least an hour before the downbeat of the session because it takes that much time to not only set up your kit, but also to mic the kit. This means that if your session starts at 7:00 p.m., then you need to be there at least by 6:00 to be ready at 7:00. You might even want to get there earlier (if they'll let you) to have some extra time to change your heads and tune your drums. If the session starts at 7:00, find out if that means load-in time or actual downbeat time. No one likes to be kept waiting.

**Change your heads.** Nothing will help the sound of your drums more than new heads. Get a set of new heads (at least for the tops), and either change them before you get to the studio or make sure that you have enough time to do so before recording.

**Make sure your drums are in tune.** Tune your drums as described above or hire someone who really knows how to do it. Not only will you learn something, but you'll also get a much better end result. For more information on drum tuning and drum sounds, check out my book *The Drum Recording Handbook*.

**Bring all your snares to the session.** You never know if a particular snare is right for a song until you try it. Sometimes you can be surprised about how good or how bad a drum sounds in the context of a recording, so to be safe, bring as many snares as you can to the session.

*There are always budget considerations so I generally bring six. I could bring 30 snares but then the cartage bill goes up and, to be honest, you're usually way covered with the six snares because no one is ever asking, "What else have you got?" So I bring three different sizes of wood and three different sizes of metal drums.* —Bernie Dresel

*I usually bring anywhere from five to six. At my studio I have about eight I regularly choose from. You'd be surprised; different drums bring out different spirit in the music.* —Ricky Lawson

*I have two trunks I generally bring that contain ten snare drums, plus I have an old vintage '70s Black Beauty I hand-carry with me. I generally don't use a piccolo, but I have one in my arsenal. You have to make sure you have everything because whatever you don't bring to the session is what the producer will ask for, so I like to be prepared and have plenty of options.* —Brian MacLeod

**Bring extra heads, sticks, beaters, cymbals, and batteries.** Just like when you're onstage, this is the professional thing to do. You need backups in case you break a head, or the battery on your metronome dies. Even if you usually play with only a certain type of stick, bring several kinds (plus mallets and brushes), because that could be the perfect sound for the track you're recording. Even if you think you have everything in your case or gig box, double check to make sure. It's easy to forget the last time you broke a head and that you never replaced the spare.

*I definitely bring a lot of different sticks and brushes and mallets too, because someone will always ask, "Can you do a cymbal swell?" If you look in your stick bag and you don't have them, it is embarrassing to have to tell them, "I can make some with some tissues and duct tape. (Laughs hard)" That's the part of being a session drummer where you have the most anxiety. I like to make sure that my stick bag is loaded with hot-rods, brushes and different-size sticks and mallets.* —Brian MacLeod

**Know your parts before you arrive.** This statement is a little deceiving, because it's altogether possible that your parts will change once you start recording. Until you actually hear the playback, you really don't know how a part fits with all the others. Still, you want to have a starting point, and so it's best to be well rehearsed before the session's downbeat.

**Bring the right cymbals.** Most drummers choose a heavier cymbal for playing live because it's not only louder but also will last longer. Unfortunately, heavy cymbals usually don't sound as good as thinner cymbals under the close scrutiny of recording. If possible, buy, borrow, or rent some lighter cymbals for the recording. Be careful not to mismatch weights though, because the uneven balance will make the engineer's job a lot more difficult.

**If you use electronics, make sure that everything is working.** If you're using a drum machine as a click track, or you're in charge of the sequencer for backing tracks, or you're using electronic pads as a trigger, then make sure that everything is in working order before you arrive in the studio. That includes having extra batteries, power supplies, and cables just in case something breaks down in the course of the session.

**Make any charts, notes, or cheat sheets beforehand.** Again, this comes under the heading of being prepared. You don't want to waste anyone's time for something that could easily have been done beforehand.

**Turn your cell phone off.** The session should be your main priority with as few distractions as possible. One of the easiest ways to achieve this is to turn off your cell phone. If you leave it on, you risk ruining a good take if the ringer goes off. And talking on the phone is the best way to stop the momentum of a session in its tracks. Don't even bother to put it on vibrate; this will cause you to lose your focus just as easily as when the ringer is on. Turn it off; leave it outside the studio so you won't be tempted to use it.

## THE DRUMMER'S UTILITY KIT

As Murphy's Law states, if something can go wrong, it will go wrong, so you've got to be prepared for anything to happen during a gig or session. The following list of items prepares you for just about anything. Each item should be considered just as essential to playing a gig as your kit.

Spare snare top and bottom heads
Spare kick-drum head

Cymbal felts and sleeves
Spare snare strainer
Tuning key
Lots of sticks
Mallets
Brushes
Assorted blankets, pillows, and towels
Drum rug (with a rubber bottom)
Wire snips
Needlenose pliers
Phillips screwdriver
Flat head screwdriver
A set of Allen wrenches
Adjustable wrench
A light source (like a flash light or a clip-on book light)
Masking tape (for attaching drum dampening materials)
Duct tape (for everything else)
Super glue
Can of lightweight oil (for squeaks)
Roll of twine (for securing snares)
(If you use a click, electronic pads, or play-to tracks)
At least two extra 10-foot instrument cables (1/4" to 1/4")
An extra 5-foot cable
RCA to RCA cables
Cable tester
Spare set of headphones
Various cable adapters like 1/4" to RCA, RCA to 1/4", 1/4" to XLR
Spare microphone (if you sing)
Spare microphone cable
Spare mic stand adapter
Spare 9V batteries
Spare AA batteries
Spare universal 9V wall wart
A small notepad
A pen
A magic marker
Band-aids
Throat lozenges
Aspirin or Advil
A towel
Earplugs

# CHAPTER 5

# Keyboards

The keyboard player has a unique and mostly unheralded position in the band. The keyboardist usually has more gear to haul around than the drummer, requires more setup time, needs more technical expertise to simply make his or her instruments work, is rarely a featured player in the band, and is usually the most musically educated player in the band. But even if you're a keyboard player who's used to being pushed into the background, you know how critical your role is to the overall sound of the band.

## DEFINING MOMENTS FOR A KEYBOARD PLAYER

As with every instrument, there are defining moments when the light comes on for a keyboard player.

**Defining Moment 1:** The day you figure out that you don't need to use both hands to fill things up.

If you're playing keys in any type of band that plays modern music, you will be called on to play one of the four categories of keyboard sound: piano, organ, lead sounds, and pads. Except when playing piano, most of the time the left hand rhythmically and sonically gets in the way of the bass player and maybe even the rhythm guitar player. The day you figure out that the left hand can sometimes not only be unnecessary but even harmful to a band's sound is the day you become a mature keyboard player.

Piano is a minor exception. While most schooled pianists have a naturally active left hand, once again it can really get in the way of the rest of the band and cause the low end to get muddy. By simplifying the left hand by just playing root octaves, the piano feels powerful yet still stays out of the way, and even that can sometimes be improved by playing the left hand up an octave.

**Defining Moment 2:** The day you learn how powerful simple pads are.

Let's face it: if you're an educated player, the last thing that you want to do is play a simple triad. It's boring and way beneath the talents of any knowledgeable musician. On the face of it, that's true, but simple triad pads are the glue that holds together modern popular music. So what's a pad? It's a chord with long sustaining notes (sometimes called "footballs" because they're written as whole notes, which look like footballs on staff paper). Pads are what guitar players tend to play when they play keyboards, but no matter who plays them, they're very powerful.

Pads can be very subtle, especially in the background where they don't stand out yet hold everything together (listen to "Clocks" or almost anything by Coldplay for a good example of a pad). In early rock music, pads were played initially by an organ (usually a Hammond) and were soon joined by the Fender Rhodes and Wurlitzer electric pianos. Soon afterwards, synthesizers took over the job of pad maker as a whole new world of sound opened up (they ended up emulating the organ and electric piano too).

Regardless of the sound or instrument, most pads are built around simple triads since, like many other things in modern music, simplicity usually works the best in the context of a song. The day a keyboard player learns the power of the simple pad is a defining moment.

## THE CLASSIC PATCHES

As stated above, there are four basic families of sounds that most modern keyboard players are called on to play: piano, organ, lead sounds, and pads. Maybe you'll have to play all four or maybe just one or two in the context of your band and the music you play, but this is basically what there is to choose from.

The piano sound has always been a rock 'n' roll mainstay, whether it's a variation of a grand piano sample from either a keyboard, dedicated sampler, plug-in, or sound library. There's a ton of different versions available, though none sound exactly like the real thing. That shouldn't matter too much, especially for live use. Note that we're not referring at all to an electric piano here. Because of the way it sonically lays into a track and can sustain notes, an electric piano is usually categorized under pads rather than piano.

Most organ sounds are based upon a Hammond organ with a Leslie speaker. Once again, while you might find a pretty close simulation, these sounds are no match for the real thing. But the real thing is a four-hundred-pound beast (and another hundred and twenty-five for the Leslie) that takes at least two really strong guys to move around (and four if you have to carry it up stairs) so there's usually no contest as to which one you'll end up using. Let's put it this way: I owned a really sweet Hammond B-3 that I loved to death, but even I would use some sort of a simulation for a gig these days. For recording, it's a different story all together—the Hammond wins.

As stated a few paragraphs earlier, pads started from an organ sound, expanded to electric pianos, and then finally to synthesizers. Early synths were initially trying to emulate either strings or horns, and did a really poor job of it. But a bad string sound actually makes a pretty good pad, and as synths got more sophisticated, so did pad sounds—to the point where anything you buy today has a great many not-found-in-nature sounds that do a glorious job at the task (listen to Coldplay's "Clocks" again). Pads are glue. They're subtle, and they stay in the background, but they're essential to today's music.

Lead lines came originally from the grandfather synths like the Arp Odyssey and Minimoog, which only played one note at a time (listen to Steve Miller's classic "Fly Like an Eagle" for a great Minimoog sound). Once again, these old synths have a sound which is only emulated and not truly captured today, and almost all synths currently manufactured are polyphonic, but the sound used for lead lines, solos, and fills remains the same.

While it might be tempting to buy a vintage keyboard like an Arp 2600, Minimoog, or Mellotron, the problem is that most vintage pieces are very unstable in their tuning and need to be frequently repaired. Since the electronics are ancient by today's standards, finding a technician that knows how to work on one is no easy task, and being able to pay for the repair might not be easy either.

# THE KEYBOARD PLAYER ONSTAGE

It used to be that the keyboard player had the toughest time being heard and had to resort to all sorts of wacky ways, like buying your own PA system, to get the level up to a point where not only you, but also your fellow band members and the audience could hear the sound. (I know; I was there, once.) Today it's a whole lot easier to project above the rest of the band as needed, but cutting through the mix is still the first concern of a keyboardist.

That being said, unless you're consistently playing through a fairly large sound system with some great monitors, keyboards need the best, most high-fidelity amplification in the band. This means that guitar amps definitely won't do (unless you want that Marshall sound like Deep Purple's Jon Lord used to get or Ben Folds gets now), for a number of reasons. First, the level from a keyboard is a lot hotter than that from a guitar, and so it's almost certain that you'll overload the input of the amp and get a distorted sound. Second, the speakers are probably inadequate for keyboards, because they have limited frequency response that's perfect for guitars, but will make the keyboards sound kind of "honky"—since you'll hear mostly midrange with not a lot of highs or lows.

Most amplifier manufacturers do make what they call "keyboard amps," but they're more aimed at the guy playing in a jazz trio than for keyboards in a band that has to keep up with some loud guitars and a rhythm section. Even so, if you must buy a keyboard amp, make sure you get one with as much power as you can get and with at least a 15-inch speaker and some kind of high-frequency horn or tweeter. That way, at least you'll have some fidelity and maybe enough level to compete with loud guitar amps.

In fact, the best way to approach amplification for keyboards is about the same as it was back in the "old days"—with a PA system. Not a full system, actually, just some pieces. A fairly inexpensive yet totally adequate system would consist of one or two floor monitors and either a PA head or a small mixer and power amplifier. That way, you'd never have to worry about having enough inputs if you get more keyboards or outboard gear, and you can even use the system as a small PA if needed. If monitors aren't enough, a larger PA cabinet will be more than adequate for getting your level above the band.

If the band has a PA system or always plays in clubs that have large PA systems, then you can go to a personal in-ear monitor system as outlined in Chapter 13, as long as you trust the soundman to adequately get you in the mix.

Many venues run their PAs in mono, which means that if you're relying solely on the PA for your keyboard amplification, then you should be in mono too. Many keyboards have lush stereo sounds (like grand pianos) that sound great—in stereo. Use the keyboard's "L/mono" output, however, and a lot of them start to sound really thin and cheesy. If this happens, try using your keyboard's "other" output if it has one. That's the one that is not the mono-mix output. You'll get one side of the stereo picture, but won't have two out-of-phase piano samples thinning out the sound. If you don't have an "other" output available, many new keyboards also have piano sounds optimized for mono, which will sound better than just one side of stereo or the stereo blended into mono.

## Getting to the Stage

Although guitar amps are heavy, keyboards are heavy and bulky, which make them really hard to carry. Do yourself a favor and get a hand truck, or at least a furniture dolly, to minimize the number of trips to your vehicle. Don't depend on the venue's having one. Even if one is available, it's often pretty old and rickety, or the venue is already using it to re-supply the bar.

An even better way to go is with a Rock-N-Roller Multi-Cart (see Fig. 5.1), which is purpose built for moving musical equipment. These carts adjust in length, have fold-up brackets on each end to keep the gear on the cart, and even have inflatable tires. Do whatever you have to in order to get loaded in and set up on time, so that you don't keep anyone waiting. A good dolly or hand truck will really help a lot (and help your back too).

*Fig. 5.1. Rock-N-Roller Multi-Cart.*

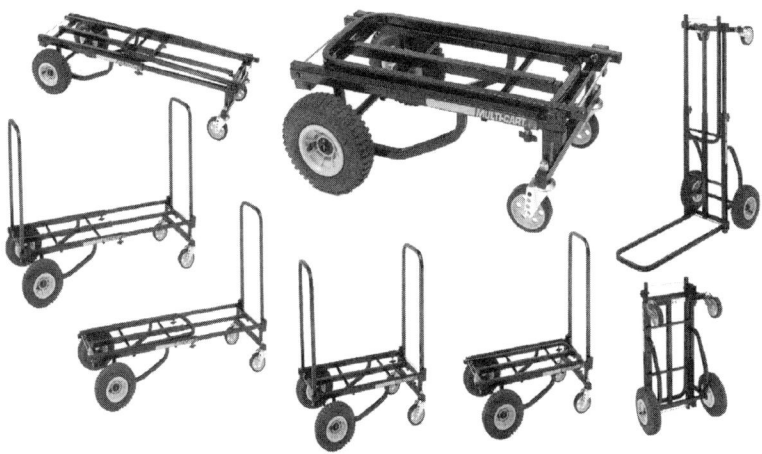

### The Quick Set-Up

If you have an extensive keyboard rig, there are some tricks that you can use to make setup go a lot faster and be more reliable. The more setup you can do offstage, the easier it will be for everyone onstage. Nothing's harder than trying to set up with a bunch of empty cases lying around. Try these tips to make your setup easier:

- ▶ First, place all your power strips and extension cords at the point where you'll be setting up, even before you set your boards onstage.
- ▶ Next, place your amplification on the stage. This includes any mixer, power amp, speaker cabinet, or amplifier. Connect as much of the gear as you can (like speaker cabinets to head, or mixer to power amp).
- ▶ Run any cables from the mixer or amp to where the keyboards will be. To make your cable runs easier, consider either buying prefab snakes or making one by bundling the cables that you normally use together, using plastic cable ties or a plastic cable conduit like the ones that AudioSkin makes. Avoid running audio cables and power cables together in the same bundle; that could cause noise or hum in the audio. Make sure you label everything so that you know which cable goes to which keyboard.
- ▶ Place your keyboards on their stands. To make this go faster, make sure you mark exactly where the height adjustment on the stand is for your playing style, so that you'll always set it back to the same place.
- ▶ Connect the cables to the keyboards. Avoid winding your cables around the stand like a barber pole, because it will take a lot of extra time to break down, and you'll hate yourself if you have to replace a cable during the show. Some Velcro straps like the ones used for mic cables can attach your cables nicely.
- ▶ Have a few pedals? Make your life easier by taking a cue from guitarists and mount your pedals on a pedal board. That way, setup and tear down will be easier, and your pedals will always stay in the same place. You can make one yourself, or just buy one from any number of vendors.

## THE RECORDING KEYBOARD PLAYER

As stated in other chapters, the approach and mindset for a recording session is different from that for a live situation. While many of the following rules also apply to a live gig, there's a slightly different emphasis on preparation. Everything below applies to every recording session, with the possible exception of recording in your own studio.

**Arrive early.** This goes without saying, but I'll say it yet one more time to reinforce it. You should always arrive at least a half-hour before the downbeat of the session, and earlier if you have sophisticated setup. This means that if your session starts at 7:00 p.m., you need to be there at 6:30 to be ready for 7:00. Getting there at 6:55 doesn't cut it. If the session starts at 7:00 p.m., find out if that means load-in time or actual downbeat time. No one likes to be kept waiting.

**Turn your cell phone off.** The session should be your main priority with as few distractions as possible. One of the easiest ways to achieve this is to turn off your cell phone. If you leave it on, you risk ruining a good take if the ringer goes off, and talking on the phone is the best way to stop the momentum of a session in its tracks. Don't even bother to put it on vibrate as this will cause you to lose your focus just as easily as when the ringer is on. Turn it off; then leave it outside the studio so you won't be tempted to use it.

**Know your gear inside and out.** It's important that you know your gear so well that you're able to get a sound up as soon as you can. Nothing stops a session cold like a keyboard player hunting and pecking around for a sound.

**Turn the plug-ins off unless you're specifically asked to add them.** Reverb, delay, compressor, and limiter plug-ins should be avoided while recording unless the engineer or producer asks you specifically to dial one up. Most of the time, the engineer has a better sounding one available and is more proficient in dialing up a sound than you are.

**Make sure the piano is in tune.** If you're going to a studio that has a real piano that you intend to play, call ahead and make sure that it's been recently tuned. If it hasn't, consider getting it tuned specifically for your session and make sure that it's tuned to A-440. This is a worthwhile investment if the piano will be an integral part of your sound.

**Bring all your keyboards to the session.** A recording is made interesting by multiple layers of different sounding instruments. You'll never know when something that you haven't used in years will be just the right sound for the song. Even though most modern keyboards have a wide variety of sounds, they do tend to have a similar tonal quality due to using the same analog-to-digital converters and output circuitry. Each keyboard has at least one patch that's unique, and you'll never know when it'll be just the right thing to make a song special. To truly get a distinctive sound on the recording, bring any keyboards that you have, even if you don't normally use them. The exception here is if the studio is so small that you can't fit everything or the producer or engineer specifically tells you what to bring or what not to bring.

**Bring extra pedals, tubes, cables and batteries.** Just like onstage, this is the professional thing to do. You have to have backups in case a volume pedal gets scratchy or a tube or battery dies. Even if you think you have everything in your case or gig box, double check to make sure.

**Know your parts before you arrive.** This is a little deceiving in that it's altogether possible that your parts will change once you start recording. Until you actually hear the playback, you really don't know how a part fits with all the others. Still, you want to have a starting point, so it's best to be well rehearsed before the session's downbeat.

**Have your amp tuned up.** Keyboard players don't tend to use tube amplification, but if a tube amp or Leslie is part of your sound and you plan on using it to record, you'd better make sure that it's working its very best. While you might be able to get away with it onstage, you'll never be able to successfully record with an amp that is either buzzing, farting, or randomly spitting and quitting. If it's good enough to play through, then it's good enough to have in good working order. If not, the tracks you put down will only have to be redone later. You always want the amp to sound the best it can.

**Make sure your cables are good.** It's easy to keep playing with a cable that cuts out or makes noise occasionally, but anything less than a perfect cable is a definite no-no for recording.

Having to redo the perfect take because your cord cut out is bound to upset you and everyone else in the studio. Cables are cheap. Buy a new one if you have any doubts about what you have.

**Make any charts, notes or cheat sheets beforehand.** Once again, this comes under the heading of being prepared. You don't want to be wasting anyone's time on something that easily could have been prepared beforehand.

## THE KEYBOARD PLAYER'S UTILITY KIT

As Murphy's Law states, if something can go wrong, it will go wrong, so you have to be prepared for any eventuality during a gig. Things break, but a pro is always ready. The following list of items prepares you for just about anything. Each item should be considered just as essential to playing a gig as your keyboard. Don't forget the hand truck or furniture mover to save your back—and your band mates'.

- 2 spare power tubes (if you use a tube amplifier)
- 2 spare 12AX7 preamp tubes (if you use a tube amplifier)
- Package of fuses
- An extra volume pedal
- An extra sustain pedal
- Spare keyboard stand
- A hand truck or furniture mover
- A light source (like a flashlight or a clip-on book light)
- Gaffer's or duct tape
- Super glue
- One extra MIDI cable if you don't usually use MIDI (two if you use it all the time)
- An extra USB cable
- At least two extra 10-foot instrument cables (1/4" to 1/4")
- An extra 5-foot cable
- RCA to RCA cable
- Various cable adapters like 1/4" to RCA, RCA to 1/4", 1/4" to XLR
- Cable tester
- Direct box with a ground lift switch
- Extra power cable
- Extra power strip
- An AC extension cord (or two)

Spare microphone (if you sing)
Spare microphone cable
Spare mic stand adapter
Spare 9V batteries
Spare AA batteries
Spare universal 9V wall wart
A small notepad
A pen
A magic marker
Band-aids
Throat lozenges
Aspirin or Advil
Earplugs
A towel

# CHAPTER 6

# Vocals

Vocals are the one instrument in the band that is usually left to chance and luck. While most players spend hours and hours learning their instruments, vocalists and players who sing spend little time developing their instruments. As a result, there are a lot of simple things that can really help your performance, but usually are taken for granted or just overlooked.

## THE THREE PS—PITCH, POCKET, PASSION

In the studio, the three Ps are what a producer lives by. You've got to have all three to have a dynamite vocal. And while pitch and pocket problems can be fixed by studio trickery, if you don't have passion, you don't have a vocal. On stage, the three Ps are just as important—maybe even more so—because you don't have any of the advantages of the studio. Let's take a look inside the three Ps.

### Pitch

Staying in pitch means singing in tune. And not just some of the notes—every single note! They're all equally important! Singing in tune requires real concentration and awareness. If you know that you have a constant pitch problem (singing either sharp or flat), then there are some really simple things to try that might help.

- ▶ Singing sharp is usually caused by the power of your voice blanking out any background pitch reference. You're singing too hard to hear yourself! The fix is easy: Just ask for more vocal in the monitors or headphones.
- ▶ Singing a touch flat is easily fixed by simply lifting your eyebrows or smiling. Smiling is not only recommended, it's required, because it provides proper relaxation of the facial, cranial, and neck muscles.
- ▶ Correct head position and correct position of the abdomen is needed to have enough air to stay on pitch. It's beyond the scope of this book to show you how, but you can consult a vocal coach for help.
- ▶ The more relaxed you are, the easier it will be to hit the higher notes in your range. Yawning is a recommendable warm-up because it promotes relaxation.

Pitch also means following the melody reliably. There's a trend these days to scat sing around a melody, and while that might be desirable in some genres, it doesn't work in any genre if you do it all the time. Scatting might show off your technique and ability but a song has a melody for a reason. That's what people know, that's what they can sing to themselves, and usually that's what they want to hear.

### You've Got to Hear Yourself

In order to stay in tune, you've got to hear yourself. How much you hear yourself will actually determine whether or not you stay in pitch.

As I stated previously, some singers sing sharp when they sing too hard. They push themselves over the top of the correct pitch when they can't hear themselves in the monitors or headphones. *The secret is to have either more vocal or less of everything else in the monitors or phones. But be aware: pitch and timing problems also occur if you hear too much of yourself in the mix.*

If you're singing flat, get a little less of yourself (or more of everyone else) in the mix, because it's not unusual for pitch to change with intensity. Less vocal makes you want to sing harder (and possibly raise your pitch slightly) and vice versa.

Sometimes there's too much in the mix, and thinning it out a little can help with pitch problems. First, ask for more bass (the root of all chords) and kick (the root of all rhythm) to help with pitch and pocket. Next, turn down anything that is heavily chorused and turn up anything that has a more "centered" tonal frequency (like a piano). Sometimes listening to only the rhythm guitar instead of two guitars (if you have two in your band) can be helpful; some singers can hear their pitch better from a simple tonally centered instrument than from screaming guitars or airy synth patches.

## Pocket

Singing "in the pocket" means singing in time and in the "groove" (the rhythm) of the song. You can be on pitch, but if you're wavering ahead of or behind the beat it won't *feel* right. All of the things advocated elsewhere in this book that help instrumentalists also apply to vocals. Concentrate on the downbeat (on beat 1) to get your entrances. Concentrate on the snare drum (on 2 and 4) to stay in the pocket.

> *Quincy [producer Quincy Jones] used to say that some singers have it in the pocket of their voice. Supposedly Michael Jackson has such an amazing pocket that he could sing a line and you could build a groove around it.*—Frank Fitzpatrick

## Passion

Passion is not necessarily something that can be taught. To some degree, you either have it or you don't. What is passion? It's the ability to sell the lyrical content of the song through performance. It's the ability to make me, as a listener, believe in what you're singing; that you're talking directly to me and not anyone else. And passion can sometimes trump pitch and pocket. A not-all-that-great singer who can convey the emotion in his or her voice is way more interesting to listen to than a polished singer who hits every note perfectly but with little emotion. In fact, just about any vocalist that you'd consider a "star" has passion, and that's why he or she is a star.

Onstage, passion can sometimes take a back seat to stamina, since you have to save yourself for a whole show and you can't blow it all out in one song. That's why many singers have only one or two big production numbers where they totally whip it out. This means that you have to learn the limits of your voice, learn how much of you goes into just cruising and when you can do it, and how much you need left in the tank to do your biggest, most effective show stoppers.

In the studio, there's never any cruising—you've got to give all the passion you can give for every song. A few paragraphs ago I said that you either have passion or you don't, but sometimes you really have it and you don't know it, and it's the job of the producer to pull it out of you. That could mean getting the singer angry to stir some emotion, building him up by telling him how good he is, or making him laugh to loosen him up—anything to sell the song! But once you know how to summon it up from inside you, you can do it again and again.

*You're telling a story that's real to you. Do you believe in what you're singing about? You have to convey it from a place other than your memory of a bunch of words and chord changes.* —Frank Fitzpatrick

## CHANGE THE KEY

This is the number-one problem of many cover bands—trying to sing a song in the wrong key for the singer. It's no badge of honor to play a song in the key of the record. The audience doesn't care. They just want you to sound great. Change the key to one that's in your range and showcases your talent.

Now some songs that are E or A guitar songs naturally sound better in those keys, but if the guitarist has a second guitar, now is the time to break it out and retune it to E♭ or D, or use a capo if an open E or A sounds that much better. That's what the pros do.

## TAKE CARE OF YOURSELF

Since the vocalist is the only musician who can't put their instrument away in a protective case after the gig or rehearsal, it's important to take very good care of it. Eventually every singer has some vocal trouble, and if you're not careful, it can really lead to long-term damage. That's why it's important for a singer to learn to be especially aware of the need to take care of his or her voice.

Aside from being sick, the number one cause of vocal problems is not getting enough sleep. When you're tired, all the parts of your body needed to support your vocal cords tend to weaken a bit, which leads to improper breathing and thus throat problems shortly after you begin to sing. Get as much sleep as you can (preferably seven or eight hours) the night before a gig, or at least take a nap on the day of the gig so you can feel somewhat refreshed.

The next thing is to avoid milk (or any dairy products, for that matter) for three to six hours before you sing. Anything with milk in it will cause an excess production of phlegm around your vocal chords, so that's a definite no-no. The old remedy of milk and honey for a rough throat is very soothing—but have it after the gig, not before!

If you are hungry before a gig, don't be afraid to eat, but just eat until you're satisfied and don't stuff yourself with a seven-course meal. Try not to eat in the last hour before your performance in order to avoid that excess phlegm. You may be tempted to clear your throat (which can be harmful) immediately after eating, but waiting an hour is usually enough time for your meal to settle.

Speaking of clearing your throat, there are some who say that you should never try to clear your throat because it can cause damage, but it's usually necessary because excess mucous inhibits—really inhibits—your singing. The trick is to find a way to clear your throat without irritating it. The best way is to do a gentle "whispered cough," and then swallow and repeat. If this doesn't work, you need to deal with the excess mucous production. Squeeze a quarter of a lemon into a tall glass of water and sip over a period of about twenty minutes. This should cut through a lot of the excess mucous.

Other things to avoid are alcohol, tea (despite popular belief), coffee, cola, and anything else with caffeine, since these actually have a dehydrating effect, which is quite the opposite of what you really need.

One thing you should do is drink lots and lots of water (ideally two to three quarts a day—the more the better) because a dry throat leads to a sore throat. If you live in an arid climate like Arizona, sleep with a humidifier next to your bed and try to warm up your voice in the shower. The moisture can be an incredible help for your voice. Also, learn to breathe in through your nose as much as possible. This will help moisten the air before it reaches your vocal cords.

Finally, some singers swear by Entertainer's Secret (see Fig. 6.1), a spray mixture that lubricates the vocal cords and was developed by an ear, nose, and throat specialist. You can get more information at entertainers-secret.com.

*Fig. 6.1 Entertainer's Secret.*

### *If You Get a Sore Throat*

Maybe you have a sore throat from a cold or you just sang too much last night, but if you have to go out and sing again you're going to have to take some precautions to be able to get through the gig. Here are some things to try as soon as you feel yourself getting sore.

- Warm drinks (act as decongestants)
- Fruit or fruit drinks (but not too acidic)
- Use your voice as little as possible (that includes speaking and singing)

Try this little mixture to make your voice feel better: Squeeze one fresh lemon into a glass, and add a couple of teaspoons of clear honey and a little bit of water to mix. Gargle; then swallow. The honey coats the vocal chords and the lemon makes you salivate, thus stopping them from drying out.

Another remedy that you can use for a sore throat (and other cold symptoms as well) is to add a mixture of honey and apple cider vinegar to hot water. Alone, the vinegar would probably hurt the throat because of its acid nature, but mixed with the honey it becomes a source of energy. The exact mixture depends on your taste and the size of the cup. First add the honey to the water until it tastes sweet enough and then add the vinegar until it tastes like a hot apple cider (more or less). Take it a few times a day, the more the better.

And again, avoid tea, coffee, and alcohol before singing, as these can have a dehydrating effect.

And above all, *rest*!

## TAKE SOME VOICE LESSONS

Don't be afraid to take some lessons to help you get your vocal chops together. It's not uncommon for vocalists (especially hard rock singers) to be terrified that a singing coach will change them into an opera singer, but that's not what's going to happen. A good singing coach wants to get you to use the proper technique to enhance your range and sing free of throat damage—not to change your style. There are a lot of benefits to a good coach, not the least is being able to sing for long periods of time with ease. No one wants to lose it before the set or the gig ends. A good coach can also give you some tips to cope with those times when your voice is not up to par because you're under the weather. As we said before, that's the time when you're most vulnerable to long-term vocal damage.

A singing coach will help you get:

- ▶ more power with less effort
- ▶ better pitch
- ▶ higher range
- ▶ more stamina
- ▶ a healthier voice
- ▶ the best warm-up technique for your voice

So give it a try. Even just a few lessons can make a big difference.

## MIC TECHNIQUE

Having good mic technique means two things: understanding that a microphone's diaphragm reacts with varying sensitivity to your vocal performance, and knowing how to adjust your body to take advantage of it. Microphones can be used effectively to hide as well as enhance a singer's faults. One of the most common techniques used to hide a lack of sustained breath control is to hold the microphone away from you when starting a sustained note and bringing it closer to the mouth as the note diminishes. To the audience the note appears to maintain its volume, although it is important to keep on pitch and not attempt to hold the note for longer than is comfortable!

If you're going to deliver a quiet, intimate vocal from start to finish, you can afford to position your mouth just a few inches (or even less) from the microphone. If the vocal is to be sung full volume throughout the song, it may be better to back away six inches. Quite often though, a song is dynamic enough to require different amounts of air to be pushed at different times. Singers with good mic technique will move their body closer to or farther away from the mic as the song unfolds. Ideally, your mouth is as close to the mic as possible before overloading it with level (which may cause it to distort or, with some super-sensitive condenser microphones, even temporarily shut down).

Tip: don't be afraid to move your head back a couple inches for just a phrase or even a syllable. You can also aim your mouth slightly above or to the side of the mic for particularly loud moments.

# HARMONY VOCALS TAKE MORE TIME

While a band can begin to sound reasonably good together within two or three months of playing on a regular basis, vocals seem to take about twice as long to really meld together. Ideally, you want any background vocals to blend so well that they sound like one entity, but unless you actually put the singing time in, it usually just sounds like a bunch of individual voices in the beginning. If vocals are a big part of your band, my suggestion is to spend as much time rehearsing vocals as you rehearse your instruments. This will speed up the process of tightening your vocals.

### Rehearse Without the Band First

The best way to get the harmony vocals together is to have vocal-only rehearsals. This means that you just sit around your rehearsal space or someone's house or bedroom even, working on only the vocals. This is almost essential for complex harmonies since it's sometimes impossible to hear the nuances that you need to hear during a full-volume rehearsal. It's also great for the lead singer because it's easier to hear any pitch or pocket problems at this level rather than with a roaring band behind him. An acoustic guitar or keyboard (with the drummer hitting a practice pad for time) is all that you need as a chordal reference.

While it's easy to sing simple or complex harmonies when you're not playing an instrument, it gets a lot harder when you actually have to play your instrument and hear all the other parts. The way to make it easier is for the band to play at half-volume while you repeat the sections that have harmonies. In other words, you'd repeat the chorus over and over until playing and singing the harmony becomes second nature. When this happens, you can proceed to a full-volume rehearsal, confident that you'll be able to hear your part and sing it in pitch and in time.

# PHRASING IS EVERYTHING

Singing together really means that you have to sing together—exactly. Every vocalist has to sing exactly the same way with the same inflections, slurs, and the same attacks (starts) and releases (stops). Usually this means that one vocal part will be the reference part and all others will follow the lead. The way that I've seen great background singers work is for one to say, "Sing it to me. Show me what you're doing," and then they'd try to match it exactly. It works for them and it will work for you too.

## Attacks and, Especially, Releases

Attacks and releases are the secret to tight music, whether you're playing it or singing it. While it's usually easy to get the attack part (where everyone starts at exactly the same time), the release part (everyone ending at the same time) is usually overlooked. The releases are just as important as the attacks, and just tightening up this one area will make your group sound so tight you won't believe it. So remember, everyone starts and stops at the same time. A great example of background vocal with a tight release is the very end to the theme song for the television show *American Dad*. Listen to how tight "Good morning, USA" is. That's what you're going for.

## Background Vocals Need Attention, Too

It's too easy to say, "Just throw a background part on this," or "Hey, sing a little background here." It's true that background vocal parts are taken for granted, but they really shouldn't be. In fact, background vocal parts are so important that it can make the difference between your band sounding polished or like it just came out of the garage. Background parts are integral parts of the song that require the exact same attention as the drum, bass, guitar, keys, or lead vocals. In fact, a bad background vocal part can easily sink a song that otherwise sounds great.

You can't have someone sing background just for the sake of singing background, either for ego's sake or because there's another vocal on the record that you're covering. If it's a part worth doing, then it's a part that must stand on its own. It either sounds great or you can't do it!

If the bass player can't remember the harmony, or the drummer always sings flat, you've got to work on it until they do a better job or lose the part all together. Believe me, people won't care if a part is missing, but they'll notice if a part is there that sucks.

## Gang Vocals

Gang vocals are when all the background vocals sing the same thing in unison that the lead singer sings. This usually happens in the chorus. An example would be a song like Kiss's "Rock and Roll All Night." It's not uncommon for a band to get some of its members who don't usually sing, to sing for a gang vocal. It's easy because you don't have to worry about a harmony. This can be a big mistake, because you still have to be concerned about pitch and phrasing, just as with harmony vocals. Don't make this mistake. Work on all of your vocals, even if you don't think they're important. They are, and every single part needs the same attention as the lead vocal. Remember, if it doesn't sound great, eliminate it!

## THE RECORDING VOCALIST

As stated in the previous chapters, the approach and mindset for a recording session is different from a live situation, and most of the items are the same.

**Arrive early.** Once again this goes without saying, but I'll say it again to reinforce it. You should always arrive at least a half-hour before the downbeat of the session. This means that if your session starts at 7:00 p.m., then you need to be there at least by 6:30 or earlier to be ready for 7:00. Just because you're the singer and don't have any gear to set up doesn't mean that you should show at 6:55. In fact, you need to get there early, so that you can warm up and be ready when it's time to record.

**Turn your cell phone off.** The session should be your main priority with as few distractions as possible, so turn off your cell phone. If you leave it on, not only do you risk ruining a good take if the ringer goes off, but talking on the phone is the best way to stop the momentum of a session in its tracks. Don't even bother to put it on vibrate since this will cause you to lose your focus just as easily as when the ringer is on. Turn it off; then leave it outside the studio so you won't be tempted to use it.

**Make sure you warm up before singing.** Make sure that you've properly warmed up before you begin to record, especially if you're going to sing aggressively or scream (good advice for singing live as well). You can cause serious damage to your vocal chords as well as blow yourself out before you get a good take.

**Have something to moisten the throat handy.** Warm water, some mild fruit juice, or Entertainer's Friend are always good to have on hand. Warm water with a little honey and lemon with both coat your vocal cords and cause you to salivate.

Stay away from beer, cola, tea, and coffee, as these will actually dehydrate you.

**Be sure to get your headphone mix right.** The phone mix is really important to your overall performance. Your pitch can suffer if you can't hear yourself enough but if you hear yourself too much you might not sing aggressively enough. Try listening with one earphone off your head to see if it helps.

**Know your parts before you arrive.** This is a little deceiving in that it's altogether possible that your parts will change once you start recording. Until you actually hear the playback, you really don't know how a part fits with all the others. Still, you want to have a starting point so it's best to be well rehearsed before the session's downbeat.

**Make any charts, notes, or cheat sheets beforehand.** Once again this comes under the heading of being prepared. You don't want to be wasting anyone's time on something that could so easily have been done beforehand. It usually helps to have the lyrics typed out for a reference, with any marks to illustrate special attention to either the lyrics themselves or how they're sung.

# CHAPTER 7

# Percussion, Horns, DJs, and Others

Although it may seem like this book is slanted toward rock 'n' roll bands, all of the tips, tricks, and rules apply to almost any kind of band doing almost any kind of music, so it's important to include a section for musicians who play instruments other than the traditional guitar, bass, drums, keys, and vocals. While much from previous chapters can be applied here, each instrument in this chapter has its own set of considerations.

## FOR PERCUSSIONISTS

Most young bands don't consider a percussionist an essential element to get the sound they want, but a good percussionist adds a great deal to a band. A percussionist's contribution is usually subtle—you only notice when it's not there—but essential to so many records that you probably don't notice until it's pointed out. Indeed, almost every producer considers percussion to be the final, yet essential, icing on the cake. The cake without it is still good cake; the cake with it is fantastic.

Percussion adds motion to the song and emphasizes beats and accents. Listen to the double-time maracas and the congas on the Stones' "Sympathy for the Devil." Listen to Jack Ashford's tambourine on just about anything from the Motown of Detroit. These are prime examples of how percussion can really add something to a song.

A percussionist must be deeply tied to the groove of the drummer. They almost have to think like one person to complement each other to the fullest. The level of communication has to be on an almost unconscious level, so both drummer and percussionist have to respect one another as players, can't be insecure about their job or their playing, and can't be rivals for the groove or attention. If that happens, you're eventually going to have something like the "clash of the guitar players" discussed in Chapter 2.

## The Percussionist's Utility Kit

While we won't get into the percussionist's utility kit as deeply as the other instruments, there's one major area that every percussionist should not leave to the random selection of the house soundman, and that's microphones. It's extremely important for you to invest in a set of microphones and (if needed) stands to ensure that you're adequately covered. It's not even a bad idea to invest in your own mixer, so that you always have enough inputs available to the house console. Usually a soundman will give you whatever mics he has left over after miking the vocals, drums, guitars, and bass, but you can't always be sure that the mics he gives you will be working well. So do yourself a favor: if you're serious about being a percussionist, invest in some mics so you're always covered and sound the same from gig to gig. Any of the clip-on mics from Shure (see Fig. 7.1), Audio-Technica, or Sennheiser will work fine. Get rid of those nasty stands that always get in the way, but you'll probably still need at least one mic on a stand (an SM58 will work fine and can double as a vocal mic) for tambourine and shakers.

Also, you can use most of the Drummer's Utility Kit described in Chapter 3.

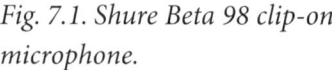

*Fig. 7.1. Shure Beta 98 clip-on microphone.*

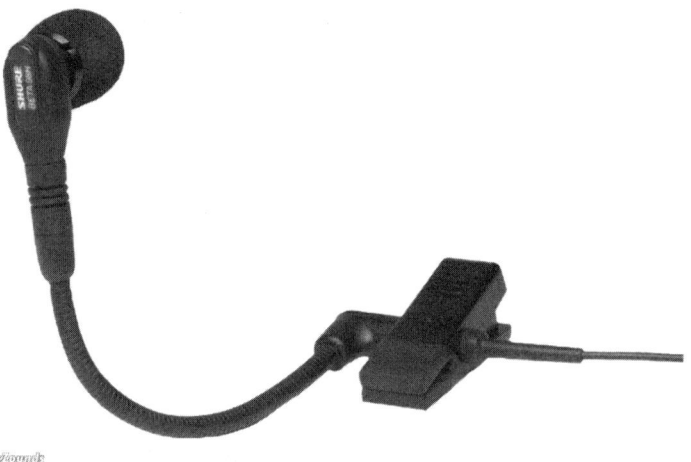

# FOR HORN PLAYERS

One of the biggest pains for a horn player is being miked onstage. Although standard vocal mics like Shure SM58s work well for both brass and reed instruments, most players hate playing into one on a fixed stand since it limits playing comfort. As with the other instrumentalists referred to in this book, it's almost always in your best interest to take matters into your own hands.

Clip-on mics are now available from a number of manufacturers, and they have the dual function of sounding great while increasing your playing comfort (see Fig. 7.2). That being said, clip-on mics are likely to cost you more than stand-mounted mics and most of them are condenser mics, which means they need to be powered to make them work. While most house mixing consoles can supply power (called phantom power) to the mic, you might want to purchase an external AC or battery power supply just to be sure you're covered for any situation.

*Fig. 7.2. SD Systems LCM89 clip-on mic.*

While most clip-on mics are condensers, SDS Systems (www.sdsystems.com) is one of the few companies that offer a dynamic (non-powered) mic. They also offer a wide range of condenser clip-on mics, all designed specifically for musical instruments.

The next big problem is hearing yourself. Luckily, there's an inexpensive solution called a sound reflector, which is a piece of clear Plexiglas that mounts either directly to the bell of the horn or on a mic stand (see Fig. 7.3). The idea is to reflect sound back at you so you don't have to rely on monitors. You can easily make your own or buy one of the many commercial versions available: the Ploeger Sound Mirror, Soundback reflector, or Note Bandit.

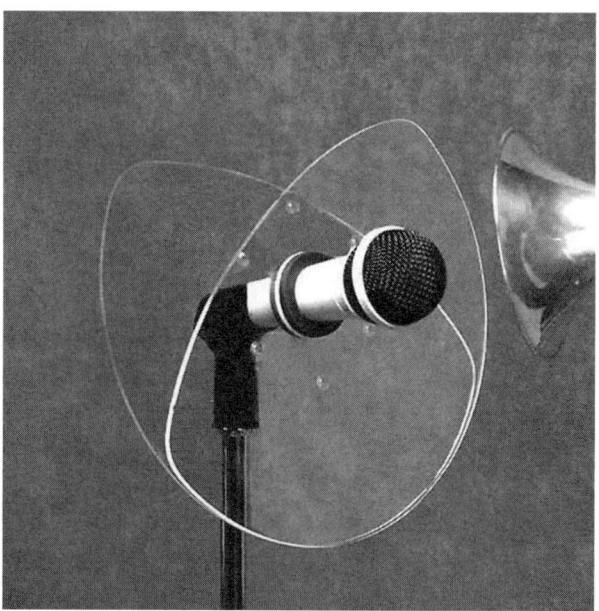

*Fig. 7.3. Soundback reflector.*

Another way to improve your monitoring is to use a personal monitoring system as described in Chapter 13.

## THE HORN PLAYER'S UTILITY KIT

Nearly every horn player brings most of these items already, but it's always good to have a list.

> Horn mutes
> Valve oil
> Extra straps
> Cork grease
> Swabs
> Oils, powders, and maintenance materials

Horn stands
Reed holders
A couple of mouthpiece patches
Batteries (if you need to power a personal mic or wireless battery pack)

## FOR DJS

We're counting DJs in the context of a band here, and not the kind that spin discs by themselves at parties. DJs are similar to keyboard players in that their gear can be complex, especially if a computer is involved. Their function in the context of a band is usually more like a percussionist adding subtle flavors that enhance the mood and push the groove.

That being said, it's important to know who's driving the bus. If it's the DJ, it's important to choose tempos that are pitched to A-440 or the band will never be in tune with what he's spinning. Choosing a time "in between the cracks" might match the beats from record to record, but the band can't tune on the fly, so everything will tend to sound like a jumbled mess. Of course, matching the band's tuning is just as important if the DJ is spinning to the bands.

### The DJ's Utility Kit
Extra set of headphones
Extra cartridge and stylus (if you're using real turntables)
Extra turntable
Extra slip mats
Most of the electronic items in the Keyboard Utility Kit from Chapter 5

## FOR OTHER INSTRUMENTS

For sure, any other instrument you can think of has been or is being used in the context of a band. Violins, cellos, fiddles, pedal steel, blues harp, banjo, you name it—the list goes on and on—but the playing considerations are all the same as the ones described in the previous chapters. In short, play in time, in the groove, and in tune. You can refer to chapters 2 through 5 for details; you'll that find most of the info will apply to other instruments.

### Utility Kit for Electric Players

If you play a stringed instrument, refer to the Guitar Utility Kit in Chapter 2.

### Utility Kit for Acoustic Players

If you play a stringed instrument, refer to the Guitar Utility Kit in Chapter 2 and also consider owning your own miking equipment, as with percussionists and horn players above.

# Part Two

## How Do I Make My Band Sound Great?

# CHAPTER 8

# The Keys to Greatness

Now that you have a better idea of how your individual skill as a player determines how your band sounds, let's get down to the nitty-gritty of putting all the pieces together to make your band sound great.

This entire section has tips for taking your band's performance to the next level. I promise you that if you spend even a little time on each of these items, you'll see positive results immediately. As with everything in life, the more work you put in, the better the result will be.

## DYNAMICS

If you learn only one thing from this book and DVD it's that playing with dynamics is the key to making your band sound great, especially when playing live. It's an improvement that both you (the band) and your audience will notice immediately, and will automatically separate you from about 90 percent of the other bands on the planet.

So what are dynamics? Simply, it means playing quietly or with less intensity in certain places in a song, and louder or with more intensity in other places. Most bands are oblivious to dynamics and play at one volume throughout the entire song—song after song, set after set. This gets boring and tedious for the audience very quickly.

Generally speaking, here's how you do it.

When the song starts, the band plays fairly loudly—at about 7 or 8 on a scale of 1 to 10.

When the vocal or lead instrument (if the group is instrumental) comes in at the verse, the band drops down to about 4 or 5.

When the chorus comes in, the volume level comes back up to a 7 or 8.

When the second verse begins, the band drops down to a 5 or 6 level (notice it's a little louder than the first verse, but not as loud as the chorus).

When the second chorus begins, the band comes back up to a 7 or 8.

At the bridge, or whatever section is the peak of the song, the band comes all the way up to 9 or 10.

The band drops down to 7 or 8 for the outro of the song.

If the song has a breakdown, the level might come down as low as a 1 or 2.

While the level of intensity (and as a result, the volume level) may change, depending on the song and what finally feels the best for it, that's basically how it's done. If the band plays the song dynamically, the song breathes, volume-wise. Going from loud to quiet or quiet to loud is called "tension and release," and it's a basic quality of all art forms (for example, in painting it would be dark to light colors; in photography it would be light to shadows). Tension and release keeps things interesting.

> **The Secret to Dynamics**
>
> When you play loudly, play as loudly as you can.
> When you play softly, play as softly as you can!

There are a few byproducts from playing dynamically, too. The vocals can be better heard because there's more space and fewer loud instruments to fight against (which is easier on the singer as well). Songs become more fun to play because there's true interaction with the other players to make it work, and as a result, the band automatically gets tighter. And the audience perceives dynamics in a way that you wouldn't expect; suddenly they'll start telling you how tight you sound.

Dynamics also applies to a set or show as well. You might start off with a couple of songs that are a 7 or 8 in intensity, back off to a ballad or something acoustic in the middle of the set that's a 3 or 4, then end the set with an 8 or 10. Once again: tension and release.

For a really great example of dynamics, listen to "Smells like Team Spirit" by Nirvana where the verses are at about a 5, the pre-chorus at 7, and the chorus just roars at 10.

## How to Learn to Play Dynamically

Most bands learn to play dynamically naturally without thinking; if just one player is dynamics-aware, the others follow (it helps if that one aware person is the drummer). Usually if a band is together for a long enough time and plays enough gigs, dynamics will magically seep into its playing after the band begins to get some self-awareness of just what it takes to get a crowd going. You can bypass years of waiting for these things to happen by themselves by just using the following method.

When the band learns a song, *treat the dynamics as an integral part of the song* (because they are) and spend as much time learning them as you would the chord changes and groove. As shown above, map out each section of the song on a loudness scale of 1 to 10, with 10 being the loudest.

The next step is the most important: *make sure that each band member agrees on how loud or quiet each dynamic number is.* In other words, be sure that the drummer's level 8 is the same as the rhythm guitar player's level 8, and that the bass player's level 2 is the same as the lead guitarist's. After that's commonly agreed upon, rehearse the dynamics of a song until they're second nature; then watch the audience take notice.

## Don't Confuse Volume Level with Intensity

A common complaint from a band that's being taught dynamics is, "The song just doesn't drive when we play the verse (or any other section) quietly." That's because it's easy to confuse volume level with intensity.

Most bands tend to get sloppier the softer they play. They begin to play the individual beats at slightly different levels and even have slight tempo variations between beats. As a result, their playing softly sounds wimpy. Another thing that happens is that the band is so used to playing at one (usually loud) level, that anything compared to that level sounds so different that it's perceived as less exciting. The same thing happens when you drive your car at 80 mph for a long time. When you bring it back to 65, it feels slow even though it's not. And finally, the internal dynamics of each individual (remember those from back in Chapter 1?) usually go out the window. Instead of playing crisp yet quiet, with the same attacks and releases the band had at the higher volume level, the attacks and releases get relaxed so the playing becomes less precise.

> **To Play at the Same Intensity at a Lower Level**
>
> Make sure the attacks and releases are the same.
>
> Make sure the tempo is the same.
>
> Make sure the internal dynamics of each individual player are the same.

The real trick is learning to actually play with the same intensity at lower levels. Make sure the tempo is even, the groove stays the same as at the higher volume, and the attacks and releases are crisp; you should be powerful at any volume level.

### Builds

Another part of playing dynamically is paying attention to builds. Builds usually occur during turnarounds (like the two or four bars between the verse and chorus), but can sometimes occur at the beginning or ending of a song too. For a good example you'll find a build at the beginning of each section of Rush's "Spirit of Radio." Once again, all band members have to play the build the same way, starting from the same low volume to about the same high volume. Builds are easy to overlook, and many times a band will think that it's performing one well if it just plays the rhythm of the build cleanly. But a build is called that for a reason, since just playing it cleanly doesn't mean much unless there's an actual volume difference.

## PLAY TOGETHER—LISTEN TO EACH OTHER

One of the fundamental errors that band members frequently make is not listening closely to the rest of the band. It's easy to just focus on your own playing, but in order to play well together it's listening to everyone else that really counts. *This is the single most important action you can take when playing with other musicians.*

So what do you listen for? You listen to how the other musicians are playing or singing a phrase or part. How loudly are they playing? What are their dynamics like? How do they start and end each phrase? (More on this later.) Where are they accenting? How are they playing the accents? Are they playing ahead or behind the beat? Does their tempo speed up when they play louder or slow down as they get softer? All these items require your close attention. The more you listen to each other and how each of you play or sing, the tighter you become. It's that simple.

> **Things to Listen for When Playing with Others**
>
> How loudly are they playing?
>
> What are their dynamics?
>
> How do they start and end each phrase?
>
> Where are they accenting?
>
> How are they playing the accents?
>
> Are they playing ahead or behind the beat?
>
> Do they speed up when they play softer or louder?

That being said, it does require some work. During rehearsal, if you notice that you're not playing a phrase or part the way everyone else is (or if just one of you doesn't seem in sync with everyone else), stop immediately and ask, "How are you playing that?" Then determine which way sounds best and just rehearse that phrase or part until you're all playing it together.

During a gig you sometimes get a different perspective on how things sound since the environment is different and you're probably set up differently from your rehearsal setup. As a result, you'll probably notice problems that got by during rehearsal. Make a mental note of the parts that aren't being played well together and address those items first at the next rehearsal.

> **Things to Work On During Rehearsal**
>
> Tempo
>
> Dynamics
>
> Phrasing
>
> Overall Volume Level

# TIMING IS EVERYTHING

A big part of playing together is timing. In Chapter 1 we talked about how playing in time means playing with the pulse of the song and how it applies to each individual band member's performance. Now we'll look at it from the band point of view. There are three parts to timing: starts and stops, the groove, and attacks and releases. Let's look at each one.

## Starts and Stops (Beginnings and Endings)

You could call starts and stops beginnings and endings except for the fact that there are sometimes starts and stops in the middle of a song. The trick here is to make sure that everyone starts and stops the song at the same time. These cannot be left for later, or treated with an "it will be better on stage" attitude. Rehearse each start and stop until you are all locked in and know it like the back of you hand! If it still doesn't sound right after five or six tries, ask the reliable "how are you playing it?" question. As is the case with most things that don't lock in tight, there's at least one player who may be playing things slightly differently from the rest. Everyone has to play them the same way—no exceptions.

## Accents

Once again, any time there is an accent in the song, everyone has to play it the same way. This means with the same feel, timing, and phrasing. If it just doesn't seem to sound right, make sure that everyone is playing it the same way.

## The Groove and the Pocket

All good music, regardless of whether it's rock, jazz, classical, rap, or some new space music that we haven't heard yet, has a strong groove. You always hear about "the groove," but what is it?

> **The groove is the pulse of the song and how the instruments dynamically breathe with it.**

To your audience, the groove is an enjoyable rhythm that makes even the people who can't dance want to get up and shake their booty. And while the concept of the groove is very subjective, the idea is well understood by experienced musicians at a practical, intuitive level. Funk and Latin musicians refer to the groove as the sense of being "in the pocket," while jazz players refer to the groove as the sense that a song is really "cooking" or "swinging."

A common misconception of a groove is that it must have perfect time. *A groove is created by tension against even time.* That means that it doesn't have to be perfect, just even, and all performances don't have to have the same amount of "even-ness." In fact, if the groove is too perfect it feels stiff. This is why quantizing parts perfectly and lining up every hit in a workstation when you're recording frequently takes the life out of a song. It's too perfect because there's no tension. It's lost its groove.

> *The groove can start from any element. You can build a groove off something like a rhythm guitar and build around it, but ultimately it comes down to the bass and drums being locked right there with it. It doesn't mean that it's square and machined out, it just means that there's some basic factor in the track that has this irresistible feel to it and everybody in the band adheres to it.*—Producer Frank Fitzpatrick

Just about every hit record has a great groove and that's why it's a hit, but if you really want to study what a groove is, go to the masters: James Brown, Sly Stone, George Clinton, and Prince. Every song is the essence of what a groove is.

We usually think of the groove as coming from the rhythm section, especially the drums, but that's not always the case. In the Police's "Every Breath You Take" the rhythm guitar establishes the groove while in most songs from Motown's golden age by the Supremes, Temptations, and Four Tops, the groove was established by James Jamerson's bass.

## How to Find the Pocket

The phrase "in the pocket" is used to describe something or someone playing in such a way that the groove is very solid and has a great feel. When a drummer keeps good time, makes the groove feel really good, and keeps it up for an extended period of time without wavering, this is often referred to as a "deep pocket." It should be noted that it's impossible to have a pocket without also having a groove.

Historically speaking, the term "pocket" originated in the middle of the last century when a strong backbeat (the snare drum striking on beats 2 and 4) came to the forefront of popular music. When the backbeat is slightly delayed creating a laid back or relaxed feel, the drummer is playing in the pocket.

Today, the term in the pocket has broadened a bit, suggesting that if two musicians (usually the bass player and the drummer) are feeling the downbeats together and placing beat 1 (the downbeat) at the exact same time, they are said to be in the pocket. Whether you are playing ahead (in front) of the beat, behind (on the back of) the beat, or right on top (the middle) of the beat, as long as two musicians (i.e., bassist and drummer) feel the downbeat at the same time, they'll be in the pocket.

In terms of bass and drums locking to create a cohesive part, there are three areas of focus for me. You have to know where your drummer is most comfortable in terms of the beat. Is your drummer very straight, playing right on top of the beat (which can sound like disco music or a machine)? Is he or she laid back, sitting in that area way on the back of the beat (like Phil Rudd on AC/DC's "Back in Black," Led Zeppelin's John Bonham on anything, or Clyde Stubblefield on James Brown's "Cold Sweat" or "Funky Drummer")? Does your drummer's playing have that urgency of a musician who plays on top of the beat (like Stewart Copeland of The Police)? This is crucial to know because the bass and drums have to function as a unit. You don't have to play everything the same, but you have to know and understand the way the other thinks and feels.

Getting the rhythm section to groove with the rest of the band is much more difficult than you might think since guitarists don't always listen to the drummer, a keyboardist may have metronomic time yet have a difficult time coordinating his/her left hand with the bass player, and vocalists will often forget that there's a band playing behind them altogether. *The key is for everyone in the band to listen to one another!*

Many people feel that the question is not so much what the pocket is as much as how you know when you've achieved it, yet I guarantee that you'll know it when you feel it because the music feels like it's playing itself. It feels as if everything has merged together with all the rhythmic parts being played by one instrument. Whichever definition you choose to go with or use, having a pocket is always good thing!

### Attacks and Releases

Attacks and releases are one of the most overlooked yet most important elements in playing together. Attacks and releases usually refer to a phrase that you're either playing or singing. The attack part is usually easy; everyone starts to play or sing at exactly the same time in the same way. The releases are overlooked. *A release is how you end a phrase* and is as important as how you start it. Once again, everyone has to end it at exactly the same time in exactly the same way. Listen to "Hotel California" for an example of both attacks and releases (and phrasing) in both the guitars and vocals. Getting your attacks and releases are one of the essential parts of making a good record (you hardly ever hear one off anymore) and they're essential to making you sound tight as well.

## TURNAROUNDS

Another portion of a song that needs to be tight is the turnaround between sections like the one or two bars between the verse and chorus, chorus and verse, verse and outro, or chorus and bridge. This part requires a lot of focus, because it's usually played a little differently from the rest of the section. For the drummer, it's usually a tom or snare roll into the next section, but unless it's a build, most of the other players usually just randomly play something over the roll. If you're covering a song from a recording, listen carefully to exactly what's going on in the turnaround. You'll find it's a precise line that you have to play in order to stay tight with the drums. Listen to "Sweet Home Alabama" as an example.

If you're playing a song that you've written, chances are that you've not thought about the turnaround too much, so *now* is the time. Make sure that every player has an exact part to play and that all parts work together and sound tight (a good idea for the rest of the song as well).

# TEMPO

Every song needs the perfect tempo to groove. One of the things we discover when making records is that as little as a single bpm (beat per minute) can make a big difference in how a song feels. Just a little slow and the song seems to drag; a little fast and it feels uncomfortable or becomes difficult to play. Therefore, it's really important that you establish the song's bpm before you even begin playing it.

This is pretty easy if you're learning a cover song since the tempo is already established, but if you're working out a song that you've written, finding that perfect tempo can be a challenge. I've found that the best way is for the writer of the song to play it by him or herself and establish the tempo that feels right. After you determine the bpm that the writer has established (you need some sort of metronome or click for this), the entire band should play the song at this tempo a few times. Even if the song feels just fine, it's still best to move the song's tempo up a couple of bpm, then down a couple, just to see how it feels. You might find that just that little bit slower or faster can make a big difference. If the song is difficult to perform, backing it down a few bpm might make it easier to play while playing it faster might give the song more urgency.

## Faster Does Not Create More Excitement

It's really important that you don't get sucked into the "faster is more exciting" syndrome. Usually the only thing you get from playing a song faster than its established tempo is sloppy playing, lack of dynamics, and no groove. And young bands are not the only ones that fall into this trap; even seasoned concert acts do this sometimes and those are usually during what they'd classify as off nights.

Playing at the correct tempo, especially something that is already slow like a ballad is especially difficult because it requires a lot of concentration to play slowly with precision and stay in the pocket. Once again, the best way to overcome any anxiety about losing the excitement is to relax, exaggerate the dynamics, concentrate on the starts and stops and attacks and releases.

## Calm Down on the Gig

If a band is playing a special gig or doesn't gig that much (once or twice a month or less), or only plays single-set shows instead of a three- or four-set night, it's easy to get amped up to play. It's just human nature that you get excited, but it's important to fight the urge and stay with the ideal tempo. If the song feels slow or unexciting, it usually means that you've lost the groove because you're not playing dynamically. When this happens, stress the dynamics (make the quiet parts softer than normal and the loud parts louder), the groove will come back, and everything will get exciting again.

## A Click Can Help

The age-old argument about playing to a click is never going away, but it's easier to do now than it ever was before because most players (especially drummers) learn to use one so early in their musical education. Some players play to a click better than others; that's just a fact. The most widely used session drummers work so much because they make playing to a click sound like they're not, which is the big trick.

> *I realized at that moment that I really could play to a click and make it breathe at the same time, and that really is an important thing for drummers to learn. If you play to a click, don't be so focused on the click that you lose sight of the fact that you're actually playing a song.*—Brian MacLeod

While recording, I'd recommend using a click if at all possible. This makes the job of the producer, engineer, programmer, editor, and anyone doing overdubs a lot easier in so many ways. It even makes your mix better because it's cleaner and easier to time delays and reverbs. That said, if you just sound too stiff while playing to a click, use it only to get a feel for the tempo for maybe the first sixteen bars and then turn it off. Sometimes just having it for the intro of a song can do wonders in keeping the tempo locked. Also remember that it's not uncommon to up the tempo a bpm during the chorus to push the band a little. This requires that the tempo be pre-mapped in the DAW, but this trick successfully mimics what a player might naturally do without a click and is used all the time in record making.

During a live show, a metronome or click is helpful as a count-off to establish the tempo. Once again, it's great if your drummer can play to a click and sound solid and natural since it now opens up the possibility to playing with backing tracks that can fill in around the edges of your show.

## PLAY BIG, NOT LOUD

I don't know if you've ever had a chance to hear a concert act play in a club, but the first thing you would notice is how big they sound. Not loud, BIG. A band that plays on large stages has to turn it up just to hear themselves. Sure they have monitors and side fills (speakers that shoot across the stage), but if you're standing twenty feet away from an amp, it's a lot harder to hear and feel than the three to five feet that you usually get in a club. Although when you see a player with two amp stacks, one is usually a spare, and you can be sure that either the main amp or its monitor feed is cranked. The point is that the stage volume comes up by virtue of the fact that they're playing on large stages. That doesn't necessarily mean it's loud; the sound is big.

So what does big mean? It's controlled loudness. When something is too loud, it's a deafening roar that usually has a frequency or two that can best be described as ear piercing. A big sound is powerful yet not uncomfortable to the listener.

Playing big is a by-product of playing large venues. A band just starting to play larger venues soon discovers that their playing style and stage performance has to change simply to be seen and heard in the very last row of the stadium. They find that everything they do requires exaggeration, such as movements on stage. The songs are played a lot straighter and a lot less busy to make sure that each note is heard at the back. The dynamics are exaggerated. Songs might even slow down a little.

Learning to play big is one of the things that can't be learned in just a few rehearsals. While playing with dynamics, being aware of starts, stops, attacks, and releases can help a band show immediate improvement in a band almost magically. Playing big does require some experience, and it's especially difficult if you're not exposed to large venues. The best way to practice this is to really imagine that you're playing in Madison Square Garden. Exaggerate all your stage moves and dynamics and try to eliminate as much excess playing as possible. Watch your favorite concert video of a superstar act (the bigger the act, the better) and key in on how they're moving and playing. Little by little your band will start to play this way too.

## YOU DON'T HAVE TO SOUND JUST LIKE THE RECORD

One of the mistakes that cover bands sometimes make is playing beyond their ability in order to sound like the record. While it's nice to be able to be a sound-alike, your audience never demands it. All they want is for you to groove so they can dance. Change whatever you have to change in order to play the song as well as you can. Change the key if you can't sing it. Simplify a line or solo if you can't play it. Don't sing the harmony if you can't hear it. Be rigorously honest with yourselves as to what really sounds good and what doesn't. The key here is to do and play whatever you have to in order to sound really great. Know your limitations and just play what you play well.

## PLAY IN TUNE

We've covered this a little in Chapter 1, but now it's important to look at being in tune from a band level. Having an instrument that's in tune with itself is only half the battle. You're not really in tune until all the instruments in the band (except for the drums, of course) are in tune with each other.

You might think that just because everyone uses a tuner that you should all be in tune. Not so fast; there are a couple of complications. First of all, every tuner is slightly different, and even though it says that your E string is in tune, it can be ever so slightly out, either because of the way you read it, or because some of its internal settings have been accidentally adjusted incorrectly to something other than the standard 440 Hz A note. The easy way around that is for everyone to either use the same tuner, or own the same brand and model.

But that's not enough. Everyone who's going to use the tuner (guitar and bass players, horn players) should get together to make sure that you're all reading the meter the same way. That way there'll never be any confusion as to exactly what an E really is.

Finally, after everyone tunes, it's best to all play a couple of chords just to make sure that nothing sounds sour. If it does, go back and look at how each player is using the tuner, and I bet you'll find someone reading it a little differently from everyone else. I'm not suggesting that you do this on a gig; a few times at rehearsal will probably tell you exactly what you need to know to make sure that you'll always be in tune from then on. But in this day and age, with an abundance of inexpensive and accurate electronic tuners available, there's no excuse to be ever out of tune!

# CHAPTER 9

# It's All in the Song

It's important to dig deeper into the songs you're playing to see if the song structure or the arrangements are getting in the way of your ability to perform them well. Whether you play covers or original songs, the arrangement is integral to making that song really cook, so we'll look at that first.

## THE ARRANGEMENT IS THE KEY

How you arrange the song is the key to how it will ultimately sound. You can play it with great precision and dynamics, but it will never catch fire sonically unless all the instruments complement each other in such a way that the sum of the band's parts sound bigger and better together than do the individual instruments and voices. Here are some things to consider.

### Sonic Arrangements

When two instruments with essentially the same frequency bandwidth (like guitars) play at the same volume at the same time, the result is a fight for attention. Think of it this way: you usually don't hear a lead vocal and a guitar solo at the same time, do you? That's because the human ear isn't able to decide which to listen to and becomes confused and fatigued as a result.

How do you get around instrument "fighting"? First and foremost, it is a well-written arrangement that keeps certain instruments out of each other's way right from the beginning. The best writers and arrangers have an innate feel for what will work, and can create arrangements that automatically lay together without much help. They're the lucky ones. Most of the rest of us have to use our experience and trial and error to make everything work together.

## Clash of the Guitar Players

In Chapter 2 I talked about the clash of guitar players, but it bears repeating since it's so important. Most bands have more than one guitar player, so it's important to learn how to refine your sound so your band sounds big and fat, instead of loud and thin. The tone controls on your amp are the first place to start to carve your sound, so that it's not covered up by the other guitar (or other band instruments for that matter), and that you don't cover up anyone's sound, either.

With two guitar players in the band, you have to take things to the next level. Make sure that the songs are arranged so the guitars stay out of each other's way. If you listen closely to just about any recording by a popular artist, you'll see that this is what's happened in the studio already. If you can hear within the song (which isn't always easy with certain types of music or MP3s), this is what you'll hear.

> **Each guitar is playing something completely different.** One guitar might be playing full chords while the other is playing a line, as in the Eagles' "Already Gone."

> **Each guitar is playing in different registers or voicings.** If one guitar is playing an A chord on the second fret, then the second guitar is playing it on the fifth fret. If one guitar is playing a line on the fifth and sixth strings, then the second guitar is playing the same thing up an octave on the first and second strings. Again, Lenny Kravitz's "Are You Goin' My Way" is a perfect example.

> **Each guitar is playing a different rhythm**. If one guitar is playing long sustained chords (called power chords, or in the studio footballs, because they're whole notes that look like footballs when transcribed), then the second one is playing a faster rhythm like quarter or eighth notes, as in the intro to "Already Gone."

If you're playing in a cover band, you've got to start listening extra closely to the arrangement to hear these different lines, rhythms, and voicings. This is where a high-quality playback system and a CD really come in handy, because sometimes you just can't hear the detail on an MP3.

If your band is writing its own songs, you'll find that by employing these techniques, the guitars will lay in better with the track and better support the vocals and rhythm section—and make the song a lot more interesting to boot.

## COVER SONG ARRANGEMENTS

Cover song arrangements can be pretty easy; they're already laid out for you. The exception is in a well-produced song with multiple support parts that can't be readily heard unless you listen on headphones or a high-quality playback system. An example would be The Police's classic "Message in a Bottle"—there are at least four different guitar parts yet it sounds like only one, unless you listen closely. The problem is determining which parts are most integral to the song and which ones will sound best in the context of your band. The solution is for the person in the band with the biggest ears (the best at picking out parts) to learn all the parts and see which ones work best given your band's instrumentation and talents. Sometimes the least obvious part is the one that sounds the best. You also might want to use the next section as a guideline.

## ORIGINAL SONG ARRANGEMENTS

While a cover song already has the arrangement worked out so all you have to do is listen to it, it's up to you to create the arrangement for a song that you've written. Some songwriters already have the arrangement—and how they want the rest of the band to play—worked out in their head, but for most songwriters (even the most accomplished), that's a skill that has to be developed or passed on to a specialist. In order to understand how arrangement influences the song, we have to understand the mechanics of a well-written arrangement first.

Most well-conceived arrangements are limited in the number of elements that occur at the same time. An element can be a single instrument like a lead guitar or a vocal, or it can be a group of instruments like the bass and drums, a doubled guitar line, a group of backing vocals, and so on. Generally, a group of instruments playing exactly the same rhythm is considered an element. Examples: a doubled lead guitar or doubled vocal is a single element, as is a lead vocal with two additional harmonies. Two lead guitars playing different parts are two elements, however. A lead and a rhythm guitar are two separate elements as well.

## Arrangement Elements

**Foundation—the Rhythm Section.** The foundation is usually the bass and drums, but can also include a rhythm guitar and/or keys if they're playing the same rhythmic figure as the rhythm section. Occasionally, as in the case of power trios, the foundation element will only consist of drums since the bass will usually have to play a different rhythm figure to fill out the sound, so it becomes its own element.

**Pad.** A pad is a long sustaining note or chord. In the days before synthesizers, a Hammond organ provided the best pad and was joined later by the Fender Rhodes. Synthesizers now provide the majority of pads but real strings or a guitar power chord can also suffice.

**Rhythm.** Rhythm is any instrument that plays counter to the foundation element. This can be a double-time shaker or tambourine, a rhythm guitar strumming on the backbeat, or congas playing a Latin feel. The rhythm element is used to add motion and excitement to the track.

**Lead.** A lead vocal, lead instrument, or solo.

**Fills.** Fills generally occur in the spaces between lead lines, or they can be a signature line. You can think of a fill element as an answer to the lead.

That's not to say that each individual instrument is a separate element, however. In Bob Seger's radio standard "Night Moves," there are bass and drums, acoustic guitar, piano, Hammond organ, lead vocal, and background vocals. This is how they break out.

> **Bob Seger, "Night Moves"**
>
> **Foundation**—Bass, drums, acoustic guitar
>
> **Pad**—Hammond organ
>
> **Rhythm**—Piano
>
> **Lead**—Lead vocal
>
> **Fills**—Background vocal answers, and sometime the piano fills in the holes.
>
> Usually an acoustic guitar falls into the rhythm category as the strumming is pushing the band and creating excitement. In "Night Moves," however, the acoustic guitar's level is pulled back in the mix, so that it melds into the rhythm section, effectively becoming part of the foundation element.

Alanis Morissette's "Thank U" contains several good examples of both rhythm and pads. There are two sets of each; one for the intro and chorus, and a different set for the verses.

> **Alanis Morissette, "Thank U"**
>
> **Foundation**—Bass, drums
>
> **Pad**—Synthesizer in intro and chorus behind the piano; different synths in chorus
>
> **Rhythm**—Piano; "breath" sample in the verse
>
> **Lead**—Lead vocal
>
> **Fills**—Guitar fills in the second verse
>
> Of course there's much more going on in this song, but any additional tracks are either replacing or doubling the above elements. The number of elements remains constant.

Gnarls Barkley's "Crazy" is a very stripped-down song with very few layers, but the four main elements are always there.

> ### Gnarls Barkley, "Crazy"
>
> **Foundation**—Drum machine
>
> **Pad**—Synth playing voice sample to chorus, where a second set comes in an octave higher
>
> **Rhythm**—Bass with the doubled guitar line
>
> **Lead**—Lead vocal
>
> **Fills**—String lines during chorus
>
> This song is unusual in that the bass and the doubled guitar line push the song forward and actually become the rhythm.

Rascal Flatts' "What Hurts the Most" is an example of the new country music, which closely resembles layered pop music except with the addition of traditional country instruments (steel, banjo, fiddle).

> ### Rascal Flatts, "What Hurts the Most"
>
> **Foundation**—Bass, drums
>
> **Pad**—Steel and guitar in chorus
>
> **Rhythm**—Acoustic guitar in verses to banjo and shaker in chorus
>
> **Lead**—Fiddle in intro, lead vocal, lead guitar in solo
>
> **Fills**—Steel answer to fiddle in intro and harmony answer vocal at the beginning of the outro.
>
> This song is unusual because it has no fills in the intro and outro (and only in one spot for each). The bass is also mixed very loud and takes up a lot of space in the mix.

> **Garth Brooks, "Two Piña Coladas"**
>
> **Foundation**—Bass, drums
>
> **Pad**—Steel guitar
>
> **Rhythm**—Acoustic guitar and shaker
>
> **Lead**—Lead vocal
>
> **Fills**—Electric and acoustic lead guitar; occasional steel fill
>
> This song is different because there's no true pad in the traditional sense, but the steel guitar playing softly in the background acts the part well and shows that it's possible for non-traditional instruments to play that role.

## RULES FOR ARRANGEMENTS

There are a couple of easy-to-remember rules that will always make even the densest arrangement manageable.

### Limit the Number of Elements

Usually there should not be more than four elements playing at the same time. Sometimes three elements can work very well. Very rarely will five simultaneous elements work.

### Everything in Its Own Frequency Range

We covered this a few pages back, but this rule is so important that it needs to be stressed. The arrangement will fit together better if all instruments sit in their own frequency range. For instance, if a synthesizer and rhythm guitar play the same thing in the same octave, they will usually clash. The solution would be to either change the sound of one of the instruments so they fill different frequency ranges have one play in a different octave, or have them play at different times but not together.

We could spend the entire book on modern arranging, but if you follow these two simple rules you'll be ahead of 90 percent of bands with original songs; these are the first things that tend to get fixed when a young band first enters the studio with a professional producer.

# LET'S DISCUSS YOUR SONGS

While this book is not a songwriting handbook, let me point out a number of common problems that stick out when I hear a band that's inexperienced at songwriting or arranging. Keep in mind that we're talking about songs from any genre of music. No matter what it is—from rock to country to goth to rockabilly to alien space music—you want the song to be interesting to your particular audience, so most of the suggested fixes usually apply.

**Too Long.** I hear a lot of songs with sections that are way too long. Two-minute intros, three-minute guitar solos, and five-minute outros are almost always boring. The idea is to keep everything interesting and to the point. You are always better off having a section that is too short rather than too long. The exception is if you can actually make a long section interesting, which usually takes a lot of arranging skill and even then, still might not keep the audience's attention. One really long outro that does work, for example, is the outro to Lynyrd Skynyrd's classic "Free Bird," with slight arrangement changes, kicks, and accents every 16 bars. A great band, great performance, and great arrangement all keep the listener's attention to the very end, and that's your goal, after all.

**No Focus.** Beginner songwriters often have no focus to their songs, which means that the song meanders from chord to chord without an apparent structure and no clear distinction between sections. This is usually the result of not honing the song enough and thinking that it's finished way before its time. Sometimes there's really a song in there if you peel it back a bit, but usually the only way to fix it is to go back to the drawing board for a major rewrite.

**Weak Chorus.** I hear many songs in which it's hard to tell when the verse stops and the chorus starts; they're basically the same. An interesting chorus has something different from the verse. It may be just a little different, with added background vocals or another instrument, or an accent or anticipation to the same chord changes and melody (like Robert Palmer's '80s hit "Addicted to Love" with the harmony vocals, or Stevie Ray Vaughn's "Crossfire" with the horn hits and guitar fill). Or it may be a lot different, like having a different set of chord changes or melody combined with the arrangement changes previously mentioned, such as in "Vertigo" by U2, "This Kiss" by Faith Hill, or our often-cited favorite, "Hotel California." Either way, something has to change in the chorus to lift the energy and keep the song memorable.

**No Bridge.** Another common songwriting mistake is having no bridge. In songwriting, a bridge is an interlude that connects two parts of the song and builds a harmonic connection between those parts. Normally you should have heard the verse at least twice. The bridge may then replace the third verse or precede it. In the latter case, it delays an expected chorus. The chorus after the bridge is usually the last one and is often repeated in order to stress that it is final. If and when you expect a verse or a chorus, and you get something that is musically and lyrically different from both verse and chorus, it is most likely the bridge (Van Halen's "Panama" comes to mind).

A bridge is important because it provides tension and release. It's sometimes the peak of the song where it's at its loudest and most intense (check out the bridge of the Police's "Every Breath You Take"), or it could be its quietest and least intense point (the Who's "Baba O'Riley" where Pete Townshend sings "It's only teenage wasteland," or The Doobie Brothers' "Black Water").

Almost every great song has a bridge, but there are the occasional exceptions. Songs that are based on the straight 12-bar blues frequently don't have bridges but might use dynamics or arrangement to provide the tension and release. An example would be the ZZ Top classic, "Tush." There's no bridge in the song, but the snare fill by itself after the last verse into the outro guitar solo supplies the release. Another would be the Guess Who/Lenny Kravitz song "American Woman," which uses just four bars of a different guitar rhythm and a stop.

And then there are the songs that can get by without a bridge because of how they're arranged or how long each section is. Fleetwood Mac's "Dreams" has only two verses and three choruses, but listen to how everything builds so that the peak of the song is the last chorus.

**Poor Arrangement**. Even with great songwriters, poor arrangement is the most common mistake I hear. Usually this means that the guitar or keyboard will play the same lick, chords, or rhythm throughout the entire song. While this can work perfectly well (and might even be a great arrangement choice if you want that part to sound bigger and if another instrument plays a counter-line or rhythm), it usually means that the arrangement will be boring. You've got to make sure that the song stays interesting, and that means the addition of lines and fills. An example of where a structure like this works is, again, "American Woman."

**No Intro/Outro Hook.** If we're talking about modern popular music (not jazz or classical), most of the songs have an instrumental line (or hook) that you'll hear at the beginning, maybe again in the chorus, and any time the intro repeats in the song. In many cases, this hook becomes the signature of the song. A great example would be the opening guitar riff to the Stones' "Satisfaction" or the piano in Coldplay's "Clocks." If you want to make your producer happy, develop your hooks before you do your demos or hit the studio.

**No Song Dynamics.** As I've said before, dynamics are the one thing that can change how your band sounds and plays overnight. Yet many players and songwriters who know this still don't write dynamics into their songs. Again, one of the secrets to an interesting song is tension and release. In the case of dynamics, it's getting loud and then soft (or vice versa). Grading the volume level on a scale of 1 to 10 (10 being the loudest), the typical song will look something like this:

Intro—8
Verse—5
Pre-chorus—7
Chorus—9
Intro—8
Verse—6
Pre-chorus—7
Chorus—9
Bridge—10
Chorus—9
Chorus—9
Outro—9

Notice how the song breathes in volume from loud to quiet, to louder to quiet, to louder to really loud. Notice how the intensity builds. That's tension and release. Even if you don't use this song structure, try to think of the volume envelope of your song when writing it. It'll sound better and make the arrangement a lot better right out of the box.

## DYNAMICS ON RECORDS

While playing dynamically works during recording (especially if you're all recording live), the way to change intensity on a record is not only with dynamics but also by adding and subtracting instruments. A typical arrangement might look something like:

**Intro**
Drums (drummer playing on ride cymbal)
Bass
Organ
Rhythm guitar
Lead guitar playing a signature line

**Verse**
Drums (drummer playing on hi-hat)
Bass
Rhythm guitar
Vocal

**Pre-chorus**
Drums (drummer playing on hi-hat)
Bass
Rhythm guitar
Organ
Vocal
Harmony vocal

**Chorus**
Drums (drummer playing on ride cymbal)
Bass
Rhythm guitar
Organ
Vocal
Lead guitar line against vocals

**Second Intro**
Drums (drummer playing on ride cymbal)
Bass

Rhythm guitar
Organ
Lead guitar line from intro

**Second Verse**
Drums (drummer playing on hi-hat)
Bass
Organ
Rhythm guitar
Vocal
Lead guitar playing answer riffs in the holes between vocal phrases

**Second Pre-chorus**
Drums (drummer playing on hi-hat)
Bass
Rhythm guitar
Organ
Vocal
Harmony vocal

**Second Chorus**
Drums (drummer playing on ride cymbal)
Bass
Rhythm guitar
Organ
Vocal
Background vocals
Lead guitar line against vocals

**Bridge**
Drums (drummer playing on ride cymbal)
Bass
Rhythm guitar
Organ
Piano
Vocal
Tambourine

**Chorus**
Drums (drummer playing on ride cymbal)
Bass
Rhythm guitar

Organ
Piano
Vocal
Background vocals
Lead guitar line against vocals
Tambourine

**Chorus**
Drums (drummer playing on ride cymbal)
Bass
Rhythm guitar
Organ
Piano
Vocal
Background vocals
Lead guitar line against vocals
Tambourine
Lead guitar solo fills

Notice how something different happens in every section of the song. Either an instrument is added or subtracted or is played a little differently like on the drums between the hi-hat and ride cymbals. Not only does this arrangement make the song naturally dynamic, but it also makes the song a lot more interesting as well. Compare the above outline to many of the big hit songs from the last 40 years or so, and you'll find they all use some variation. If it's worked so well before, then it will work for you too.

## THEY'RE NOT "ORIGINALS"

If there's one thing that really bugs me, it's when a band refers to their songs as "originals." This is a sure sign of an amateur band that doesn't take writing songs seriously. If a band wants me to hear their originals, just that one word tells me that they're a club band and not to expect much. A tape that's labeled originals really has club band written all over it. Now this is nothing against club bands. I've played in them and a lot of my friends have played in them (and some still do) and so many musicians just love doing it. But no one is going to take your writing seriously when you refer to your songs with that word. It's much better to say, "Here are some songs we wrote," or "Here's one of our songs." You'll be taken a lot more seriously by the very people that you want listening.

# CHAPTER 10

# Rehearse Wisely—Plan Ahead

So many bands hate to rehearse, but rehearsals are a necessary evil. After all, the more you play together, the better you get. You'll find that if you plan your rehearsals so that they run efficiently then you can actually accomplish a great deal in a short period of time. The whole key is to not waste any time while you're there.

## HAVE AN AGENDA

Knowing what you need to accomplish beforehand is the single greatest thing you can do to make your rehearsal both painless and efficient. It doesn't do anyone any good to go to a rehearsal because "we always practice on Tuesday night" and then just argue about what to do when you get there. You need to have an agenda.

The best time to set an agenda is at the end of a rehearsal. That way you have the maximum amount of time to individually work on things prior to the next rehearsal. The agenda is also easier to set because you have all the band members there to agree on what needs to be accomplished. If that's not possible, someone should call or email everyone as far ahead of the rehearsal as possible.

The dialog may be something like: "Let's try to learn X this week," or "I'm still not sure of my part in X. Can we go over it at the next rehearsal?" Or, "I'm not sure we're all playing the same thing on X. Can we try it and see?" Or, "I have a new song I want us to try." If you set three basic goals for the next rehearsal, you'll be surprised at how much you can accomplish.

Also, rehearsals are not band meetings. Band meetings should always be kept separate from rehearsals, and be held, preferably, at a place other than your rehearsal spot. The rehearsal room is your workplace. It's where you go to improve as a band. If at all possible, the only thing that should be dealt with there is music, not business.

### Know Your Parts Before You Get There

Knowing what you want to accomplish when you get to rehearsal allows you to do some homework. If you're learning a new cover song, get the CD or MP3 and learn your part as best you can. If you're not that good at picking out your part, have someone in the band write the part out or show it to you beforehand so you can practice it. The idea is to know your part before you get there so as a band you can practice on the nuances of the song. Learning the nuances of the song is what will separate you from every other band out there.

> *One of the things that will really help if you're in a cover band is to work individually on your parts before you get to rehearsal because you can get so much more done. You can get through a lot of songs if everyone has done their homework because it's just fine-tuning the song in rehearsal at that point.* —Peter Thorn

If a band member wrote a new song, try to get a demo recording and a chart so you can work out some parts or ideas before you rehearse it as a band. Once again, the idea is to come prepared so you don't spend the rehearsal learning your part.

Make a list of any questions you might have pertaining to what you or the band will be playing before you get there. Every band, no matter how successful, has questions about how things are played. Even after you've played a song together for years, the part can change over time as you experiment with it (sometimes out of boredom) to where it's not as tight as it used to be. If something seems out of time, out of sync, out of tune, or just plain funny, make a note and bring it up at rehearsal to work out.

### Practice Good Time Management

Not everyone can just jump in at the start of rehearsal and play or sing at their highest performance level. It takes time for everyone to warm up, but it's more important for some players than others.

Ornery acoustic string instruments (acoustic guitars, banjos, mandolins, acoustic basses) need time to adjust to the room conditions so their tuning stabilizes. Brass players need some time to warm up their lips. Vocalists have to warm up before jumping into anything strenuous. Each player should be aware of (and plan accordingly for) how much time they need before they can really get down to the business of rehearsal.

Many bands like to begin a rehearsal with a jam to warm up. While this can be great fun and even a source of song ideas, limit it to fifteen minutes or so. It's easy to get carried away and end up with no time for real rehearsing.

Most important is to plan regular breaks to stay fresh. You should take at least one break halfway through a three-hour rehearsal, although a five minute break every hour may be better if you can hold it to that (most bands can't). It's also best to have drinks and snacks on hand, so that people aren't making store runs and losing rehearsal time. Save the alcohol for after rehearsal; you need to stay focused to give it your best.

## YOU GOTTA HEAR YOURSELF

It's hard to hear the nuances of your part and how they integrate with all the others in the band if you can't hear yourself and everyone else equally well. A problem that bands have is cranking up the volume before they really learn the song. I've found that it's best to learn the song at a low volume level, so that everyone can hear all the parts, and then play at stage volume once things are worked out. This will save time later when you're trying to figure out why something doesn't sound right, and you have to find out why player by player and part by part. .

In fact, I've been in bands where the rehearsals were only on acoustic guitars and drum pads in someone's living room. This was surprisingly effective, since it was easy to hear what everyone was playing and especially easy to hear the vocals (works great for harmonies). Once we got onstage, the song sounded as if we had rehearsed at full volume in a rehearsal hall. Of course, these bands had been playing gigs for a while so we all knew what to expect onstage.

### Practice in the Round if Possible
A really good practice technique is to set up in the round, so that everyone is facing each another, instead of setting up as you would

on stage. This allows all players to hear themselves really well. Almost everyone records this way because it's so important to have eye contact when you're doing a take. Playing in the round usually means you have to control your volume a bit, so that you don't blow out your fellow band member. But that's not such a bad thing, is it?

## A FEW REHEARSAL TIPS

No matter what kind of music you play, here are a few rehearsal tips to help things go a bit smoother.

**When you're first learning a song, stop as soon as there's a train wreck and work it out.** Talk it over to see what everyone is playing; then play just that part until you get it. Sometimes the problem may be in the middle or end of a section, so if you're able to play just that section, great. It's pretty easy to work out. Most bands just can't get into it unless they start four bars before or even at the beginning of the section to work it out. Do whatever it takes to make things sound great!

**Find the hardest part of the song and concentrate on that first.** Slow it down to where it's easy to play; then bring it up to speed when everyone can play it cleanly.

**Sometimes it's best to start with the chorus, especially the out-chorus, since it usually repeats.** It's the section of the song that you'll play the most anyway and probably has a hook so it's easy to remember. Starting with the chorus can give you confidence about playing a difficult song.

Once the band knows the form and can make it through the song, they can come back and work on the things talked about in Chapter 8 and below.

### It's the Little Things That Count

As we've been saying throughout this book it's mastering the little things—the nuances—that takes your band to another level. That's what makes your band sound great. We've talked about these things before, but let's list them again, because these are the things that you've got to have down.

- ▶ You know the part inside out
- ▶ The turnaround between song sections is defined
- ▶ You know the dynamics of the song
- ▶ All rhythms are in the pocket, and the song grooves
- ▶ Attacks and releases for each part are worked out
- ▶ All the sounds are layered so that nothing clashes either rhythmically or tonally
- ▶ All vocals are in the best range for the singers
- ▶ Background vocals are defined and tight

These are the things that you should be concentrating on during rehearsal, more than your individual parts. Or, if you must learn your parts at rehearsal, make one rehearsal for the parts and the next for the nuances, but don't take the song out of the room until you've got both down cold!

## Don't Rehearse a Song to Death

I frequently see bands that have been together for a while (especially bands doing their own material) rehearse the same songs at every rehearsal over and over. They're basically rehearsing their songs to a point where they don't want to play them any more. This starts you down the road to changing the song in small or large ways because of boredom, sometimes taking a great song and reducing it to something that gets worse as it goes along instead of better.

After you've learned a song and really have it where you're satisfied with it, I recommend you not play it again until either a gig, or perhaps the last rehearsal before a gig, just as a refresher. Then play it only once or twice at most unless something is really wrong. This way the song will stay fresh for both you and the audience. Obviously, if you hear that something is really off, then you have to work on it until it gets straightened out, or listen to a rehearsal or gig recording to remember how you played it.

In general, a song should take you at least two three-hour rehearsals (and maybe more) to get to where it is playable, if you're rehearsing it right. If you follow all the points in Chapter 8, you'll know why it takes so long. In Chapter 16, you'll find even more things to work on. If you find yourself at the end of a rehearsal with enough time left over to play your whole set list, then you're not spending enough time refining each song. But once you have that song ready to play, set it in stone and move on; only go back to it if you hear something's not working on a gig recording. You do want each song to sound great, don't you?

## PRODUCTION REHEARSALS

All major touring acts have production rehearsals before going out on tour. These are literally weeks of rehearsals where the stage show, as much the music, is rehearsed. A big show that has lots of sound, lighting, pyro, video, moving stages, guitar changes, wardrobe changes, and a host of other items needs a lot of rehearsal to pull it all off seamlessly and everyone, including the band, has to know their cues.

If big-selling touring bands do this, why shouldn't you? After everything else is worked out in your set, take a rehearsal and dedicate it just to the show. Make sure the echo is added on just the right word. Make sure the lights are soft or colored or spotted or bright so the music is accented at the right place in a song. Make sure your show is the best it can be (more on this in the Show chapter). Here are some things to work on after you have the song down cold.

- ▶ The transition from one song to another
- ▶ Any audio effects or volume rides
- ▶ Lighting cues for mood and maximum dramatic effect
- ▶ Guitar or costume changes

## THE DRESS REHEARSAL

Until you're used to playing gigs, or if you're inserting new production into your show, it's best to have a dress rehearsal before you actually take the show onstage. Play your set just like you would at the gig, complete with full lights and sound production, chatter directed to the audience, and any costume and guitar changes.

Play the songs just as if you were performing. Don't stop, and don't try to fix anything. It is what it is, and you'll learn a lot more from doing it this way than from normal rehearsing.

After the set, talk over any areas of concern and generally debrief, so that you can make a list of problems and start fixing them.

# CHAPTER 11

# You Need the Stage Time

The real secret to taking your band to the next level is stage time. The more you play in front of people, the better you get. After you become a "good" band, the more you play the larger your fan base grows. The more your fan base grows, the easier it becomes to sell things to them (like gigs, music, and band swag) so that you can make a living playing music. The longer you sell music and swag to your fans, the larger your fan base will become, and so goes the cycle. That's the whole formula for a career in a nutshell, but it all starts with playing those small local gigs.

## ALL GIGS ARE WELCOME

Until you reach a point where you're well in demand and are booked on a relatively frequent basis (say, every week), you should take any gig that you can take. Parties, gigs at schools, free concerts, free any-kind-of gig just to be in front of people—nothing should be beneath you, if you know you can pull it off.

Weddings might be the one exception, unless you're specifically a wedding band. When you play a wedding, the attention will never be on you because it's the bride and groom's (mostly the bride's) day and they'll have pretty definite ideas about what songs they want, and how and when they want them played. For the band, weddings really take a specific mindset, and unless you have it or want to develop it, it's best to pass on the gig—especially if you're a rock band.

The younger you are, the easier it is to get gigs. There's always a party to play at, or events at school or the community pool. Don't pass up playing gigs at your friends' parties, even if you set up in a basement or living room. A gig is a gig. If you're old enough to play in clubs, you probably have a lot of friends with some free time that want to come see you and hang out. The rule of gigging has always been the same: if you draw a crowd, then you'll be asked back.

The older you get the harder it becomes to initially get gigs and draw a crowd, mostly because of the limited number of your friends that have free time and are able to come to your gig to support you. The older you get, the more life seems to get in the way of hanging out, as the responsibilities of work and family become more important and pull at you. The available pool of gigs gets smaller too. If your band has been around for ten years and is a regional favorite, you still might get high-school gigs, but it's a lot harder if you're thirty years old and your new group is just getting started.

Remember, bookers, agents, and promoters don't care how good you are. They only care that you draw!

And while you're thinking about drawing people to the gig, remember that it's easy to play for people that you know. You're a lot more comfortable and they'll cut you a break if something doesn't sound right. Where the rubber meets the road is when you play for a totally new crowd that hasn't heard you yet. Your ultimate goal is to be able to make a crowd who has never heard you before into your fans, which is no easy task. When you can do that, stage time is no longer an issue and you can begin to hone your stage presentation instead (see Chapter 16, "Your Show").

## HOW NOT TO GET GIGS

The following was in a widely circulated email that went around the music community. It's from Memphis promoter Chris Walker, who explains both how to get gigs, and more important, how not to get them. If you want the hard, cold facts about club gigs for acts with original music, read on.

From a 17-year vet:

How to not get your band booked!

I've had many, many jobs in my life, from removing asbestos to strip-club DJ to pizza delivery to unloading aircraft, but the one thing I've done and never stopped doing was booking concerts. When I say "job," that would infer that I get paid to do that job. Booking concerts very infrequently pays but I'm addicted to music and have been ever since my big brother gave me my first record, *Destroyer* by Kiss. I learned a long time ago that if I don't book the bands I like ... they ain't coming. Over one thousand concerts and 17 years later of bringing bands to Memphis, I'd say I know EXACTLY how to get a band booked into any venue in the world. I didn't say I could get people to show up—I just said I could get it booked.

I've been on all sides of the live concert equation. I've been the promoter. I've been in the local band. I've been in the touring band. I've been the patron. I've been the sound guy. I've been the bartender. I've been the door guy. I've been the janitor. I've even been the groupie. So there isn't an angle I haven't seen.

Now ...

You've got a band. You've got 30-60 minutes of music to play live and you want to hit the stage—any stage. Hell, a floor! As long as it's a public place and you can get away with charging people to hear live music. Getting a show in your hometown isn't all that difficult. Most venues know that as long as you're local and especially if it's your first show, all your band members' girlfriends, friends, and family will probably show up for your first show. I've booked plenty of kids' bands on their first show and they usually draw well with decent bar sales. If you're worth a shit, they'll continue to come out. If not, those friends and family will drop like flies to future performances.

Now about playing shows out of town ...

Allow me to put things in the venue's point of view. When you're trying to book your band out of town, ask yourself this very very very (x100) important question:

HOW MUCH MONEY WILL THE VENUE MAKE IF WE PLAY THERE?

Musicians hate that money actually comes into the equation. In major markets, there are venues that make unproven bands buy 'x' amount of tickets to get a show. The band in turn then sells the tickets to their friends, family, whoever. The Milwaukee Metal Fest survived for years doing this. The response is: "Pay to play sucks, dude. It's bullshit." What no one seems to realize is that live music is always a pay-to-play proposition. It's just that it's the venue that has to pay. A mid-size music-only venue in Memphis usually has a nut of about $3K to $5K to cover monthly. I will not list the expenses here, but the fact that it's a long list should prove my point. Almost all of the venues in Memphis that I know of don't take anything out of the door for the venue itself except to pay the door guy and sound guy and maybe security if necessary, so that leaves the bar to cover that monthly nut. Risky business, eh?

Truth be told, if your band isn't on a record label, the best way you're going to get a gig out of town is to trade shows with some band in whatever city you're looking to play. MySpace is perfect for this. However, make sure that the out-of-town band you're trying to contact sets up said show for you. Odds are, that band already knows people at the venue and has already played there a few times.

Here's some perspective. The following bands have drawn right at or less than 100 people in Memphis:

Queens of the Stone Age (this was after their second major label release with massive radio airplay complete with commercial spots that we bought. The station gave away 20 tickets; 3 of the 20 showed up.)

Morbid Angel

Jeff Buckley

Deicide

Southern Culture on the Skids

There are a ton more, but you get the idea. Why do you think, if these bands can't even break 100 people, you can make it worth the venue's time to book you?

Let's look at a standard email (complete with spelling and grammatical errors) that venues get, and I'll explain what's wrong with this email below:

*Dear Hi Tone Cafe*

*I have some new talent that is looking to break into your area. They have experience, image and a great alternative rock sound and are going places (otherwise I wouldn't have pick them up). They sell sold out shows in their own area of South Carolina and are working on a getting a Major record deal within these next year. Hope to hear from you soon.*

*Enclosed is a little bio with tour dates and distribution info of their new CD coming out July 25th, 2006 plus a full bio and little info on their new album.*

*Souls Harbor is 5 piece Rock / Metal / Alternative that hails from BEAUFORT, South Carolina. Late last year the band put out their own EP entitled "Burning Souls", produced by Eric Bass. The EP quickly sparked the attention from several southeastern radio stations including 98X (Charleston, SC) and Rock 106.1 (Savannah, GA). The EP spawned off two singles and the group moved more than 2,500 units within 90 days.*

*Signed to Crash Music in January of this year, the band reunited with producer Eric Bass for the recording of their first full length album entitled "Writings On The Wall" hits stores world wide July 25. Look out for a full US tour, music video as well as more commercial airplay this summer. we already have 1000 pre-orders fye ,tower record, best buy, monster, etc world wide.*

*Played with or Supported:*
*SLAYER, KILLSWITCH ENGAGE, CHEVELLE, CROSSFADE, NON-POINT, FILTER, SEVENDUST, COLD, STRATA, AUIOVENT, EARSHOT, MASTODON, MUSHROOMHEAD, FIVE SPEED, FLAW, FIVE BOLT MAIN, ALSTON, ALLELE, TRIGGER POINT, DRYCELL, REVELATION THEORY.. AND MANY MORE REGIONAL AND NATIONAL ACTS*

Here's a list of things that a venue doesn't give a shit about:

**Who you've opened for or played on a bill with.** Unless you played in the town you're trying to get a gig with, who's name you are dropping means zilch! And even if you did, it means little. My band opened for Faith No More, Corrosion of Conformity, GG Allin, and a slew of others. Would anyone go see us because of it? No.

**Who is doing your press or publicity.** No commercial radio station is going to give away free airtime and there is no college radio here. There are only two papers of note here. The *Commercial Appeal* and the *Memphis Flyer*.

**Who produced your record.** That's like saying, "Emeril Lagasse fixed my dinner." They didn't do it for free. The biggest producers in the world will produce your record if you pay them.

**How well you do in your hometown.** Although this is completely meaningless in whatever town you're trying to play, it does matter, because if you ask a band in whatever town you're trying to play that you're huge at home and you'll be glad to trade shows with them, they'll be a lot more interested in helping you get a gig in said town.

**Press clippings.** You wouldn't send out negative reviews, would you? Of course not. No talent buyer looks at press clippings because they all know what they're going to say. "Oh, this band is wonderful. Coldplay watch out!" or whatever. I'll say this, though. If a band ever did send me multiple press clippings stating things like "This is the worst band to walk the planet," and "I'd rather have a barium enema than listen to this band," I would at least listen to their stuff and consider them just because that'd be an approach I've never experienced.

**How good you are.** Of course you think you're good. Your music is probably your life. Guess what? It's just another band setting up and making racket to the club staff. Hard to believe isn't it?
To a lesser extent . . .

**What you sound like.** The only reason the venue cares what you sound like is because they don't want to mismatch music genres or book the wrong type of music altogether. Other than that, they don't care.

Nothing listed above answers the most important questions a talent buyer has:
HOW MUCH MONEY WILL THE VENUE MAKE IF YOU PLAY HERE?
See? Here it is again. This is the number-one priority when it comes to booking shows. Always, always ask yourself that question when approaching a talent buyer regarding a show. If this pisses you off, then that means you probably can't draw.
WHAT DO I GET OUT OF THIS IF I DO BOOK YOUR BAND?
While money is far and away the number-one priority, it is not the only way to skin a cat. If booking your band will get the talent buyer laid or a favor in some shape, form, or fashion, you stand a much better chance.

That's pretty much it. Ask yourself those two questions before contacting a talent buyer.

Recently I took a chance on a band that I didn't know from Adam. All I knew was that they were from three hours away and they had a shtick. I knew they had no draw but they were asking for an opening slot on a bill that would've guaranteed that they play in front of over 100 people. This band could play here every month for a year and not be able to draw 100 people, if ever in their lives.

I liked their shtick and told them I'd put them on the bill; there was no money available to pay them, but they'd have the chance to sell merch to a crowded house. I could've left the bill alone and not put them on and still would've had the same crowd. They agreed to play for free. Once they got there, they were aloof and complained about having to play for free. Even though I'd told them the deal way in advance, it didn't matter. I will never book them again nor will I book a band sight unseen unless someone whose opinion I respect recommends them.

I would now like to give even more perspective. There's a club in St. Louis called The Creepy Crawl. I book a lot of the same bands they do. They have on their Website a list of "Top 39 Annoying Things That Bands Do." Twenty-three of these things have happened to me on several occasions. I'm going to post this list (A) because it's hilarious, and (B) so you can understand where the venue is coming from. Not all these things apply, but most do:

1. **Bands who feel compelled to bang on their drums and guitars in an annoying display of lack of talent before the doors open.** Usually this occurs when we are trying to talk to someone on the phone or give instructions to employees. There is a place for this type of behavior; it's called your basement.

*Right on, brothers! No one wants to hear you noodle around... NO ONE! Once you get your gear set up, make sure all your gear works; then STOP!*

2. **Out-of-town bands that show up and say, "We decided to bring another band with us. Don't worry; they just need gas money and pizza."**

*This only happened to me once that I can remember (I've probably blocked it out), but the one I do remember resulted in a large brawl between myself and staff and the worthless band that showed.*

You Need the Stage Time  **121**

3. **Out-of-town bands that watch you order their pizzas with "the works" and after they arrive tell you, "Oh, we're all vegetarians. Can we get buy-outs instead?"**

*I make it REAL clear that I don't do buyouts unless you're The Rolling Stones or something.*

4. **Local bands with managers.**

*This happens occasionally but I don't sweat it. I just don't book them again.*

5. **Local bands that have a girlfriend as their manager (Can you say "annoying pain in the ass"?). This usually marks the beginning of the end for most bands at the Creepy.**

*This happens too but even less frequently than above. Again, I just don't book them.*

6. **Bands that bring their own "personal" sound tech.** After seeing him try to operate the soundboard for 5 minutes, the house soundman concludes that this guy has absolutely no clue how to operate a PA. Accordingly, the band sounds like total crap.

*Most sound guys don't mind letting a touring sound tech on the board. It's less work for them and they could care less how the band sounds. They just don't want him to break the house's gear.*

7. **Bands that have more roadies than band members.**

8. **Bands that spell their names with a strange spelling twist, e.g., junkeez, katz, etc.** After meeting the band, however, we are left with the impression that they didn't intentionally try to spell their name with a twist but rather, they probably just don't know how to spell.

*I don't book those bands, period.*

9. **The out-of-town band that was lucky to get the gig, brought absolutely nobody, bitched all night long about**

their time slot, and then when told they had one song left in their set play four more anyway, and who when being paid out $50 in gas money asks, "Is this the best you can do?"

*See my above comments regarding the band from three hours away.*

10. **Bands that arrive and state that they talked to someone at the club and were told they get to play third at 10:30 and can play for an hour.** When asked the name of the person they talked to, they suddenly forget their name but are sure they talked to "someone."

11. **Bands who all arrive at the same time but no one is willing to play first, subsequently the show doesn't start until 11:30 and everyone has ten-minute sets.**

*This is so unbelievably common in Memphis because people don't start showing up here until say 11:00 p.m.—no one wants to play first. This is because no one wants to see the openers. This could be you!*

12. **Top three signs that the band will bring no one to the show:** 1) Two weeks before the show they say, "We're gonna pack your place!" 2) One week before the show they ask, "What's your capacity?" 3) Upon arriving at the gig they ask, "So how many people do YOU usually get on a Wednesday night?"

*I've only gotten number 3. I inform them that the bands are the draw not the venue. The usual response is, "Oh...bummer."*

13. **Bands whose draw is so bad that even their guests don't show up.**

14. **Bands who have no guests because they have no friends.**

15. **Bands who bring absolutely no one to their first gig and then call back relentlessly to ask for another show and can't understand why they haven't gotten asked back.** That's fine, we don't have to eat this month and we really dig watching you guys rock out to our empty club. Bands fitting

this category don't need to bother calling back because the booking guy will always be away when you call.

*The above three are basically the same.*

16. **Bands who after drawing no one at the end of the night apologize by saying, "Geez, after you booked us we booked ourselves to play at the Hi-Pointe last night and we told all our friends to go to that show. That's probably why no one came tonight. By the way, when do you think we can play here again?"** (Note: see above for our response).

17. **Bands who pester you to book their band's "side-project."** Side-project is another name for self-indulgent crap so embarrassingly bad they can't dignify it with a name, and something that gives them a cover why none of their friends will come see them perform. Note to bands: think of your side-project as a project never to get booked again.

18. **Bands who show up wearing "All Access" laminates around their neck.** Note to these bands: We honor these laminates for the bathroom and parking lot areas only. I wanted to be an astronaut when I grew up but you don't see me walking around wearing a spacesuit at the club. We're convinced these people are recovering air guitar addicts from the '80s.

19. **Bands who, right before their set, ask to play without a PA so it won't be deducted from their pay.** (This has actually happened before.) Sure, we'll just ask the sound guy to go home for a half hour.

20. **Bands that want to play in front of or at the side of the stage.**

*Usually 19 and 20 coincide.*

21. **Bands that suck and then ask if you'll swap them out a shirt.** You know, our shirts actually cost us money and I really doubt anyone at the club wants to wear your shirt. How about if we swap stickers and call it even?

22. **Band members that ask in a nasally voice for a soda or water before the doors are open.** Usually this occurs when you're in the middle of doing something important like counting down the drawer or talking to a booking agent on the phone about a future show. You can wait!

23. **Parents of bands.** This could be a whole top 39 list on its own. Parents who either a) insist on standing next to the owner all night and talking his ear off about how great their 14-year-old kid's band is (who, by the way, sound like they had never picked up an instrument in their lives before they started "playing" that night), b) insist on standing next to the sound person all night and making stupid suggestions on how to improve the sound of their kid's band throughout their set, c) go to the bar while they wait for their kids band to play, consume way too much, and then stand next to the owner and talk his ear off about how he used to jam in a band but now their kid's band is going to hit mega-stardom any day now and . . . Oh right, this is only supposed to be a paragraph.

24. **Bands that leave gear behind.** This happens at least several times each week and then we get the deluge of frantic phone calls in the following days about "Have you seen this or that piece of equipment?" like we should know where their stuff is. It's amazing how something that is so important to them the next day gets so carelessly left behind the night of the show. We're the Creepy Crawl, not Bob's Nightclub and Repository of Leftover Band Shit. Keep track of your stuff and take it with you when you leave!

25. **Out-of-town bands that show up at 1:30 in the afternoon while you're doing work at the club.** They then want to hang out with you all day and ask endlessly annoying questions while you work.

*Questions like, "Do we get free beer? Do we get dinner? Do we get a discount on either? How many guests do we get?" See why the club might get irritated?*

26. **Bands who when you tell them they have one more song left because they're running late into their set, decide to play a 45-minute opus full of self-absorbed guitar solos, which in the course of playing, covers in its entirety side 2 of Pink Floyd's** *Dark Side of the Moon.*

27. **Bands that pester you constantly to open for a particular touring band because they swear they worship their musical footprints and are the heaven-endorsed guiding light of their musical lives.** On the day of the show and after you told them, "Sorry but the show is already filled up," don't even bother to come to the show. However, someone at the show reports hearing they decided to catch the *Story of the Year* show at the Pageant instead.

*This happens constantly. It's a great way not to get booked.*

28. **Bands that cancel playing on the day of the show because, even though you've had them booked for two months, it wasn't until yesterday that someone in the band decided maybe then was a good time to try and ask off work.**

29. **Bands that can't play longer than a 15-minute set.**

*Actually I'm all for 15-minute sets.*

30. **Bands that bitch and beg to play a longer 45- to 50-minute set.** They do this knowing everyone else only gets a half-hour slot. We finally relent and rework the whole show to accommodate them and they still wind up playing the same "rush-through-it-because-we're-dipshits" 23-minute set they play every other night they play. Apparently they live in a different time dimension than everyone else on the planet. They thank you profusely at the end of the set for letting them "headline" for their fans, but we make sure they buy us and everyone around us shots at full price.

31. **Bands that give big lectures on stage about how important it is to support "the scene," but at the end of their set want to get paid ASAP and don't want to wait until the other bands get done.**

*This is a constant around Memphis. I will not pay before the show is over.*

32. **Bands that keep asking to let us let them "set up" a show.** These requests usually come from bands that can't even show up on time for their own gig, and no matter how many times you told them what time they go on, there is always one member of the band who doesn't get the message and totally screws up the band schedule for the whole night. However, they have somehow convinced themselves that if we let them book a whole night this will somehow be the secret to their success. Ninety-nine point nine percent of the time when we actually allow a band to do this, it turns into a giant train wreck, where half the bands they claim will be playing don't show up and the other half show up bitching about how they are supposed to be headlining.

33. **Bands that are booked for a show but email every 12 hours to tell you they have changed their name and to please update your advertising.** Call yourself "Bobby & the Blowjobs" for all we care. Pick a name and STICK WITH IT!

34. **Pathetic reasons why bands cancel.** Bands that cancel ten days ahead of time because they have to go to a funeral! We feel so sad for these bands. If you're going to friggin' lie, try and come up with something half-way believable please.

35. **Shows where the four local bands collectively can't outdraw the one out-of-town band you threw on the bill for gas money, but through their own initiative and hustle actually manage to outdraw the four local bands (this BS actually happens!)** We feel sorry and embarrassed for the out-of-town band who usually, when getting paid out their gas money, asks us quietly, "What's up with the locals? Why don't they have anybody come see them?" and we tell them as loudly as we can, "BECAUSE THEY ARE PATHETIC AND RETARDED LOSERS." Invariably (and we do mean invariably), there has to be the one local band who lives 20 minutes away and brought a negative number

of people (they sucked so bad they ran off our happy-hour crowd early), and asks how much did they make and we tell them zero "BECAUSE THE BAND FROM HALF A CONTINENT AWAY OUTDREW YOUR PATHETIC AND RETARDED ASS." Actually we don't say that because we're so pathetically nice. We usually say, "You guys rocked. Let us know when you want to play again!"

**36–39: Bands that don't correctly understand the definition of these terms** (Author's note: There are actually 40 items here, not 39. We'll cut them a break as long as they don't make any mistakes counting the money at the end of the night):

**Load-In Time**
CORRECT UNDERSTANDING: If a band has a load-in time of say 6:30, at that time they may attempt to enter the premises and inquire about loading in their gear. If they by chance happen to arrive early, they can occupy themselves with other activities to fill in the time, such as visiting the library, worshiping at a local church or synagogue, or beating up the homeless guy living in the dumpster.

INCORRECT UNDERSTANDING: If a band has a load-in time of say 6:30, they arrive at 1:45 in the afternoon and knock incessantly on the back door. Usually they knock while the owner is standing knee-deep in water in the basement working with a plumber to fix a leaking drain pipe. After trudging all the way upstairs to find five snot-nosed kids asking if they can load-in now (and hang out all day!), they are politely told to screw themselves and come back at 6:30.

**Promoter**
CORRECT UNDERSTANDING: This is a person who actively works to promote a show. He promotes by distributing flyers, plugging the show wherever he can, and tries to get as many people as possible to come to the show. If he has an out-of-town band booked on the show, he takes financial responsibility to ensure they get paid and are taken care of in whatever way they need. He also takes charge in organizing the show and making sure all the bands know when they are scheduled to play and how the money works for getting paid.

INCORRECT UNDERSTANDING: This is a person who, after asking repeatedly to put on a show, does the following: 1) fails to promote show in any way, 2) fails to communicate any show details like lineup or order of the bands to the club (or the bands themselves), 3) makes themselves very scarce at the show, assuming they show up (they sometimes make a pathetic phone call just before doors open to say they've just contracted a rare disease and to please take care of the out-of-town band). If they do show up, when questioned about things like band order, who's taking care of the bands etc, they only respond with a blank stare.

**Gas Money**
CORRECT UNDERSTANDING: Gas money is a term used to designate an amount of money to get a touring band to their next show. It sometimes includes a little more than that so they can buy themselves some fast-food on their way or if they're lucky enough, cover a room at a Motel 6. Generally gas money would be considered anything from $30 to $75 and depends on how well the show goes.

INCORRECT UNDERSTANDING: $200 is not gas money. $200 is "We're partying all night on the East Side" money.

**Touring Band**
CORRECT UNDERSTANDING: This is a band that is engaged on a "tour." They come to the Creepy Crawl while on their tour and often come from faraway places such as the far corners of the country, Canada, Europe, or Asia. They are on the road for extended periods of time, sometimes for several months at a time, in a van or bus, and experience many new places along their journey. These bands are always entitled to at least gas money or more.

INCORRECT UNDERSTANDING: Driving up from Festus (about 30 miles away) does not make you a touring band.

**A "Following"**
CORRECT UNDERSTANDING: A "following" is a collection of fans that attend the performances of a particular band. This is what bands try to develop and grow over time to

get ahead in the business, and is a measure of their general popularity. The larger a band's following generally means they will be booked more often and on better nights at the Creepy Crawl.

INCORRECT UNDERSTANDING: A "following" does not mean all the people who attended The Queens of the Stone Age show you opened for count as your band's following (Perhaps the rush to the bar by the entire audience and club staff when you started playing was an indicator). And, yes, this means the Jager girls at the club that night probably didn't come to see you and probably won't be following you to your next show.

Now you get the idea of how cynical and jaded booking concerts can make you.

I used to be in a band called The Diarrhea of Anne Frank. We were total noise. If you put two gorillas in a room with some instruments with heavy effects on them and gave them a really good drummer, you would be us. We didn't rehearse, we had no songs, and we had no structure. We did have a television that showed unpleasant things like graphic scenes of violence, Charlie Brown cartoons, and parts of the show *Friends*. The TV usually was smashed before the end of the set. We didn't have a record out or T-shirts or anything. It was just a release for us. We had no aspirations.

Yet we managed to play Chicago, Detroit, and the Knitting Factory in New York City.

If I would've worked harder, we could've played even more shows, but it was really a glorified vacation. If my crappy band can play the Knitting Factory, you can too. Here's how to do it:

**Develop a draw in your hometown.** That means you should play once every month to six weeks. Beg your friends to show up. MySpace the hell out of your show. If the venue can count on you bringing 20-40 people a show, you'd be amazed at how often people will ask you to play. Remember, once every month to six weeks. Don't just play because someone asks you. The best drawing bands in town maybe play at home two or three times a year.

**If you haven't left your hometown and you don't have a record, your only hope is to trade shows.** Why develop a draw at home? So you can trade shows with bands from out of town. That's another thing: make sure the band you're trading shows with has a draw in their hometown. Check that city's music message boards. Use the many avenues of the Internet. It's your only hope.

**Sling that promoter oil!** Actually save up your own money and book big acts (or as big as you can afford) in the clubs you wanna play, then stick yourself on the bill. It's a perfect way to find out if you're worth your salt. That's how my teenage band got to open for all those bands we played in front of. I saved my money, booked who I liked into a club, and threw my band on as support. The club loved me for not bugging them for a gig but instead asking for a date and ACTUALLY BRINGING SOMETHING TO THE TABLE! You'd be surprised at how some musicians think that they shouldn't be accountable; that all they should have to do is show up and play and expect money, food, and beer although they may or may not have promoted in any way or brought anyone to the show.

I'm sure there'll be some who read this and get their feelings hurt. Seventeen years can make you callous.

That email is an eye-opener. If you're a band with original material, heed what it says and you'll find you'll get a lot more gigs. If you're a cover band, many of the same things apply but remember the big one: *bring some people so the club can make money.*

## HOW LOUD SHOULD WE PLAY?

Ah, the age old question. How loud is too loud for the room? Usually the audience will complain about the volume if two things happen; the volume is the same level throughout the song and from song to song, and if there's a particular frequency that's so piercing that it feels like an ice pick through the brain.

Here's how to play at a level that feels comfortable and still isn't overpowering for the audience.

### Dynamics

We've talked about dynamics repeatedly throughout the book and about how they'll make the band sound tighter, but dynamics controls the perceived volume level for the audience as well. *If the band plays as loud as it can only at the peaks of songs while it plays at controlled levels in other sections, the audience will almost never complain about the volume.* It's the loud din that never stops that usually gets complaints.

### Play Big Instead of Loud

No matter how small the room, you should play it like it is Madison Square Garden. This means that you're trying to reach the people sitting in the farthest seats from the stage. All motions have to be exaggerated so that guy at the back can see you. Every note has to be clean and precise so it doesn't turn into sonic mud. Every note has to have a meaning, with nothing played that's not supposed to be played. Loud parts get louder while soft parts get quieter. This is a very hard thing to learn, but if you master it, the band will never sound loud regardless of the size of the amps or sound systems. It'll just sound "big."

### Even Frequency Balance

Once again, this has been discussed before but it needs mentioning again because now we're talking about your audience. Sometimes being perceived as "too loud" means that only one small band of frequencies is the culprit. This is usually from a guitar amp, which again can be turned away from the audience if that's the sound that the guitar player really has to have. The other possibility is that it's coming from the PA system, and there's no reason that has to happen, regardless of the brand or size of the system. There's plenty of technology available in even the least sophisticated sound system these days so this problem shouldn't occur. If it does, it usually means that your soundman has lost some portion of his hearing and is trying to compensate by raising those particular frequencies, or he's just bad or inexperienced. Any way you cut it, he's not going to win you many fans, and you have to fix the problems if you want to keep your audience and get another gig.

# VOLUME WARS

Volume wars (the need to turn up because someone else is playing so loud that you can't hear yourself) is usually caused by three things:

- A guitar player who can't get his sound unless his amp is at a volume level that's too loud for the room
- Playing on a small stage with the amps placed where you're not used to them
- A drummer who's not able to play dynamically

The first two items are easy to fix: simply change the position of the offending amp! Turn it sideways, face it toward the wall, get it up off the floor closer to ear level of the player, even turn it completely around so it's facing away from the audience. You can usually find a balance somewhere so that everyone is happy. Sure it will sound different, but if you have a soundman you can add some guitar back into the monitors (or side fills if you have them) to balance everything out. If you don't have a soundman or monitors, you'll get used to the sound after a tune or two.

If you have a drummer who doesn't know his own strength and can't perceive how loud he's playing, or someone who just can't play dynamically on a gig, it's back to the drawing board for the band until this gets worked out. Dynamics once again are the key to controlling the volume level and everyone, especially the drummer, has to be on the same page.

And speaking of soundmen, if you have one who regularly does your sound, he can work against you if he constantly tries to see how loud he can push the system, or tunes it to where the audience is wearing ear protectors. Get him to rehearsal a few times (see Chapter 15, "Your Show"), rehearse not only the effects you need him to add but also the levels that you'd like for him to get, and discuss the way you want it to sound, then hold him to it. Remember, he works for you.

**CHAPTER 12**

# Record Yourself

It's time to record a few songs, either for a demo of your band to get gigs, or a recording of some of the songs you and your band mates have written. While it might seem as easy as setting up a couple of mics and a portable recorder during a gig, you can bet that it will take a great deal more work than that.

Recording is so easy these days. The gear is so inexpensive that every musician should invest in some kind of recording system, if only because it makes a great personal practice tool. But recording is a lot different from live performing, and you definitely have to adjust your approach and way of thinking to get the most out of it. While recording may be easy, getting the results to sound good and getting great performances are not. Let's take a look at some different aspects of recording and how to get the most out of them.

## RECORDING REHEARSALS

Recording rehearsals should be almost mandatory for any band. You never know when either the band or an individual player will play something great, so recording everything that goes down gives you a way to capture it if it happens. Likewise, if something sounds bad, a recording may be able to tell you why. You can't always tell while you're playing the song, because you're concentrating on your playing or singing.

There are three ways to record rehearsals: simple, easy, and complex. The simple way is to use one of the many portable stereo recorders made by Edirol, Zoom, M-Audio, Yamaha, or Olympus, and experiment with its placement until you get the best balance. Be sure to set it up with the gain down fairly low or the sensitivity set to low so you won't overload the input and get a distorted recording (this means don't allow any digital overs).

Depending upon the acoustics of your rehearsal room (it might be so reflective that none of the instruments or PA have any definition), the simple way to record might not get you a clean enough recording to use, so try something a little more elaborate. This method involves taking a feed out of the PA head and into your recorder of choice (see Fig. 12.1). Almost every PA head (even the least sophisticated) now has either a Tape Out, Line Out, Alternate Out, Aux Out, or FX Out that can be used to feed the recorder. This might not be the best way to go since you might be recording only a vocal-heavy mix unless A) you have more than one vocal mic and those mics pick up some of the band, or B) you minimally mic all the instruments. Once again, the best thing is to experiment until you get a balance that you can live with, then rehearse and record away.

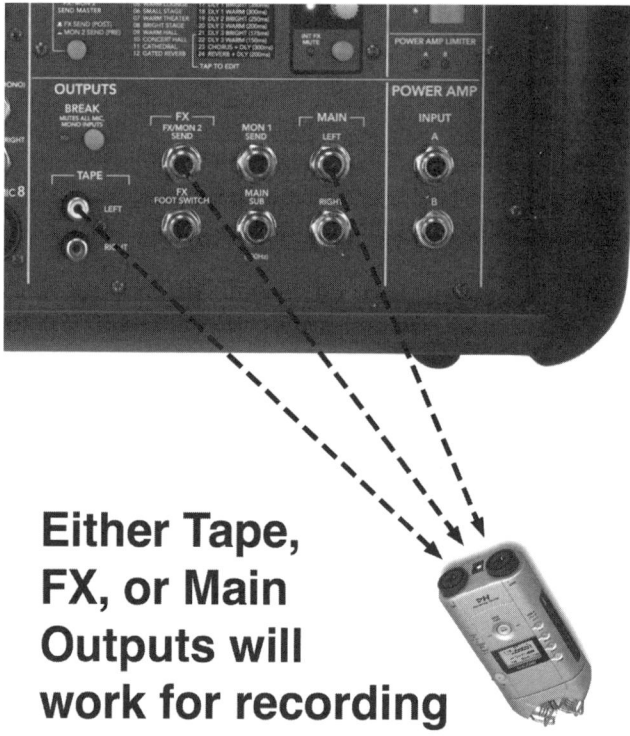

**Fig. 12.1.** *Taking a feed from your PA head.*

The complex way to record is to mic all the instruments and do a multitrack recording. Although you'll get the cleanest recording this way, I wouldn't recommend it unless you have the intention of using the recording at a later time (like as a demo). As a rule, rehearsal recordings are never made for distribution—they're only an internal working document to give you a reference point. Recording yourself this way will take a lot of time to set everything up, and may leave you with no time to rehearse. Plus, you might be concentrating so hard on getting the recording to sound good that you forget to play well. My advice: keep it as simple as possible for rehearsal, and when you want to make a real recording, head for a proper studio. You'll be a lot happier with the better result.

## RECORDING YOUR GIGS

Recording your gigs today is much easier than it used to be. Most of the hand-held stereo recorders on the market are inexpensive and sound pretty good; and it seems like everyone has DAW software on a laptop. But just because it's easy to record doesn't mean that it's easy to make it sound good. Live albums done by big-selling acts require a complicated and expensive array of recording gear to actually pull this off.

### The Problems

Assuming your performances are spot on, the problem with recording your live gig is always one of balances. Balance of the vocals against the instruments, balance of the instruments themselves, balance of the audience versus the band, or balance of the direct sound versus the reflected sound in the room. You can usually bet that at least one of these will be out of whack. Let's look at each of these problems separately.

You would think that the best way to get a great mix is off the mixing board. While this might be the cleanest signal, it's usually the least balanced, because even if all the instruments are miked, the vocals will be too loud. This is because they're the quietest thing onstage and need the most amplification. Many times the loudest stage instruments are missing from the board recording since they're not amplified in the mix. This is especially true in small venues like clubs. The larger the venue, the more balanced the mix becomes as the miked instruments have to be raised louder in the mix, but as a rule, you'll always find that the vocals are too loud in a board mix.

If a board mix won't work, consider putting a couple of mics out in the room and record the performance that way. Engineers have been experimenting with different ways of doing this since the beginning of recordings (especially in orchestral recording) and while it's possible to get a really great-sounding, balanced recording, it takes time and experimenting. It's difficult to find the place in the room where vocals and instruments are perfectly balanced. When you find that spot, chances are the sound of the room's acoustics will rear its ugly head (since most venues aren't acoustically treated) and you'll get so many reflections that the recording sounds hollow and distant.

Another problem is the spot in the room with the best balance might also have too much audience, either when you're playing (you don't want to hear the drink orders on top of the guitar solo) or too much applause when the song is over (assuming that you get applause, of course).

## The Solutions

Here's how a big-selling group does it. All the instruments, as well as the vocals, are miked onstage. The signals are split so that they go to both the house PA and monitor system, and to a separate recording rig either isolated in a separate room in the venue or located in a mobile recording studio outside (see Fig. 12.2). The audience is miked with multiple pairs of mics (the number depends on the size of the venue) usually located at the front, in the middle, and at the rear of the venue. Another pair might be located on the stage aimed

*Fig. 12.2. The three-way signal split.*

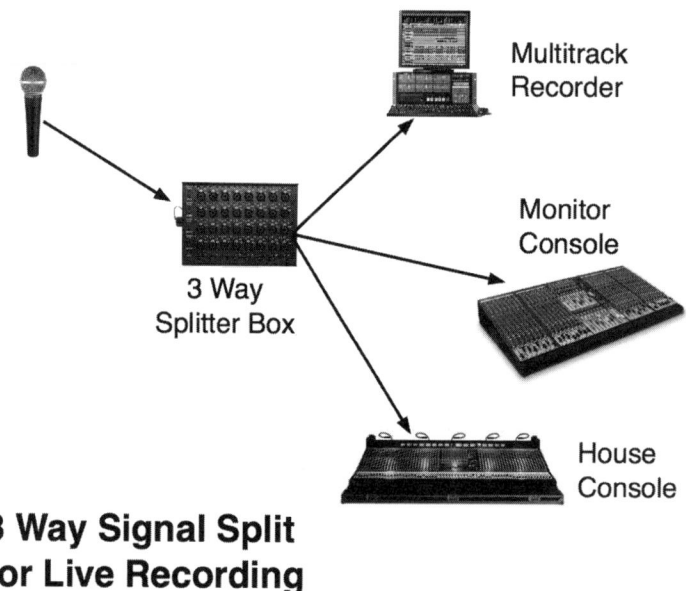

out toward the audience. All this is recorded (alongside a backup unit, should the primary one go down during the show) over a series of shows, with the best general performance chosen and mixed later, or the best of several performances edited together. Instruments or vocals might even be fixed or replaced by overdubbing at a later date if the artist just can't live with a clam or shaky performance. I've known live recordings in which everything was replaced except the drums and the audience! That's cheating to me, but if it's okay with the artist and their fans, who am I to say?

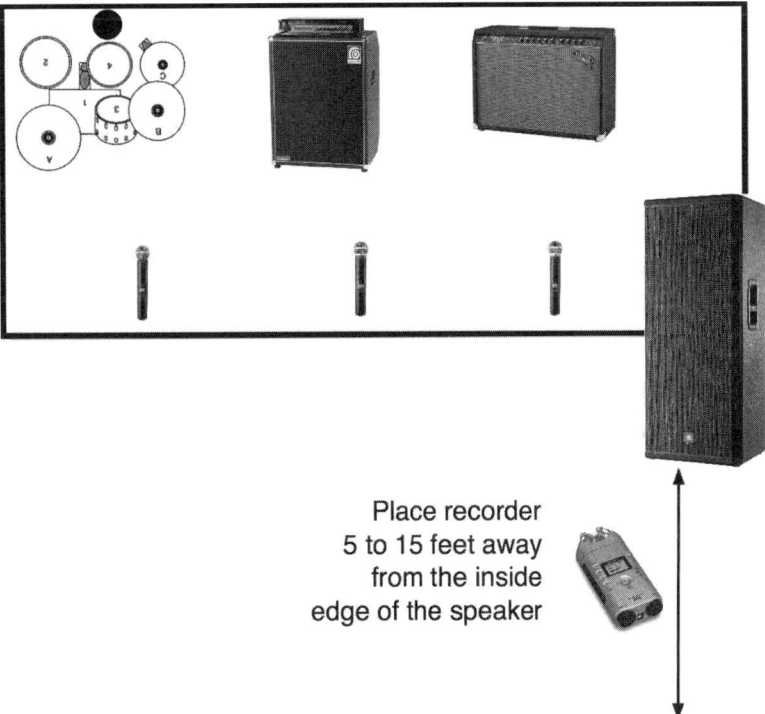

*Fig. 12.3. Positioning the recorder.*

Place recorder 5 to 15 feet away from the inside edge of the speaker

Now I know you can't afford all that, so what can you do to get a decent live recording? The simple way is to use a hand-held stereo recorder like an Edirol, Zoom, M-Audio, Yamaha, or Olympus model like you're using during rehearsal, and position it about 12 feet back from the PA cabinets, but more on the edge of the cabinet toward the stage (see Fig. 12.3). This will give you the best balance between the vocal-heavy PA and the instruments on the stage. Keep in mind that you'll have to experiment a bit to find the exact spot where the balance is right. That's because the balance depends upon the song, the room you're recording in, the volume of the band, the volume of the PA, and how large and boisterous the audience is.

The more sophisticated way to record would be a smaller version of the way the big guys do it. If you have either DAW software for your computer and a FireWire or USB interface, or a dedicated digital recorder like a Tascam DP-2 or Alesis HDR-24, then you can try this: Let's say you have a common eight-channel interface from a manufacturer like M-Audio, MOTU, or Edirol. Ideally, what you want is to get the lead vocals on one track, the background vocals (if there are any) on one track, the kick and snare on separate tracks, and guitars, bass, and keyboards all on separate tracks. Usually the rest of the drums will be picked up by the stage mics, and while this isn't ideal, it does give you a measure of control over the most important elements.

Fig. 12.4. Direct output.

How do you separate these mix elements? On all but the most inexpensive mixers there are either Direct Outs or Inserts on each input channel of the mixer or console. Direct outs (see Fig. 12.4) do just what they say. Each one sends an output directly from an isolated channel, so they're perfect for recording. Just connect one each for the lead vocal, kick, snare, and bass from the mixer to your interface. If you don't have a Direct Out, you'll probably have an Insert on each microphone channel (see Fig. 12.5). An insert jack allows you to insert a device like a compressor, delay, or reverb only on that particular channel. The insert jack can also be used as a direct output too. The trick (with mono connections like a guitar cable) is to push the plug in only *halfway*! (See Fig. 12.6.)

*Fig. 12.5. Channel insert.*

What if you have two guitars and two background vocals? You have four band elements to record but only two additional inputs. The answer comes from the sub-groups that you might also have on your mixer (see Fig. 12.7). Route the guitars to a sub-group and plug that output into your interface, then route your background vocals into a second sub-group and send that to another channel of your interface (see Fig. 12.8). Done!

*Fig. 12.6. Mono plug inserted halfway into an insert jack.*

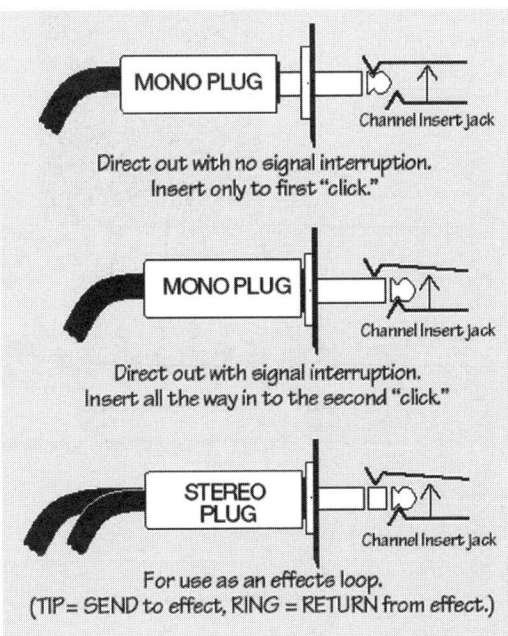

*Fig. 12.7. A mixer sub-group.*

*Fig. 12.8. Eight-channel live-recording setup.*

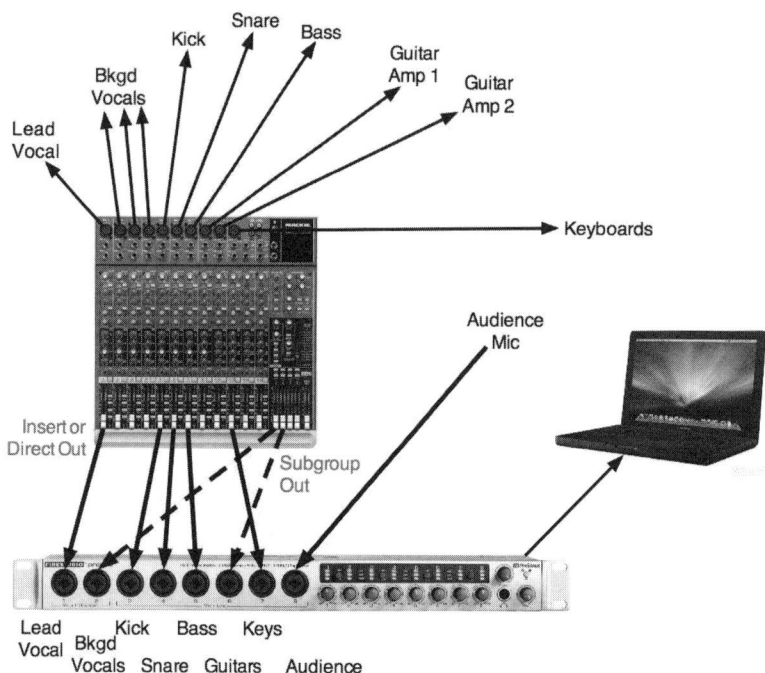

To finish the recording, place an audience mic about half the length of the room back from, and pointing toward, the stage. The audience mic will not only pick up the audience response but also should give the track a little "glue" by helping to balance everything. Don't add too much, though, as a little goes a long way. You can lose some of your bass response if you add too much.

### A Simple Track Sheet

Here's how a track sheet of the setup above would show channel assignments. Note that the first listing includes a keyboard track instead of a second guitar track.

| 1 | 2 | 3 | 4 | 5 | 6 | 7 | 8 |
|---|---|---|---|---|---|---|---|
| Ld Vox | BG Vox | Kick | Snare | Bass | Gtrs | Keys | Audience |

| 1 | 2 | 3 | 4 | 5 | 6 | 7 | 8 |
|---|---|---|---|---|---|---|---|
| Ld Vox | BG Vox | Kick | Snare | Bass | Gtr | Gtr | Audience |

### It's Time to Mix

When it comes to mixing for a studio recording, you will probably take a different approach from the one I suggested for live recording. In a typical studio recording, you'll probably start with the drums (either the kick first, but sometimes the snare or overheads), the bass, or the vocals. It all depends on the song or the particular preference of the person doing the mixing. In this case, it's probably a good idea to not be too stringent about where you start from, because you might wind up emphasizing the weakest track you have. What you're trying to do is take the attention off the weakest track.

Even though an eight-track mix is fairly simple, figure out the weakest tracks and save them for the final stage (the audience track will be last). If the drums are a little floppy execution-wise, start with the bass and keep that in front (just like in all the '60s records). If the vocals go a little sideways, keep them lower in the mix. At all times, mix to your strengths, de-emphasize your weaknesses, and bring the audience in at the end to add the glue to the track.

## NOW FOR SOME SERIOUS RECORDING

Now let's look at recording songs, either for a demo, to get gigs with or to showcase the songs you and your band mates have written. While it could be as easy as setting up a couple of mics and a portable recorder during a gig as illustrated above, it probably will take a great deal more work than that.

# THERE'S NO SUCH THING AS A DEMO

About the only thing that I would consider a demo is a sample of the songs from your set list if you're in a cover band and need to prove to a promoter or club owner that you play acceptably well. If you record these songs too well (like you might in a professional studio) you run the risk of having the recording backfire on you, with the club owner thinking that you really don't sound that good because everything was polished in the studio. That's why I always felt that a controlled example of your set, like at a rehearsal, made a lot better sense for getting a gig. You don't want to spend too much time or money on this, and luckily, you don't have to.

If you're recording some of your own songs, erase the word "demo" from your mind. A demo will always keep you in the "good enough" mindset. You have to approach each song as if it were a finished master because these days it's easier than ever to make some excellent recordings without spending a huge amount of money. So, forget about demos. They're just an excuse for a recording that's inadequate in some way.

The idea of the demo came out of practicality, since up until about the year 2000 you just didn't have the ability to make a record that sounded like a major release anywhere but in a real recording studio. Yes, it was done occasionally, but the vast majority of songs you heard on the radio were made by real pros with real pro equipment. Back then, bands would make a demo that was just good enough to get a label or producer interested in taking them to the next level. Because studios were so expensive (typically $100 to $250 an hour, plus engineer, tape, etc.), it was usually impossible to spend enough time to make a recording that was up to snuff, compared with a major label release. And if you weren't located near a reasonably high-end studio, you were forced to use whatever was available. As a result, almost everyone made a demo before moving on to a deal with a label. Once signed, you got to make a record in a professional studio with some pros who knew what to do.

Most of that has changed with the last few generations of affordable and readily available recording gear, and with the fact that the listening public doesn't care as much about audio fidelity as they once did (maybe they never did, but the record companies sure thought so). It's easy enough now to record for less money and distribute it for next to nothing. People expect every recording to be as good as you can make it, and that's part of the problem.

Just because you own a hammer doesn't necessarily mean that you know how to swing it, and the same applies to recording gear. You may have some really cool recording toys, but it takes more than owning them to make a decent-sounding recording. There's a lot of information on recording available in books (like my four prior to this one) and on the Internet, but only an ear developed by experience can bring these tools to life.

## THE WAY TO MAKE YOUR RECORDINGS SOUND GREAT

Now that we've gotten that straight, let's talk about recording your stuff so it really sounds great. I'd be shocked if someone in the band doesn't already have some sort of multitrack recording setup, so the temptation to record yourselves is going to be really great. My advice: don't do it if you can help it, at least not the basic tracks. The reason? Recording takes a lot of practice to develop the ear required to make things sound good, for one. It's usually impossible to concentrate on both playing in a band and learning how to record at the same time (believe me, I know from experience). The second reason is that you probably don't have a recording environment that's conducive to making your band sound great. My suggestion is to do what most of the pros do: record your basic tracks (all the rhythm instruments if possible, but at least the drums) in as close to a real studio as you can using the best engineer you can get. After you've gotten the basic tracks to the point that you're satisfied, bring the tracks back to your band mates with the multitrack setup and do your overdubs without feeling the need to look at the clock all the time. When you're ready to mix, go back to either the engineer who recorded your basics, or find the most experienced person you can find. Use this method and you'll find that you'll get a better product without having to spend too much of the band's time learning to record and mix.

If you decide to record yourself or if there's just no one in your area that you like and trust to record you, at least get some help. There are lots of good books out there, but of course I recommend the ones I wrote: *The Recording Engineer's Handbook, The Mixing Engineer's Handbook* (a best seller!), and the *Audio Mastering Handbook*. The first book you should get is *The Drum Recording Handbook*, because the drum sounds are the key to a great-sounding recording. If the drums don't sound great, neither will anything else.

# PROS ARE PROS FOR A REASON

In the days before home studios were affordable, people learned the art of making records mostly through an informal apprentice program. They started off in the studio as a runner or go-fer (the person that goes for coffee, sandwiches, etc.—in England they called them tea boys), moved up to tape-op (the person that operated the tape recorder—a position that was the first studio job to become obsolete), became an assistant engineer where they really learned the ropes, and then finally became a full engineer. When an engineer got enough clients he (or she) became an independent, and if he worked on enough hits, finally got a chance to become a producer. A producer didn't necessarily need to be an engineer, and was usually a musician who had some experience making records, had a good sense of what sounded good, and knew how to put songs together. Today the studio pros who can be really helpful have spent a lot of time in the control room and have developed their ears to where they're finally tuned to what needs to happen to make a recording great.

The same goes for studio musicians. Session players have enough experience to know what to play and when to play it. They know how to best interact with the artist, other musicians, the engineer, and the producer to make the session the most efficient and fun. They have a vast array of equipment to choose from, all of it in perfect working order. They know how to make you and your song sound great.

> *I tend to approach every session, whether it's in somebody's cramped little studio with Pro Tools LE or if it's in a multimillion dollar facility, the same as if I were at Abbey Road with the Beatles. They're all equally important. I'm as enthusiastic or excited about coming over to somebody's house for $50 as I am for a triple-scale record date. To me it's all the same and I think people sense that enthusiasm and excitement.*—Paul Ill

> *If I have Chad Wackerman on drums, I can tell him to lay back one more hair on the beat and he'll know what I mean, where with younger players there's only ahead of the beat, behind the beat, and on the beat. For advanced players there are a hundred variations of all of those places.*—Producer Frank Fiztpatrick

> *An important thing for me is to serve the song at all times. Try to keep an open mind and if someone has an idea in the*

*room then always let that idea be heard. If it involves you trying something different in the part that you're playing, you can't get defensive about it. You have to just let it happen because that really goes a long way toward creating a good atmosphere in the room. When everybody drops their ego and just tries to serve the song, I find that the best idea will rise to the surface and everybody will recognize it. It's human nature to want our ideas to be the best ones, but if you can be open to others' suggestions, you can learn something and maybe do something that you wouldn't have thought of doing.*—Peter Thorn

The problem now is that most of the high-level pros are concentrated in London, New York City, Nashville, and Los Angeles, and so chances are you won't have the ability to work with one of them even if you want to (although it's getting easier with musicians, since most are available via eSession or will play on a track if you send them song files).

What I'm trying to illustrate is that studio pros are pros because they spend all their time working in the studio on music, and all that experience takes their ears and ability to another level completely.

## IT'S A DIFFERENT MINDSET

It's been said over and over in this book, but it's still worth repeating. You have to think differently when you're about to do some serious recording. If you read the first part of the book about your individual instrument, then you're aware of the things that are expected if you want your recording to be successful. Once more, let's reinforce what it takes to think like a pro when it's time for a recording session.

**Arrive early.** This goes without saying, but I'll say it again to reinforce it. You should always arrive at least a half-hour before the downbeat of the session and if you're a drummer or keyboard player with a lot of gear, then figure one full hour. Remember, if you're late and you keep people waiting, it's probably going to cost you money.

**Turn your cell phone off.** The session should be your main priority with as few distractions as possible and one of the easiest ways to achieve this is to turn off your cell phone. If you leave it on, not only do you risk ruining a good take if the ringer goes off, but talking on the phone is the best way to stop the momentum of a session in its tracks. And it's disrespectful to everyone else involved. Don't even bother to put it on vibrate, as this will cause you to lose your focus just as easily as when the ringer is on. Turn it off; then leave the phone outside the studio in the lounge so you won't be tempted to use it.

**Make sure your gear works.** If you're serious about recording, then everything has to work, from the smallest guitar cable to the largest amplifier. Not only does everything have to work, but it has to be in tip-top condition as well. The better everything works and sounds, the better your recording will be.

*Make sure your gear is comfortable to you. Make sure everything's working, the cables aren't crackling, your basses are in tune and intonated, your tuner is working, and your amp sounds good. Make sure you can set everything up quickly and be zero hassle to anybody, either technically or personally. Turn off your cell phone. Make it a point that everyone sees you're turning off your phone or leaving it outside the studio so they all understand that you're not interested in phone calls while you're working. Make the session a priority.*—Paul Ill

**Be Prepared.** Know just what you're going to record. Have a plan, and then have a backup in case things don't work out the way you expect. Make any charts, notes, lyric sheets, or cheat sheets beforehand. You don't want to waste anyone's time for something that could easily have been done beforehand.

**Bring everything to the session you think you might need.** Even if there's only a remote possibility that a piece of gear might be needed, bring it anyway because you can bet it'll be the one piece that will hold everything up if you don't.

*I over-kill. I bring so much more stuff than we'll use, because that's part of the charm of hiring me. It's part of the "ooh, ahh" factor, and also it's to be of service to the muse and the spirit of the session. If you're not sure what you're going to be doing or where the music is going to go, that one extra piece that you bring can make the difference. I'll bring as many basses as I can fit in my car for that day with a B-15.*—Paul Ill

## DIFFERENT GEAR FOR DIFFERENT JOBS

It's also been said many times in this book that playing a gig is distinctly different from recording a song. What works on a gig won't always translate, either playing-wise or gear-wise. You choose your gear for a gig based on versatility, durability, and general ruggedness. The only thing that counts in the studio is the sound.

While one size might fit all on a gig, it will usually make for a boring recording, especially if you're recording more than one song. This doesn't apply if you're just trying to record some songs of your band to get some gigs, but if you're recording your own songs, then gear makes a profound difference in how you sound. You should make every effort to get a variety of the best-sounding gear that you can.

I'll give you an example. On the first record I ever made (at the tender age of fifteen) my band, except for the keyboard player, took all of our stage gear into the only place you could make a record at the time—a real recording studio. The keyboard player used the studio's Hammond and Leslie combination. When we finished the record and looked back on our experience, we were horrified to find that the one who sounded the best was actually the weakest player—the keyboard player! How'd that happen? Because he had the best pro equipment to use and all the gear we owned paled in comparison. It was an early lesson in using the right gear for the job.

## TIPS FOR A GREAT RECORDING

Whether you're recording yourselves with your own gear or are using a studio, the goal is the same: make the songs and the recordings sound as big, as polished, and as accessible to your audience (however large or small) as you can. That being said, here are some things to be aware of.

### You Hardly Ever Sound Great the First Time

Contrary to what you might have heard about hit records done on the first take, most recordings of any type require a lot of work to be any good. It takes time to get the right sounds and performances, and unfortunately, these things usually can't be rushed.

Perhaps the most difficult thing to learn when recording is not to expect gold-record-quality playing right off the bat. One of the worst ideas you can get is that you have to be perfect every time you play. It just doesn't happen that way, so don't get discouraged. Even the best studio players make some flubs or have slightly erratic time when they're playing. They just go back and fix the problems afterward, and you can too. Yes, it happens occasionally when someone gets extremely lucky and plays something terrific on the first take, but it's a rare exception—even for studio-savvy and expert musicians.

Recording is hard work. It's not uncommon for people to slave over a part for days or even weeks until it feels right in the track. So if pros won't settle for something that's not the best it can be, why should you?

I know you're probably thinking about all those hit records in the '50s that were done in just a few takes, how the first Beatles record was done in one twelve-hour session, and how in the glory days of Motown in Detroit they used to crank out three number-one hits in three hours. All true. But don't forget that all those famous 1950s artists honed their act from months and years of playing on the road, the Beatles played six sets a night for a year in Hamburg before they hit the studio, and the Motown studio musicians were the best of the best jazz musicians in Detroit with some hall-of-fame songwriters and arrangers. But besides all that, the bar is set so much higher for recording these days. Sad but true that many of those incredible tracks just wouldn't make it through the recording process if they were done today because of defects in the playing.

The fact of the matter is that recording today on any level is a demanding process, so don't expect great results right away. Just like a band learning a new song together, everything takes time before it actually gels, so be prepared to work until you get it.

As an example, I believe that a typical overdub takes at least two days to record. The first day you work the part out until it's a perfect fit for the song. The second day you perform it well, because by then you know how to play it and can concentrate on performance. The whole trick is to follow your gut. If you think deep down inside that you can do it better, then you probably can.

### It's Work

In the majority of cases, making a record is hard work. It takes a lot of time to work parts out, make them sound great, and play or sing them well. Sure, there's been a handful of records that have been done on the first take or in a couple of hours (mostly in the '50s and early '60s), but today it's a rare occurrence that involves as much luck as winning the lottery.

During the recording of one of my early band's demo tapes, we became increasingly frustrated because it seemed to take forever (a whole four hours!) to record six songs from our set. "We must really suck," is what we told ourselves from that point until the band broke up, but only later when I began to regularly work in studios did I learn the real truth. Recording is hard work and takes a lot of time to make something that will sound good.

These were songs that we'd been playing at gigs every weekend for about a year so we knew them backward and forward. Or so we thought! You never really know exactly what you're playing and exactly what you sound like until you record yourself. Almost always, you'll find that something that you thought was gangbusters is, in fact, just a buster. You might be playing a line differently from the other guitar player. Maybe your rhythm pattern is different from what the drummer is playing. Maybe you just can't hit that high like you thought you could.

The secret is to be brutally honest about your playing and singing, just like in the previous chapters. If it doesn't sound great, either rehearse it until it does or don't play it at all!

## The Importance of a Producer

Whether you're recording cover material as a demo for getting jobs or making a record of your own songs (remember, there are no demos when it comes to your material), it really helps to have an outside ear to help. I can tell you from experience, most people are incapable of doing more than one of the primary studio jobs at the same time (artist, musician, engineer, producer). Yes, Prince does it, but he's not in a band and has plenty of time and money to get things to his liking.

A producer is the equivalent of a movie director in that he has the ability to craft your songs technically, sonically, and musically. Having a producer helps your studio efficiency. He can tell you when a take is better or worse than the rest. He can tell you when something sounds good or bad and, most important, tell you why. He can mediate between opinions of band members if you let him. Just these things alone can make things go a whole lot faster and save you money and some brain damage as well.

Obviously, it's best to get a pro who produces a lot and knows his way around the studio, but someone like that will charge you. An engineer can usually help because he has a lot of studio experience, but once again, it's really hard to engineer and produce at the same time and do both well. A trusted musician friend who likes your band can be helpful as long as he has the respect of all the band members. The real key is to have a respected outside voice that can help you in your decision making.

What you don't want, however, is a control freak who insists things be done his way, someone who claims to have a lot of experience that can't back it up, or someone who everyone in the band disrespects. It's your music and he works for you (unless you're signed to a record label, in which case he works for them). He's there to facilitate your vision, not his.

## This Isn't a Party

You should never treat recording as anything other than something that must take your entire focus. Indeed, you'll need to give it 100 percent of your concentration to sound your very best. To that end, recording should never be treated as a party. It's not a place for your friends or fans to hang out, and it's not a place for a couple of six packs. Just because you might be a punk band, it doesn't mean you have to carry the lifestyle over to recording. The Pistols had to be wild, wasted, and non-conformist because that was their image, but they were deadly serious when recording. Green Day also had that persona in the early days, but they were serious when recording and that's why they climbed the ladder and most of the others from that scene didn't. If you want to make the best recording you can, don't show up wasted. Do show up on time, and show up prepared. Good music makes you a cool person, not the act.

# CHAPTER 13

# The PA

Regardless of whether you own your own PA (public address) system or rely on what you find at the venues where you gig, having a basic idea of the philosophy and workings of a modern system will help you get the most out of one. Knowledge will take away some of the misconceptions today's musicians have, and help you sound better as a result.

## VOICES COME FIRST

The softest things onstage need the most amplification, and that means vocals first. Regardless of what anyone might tell you, unless you're playing in stadiums and arenas where everything onstage needs to be reinforced, vocals take precedence and are the starting place for getting your mix together.

One of my pet peeves is a whole generation of soundmen who have learned how to mix live sound the wrong way. They concentrate more on the kick and snare, forgetting (or not knowing) that the vocal not only needs the most help, but also has to be the most prominent in the mix. Yes, you want your live audio to sound like a record, but the only way to do that is to concentrate on the vocals first (just like a on a record).

In order to get a great balance in the least amount of time, the priority of instruments should go something like this:

1. Vocals
2. Kick drum
3. Keyboards
4. Anything needing a direct box (like a computer for backing tracks)
5. Snare
6. Horns/blues harp (harmonica) if you have them
7. Guitars
8. Bass

This isn't the order in which you sound check each instrument; it's what usually needs the most reinforcement prioritized by what's the quietest onstage. (There are exceptions, of course; someone might be playing a mandolin, for instance). Even though the DI'ed (direct injected, or plugged directly into the mixer without being miked) backing tracks from a computer usually don't have any amplification onstage and are technically quieter than the vocals, if you have singers, then vocals are still the priority.

You also should beware of any soundman who spends an inordinate amount of time working on the kick drum and who mixes it louder than everything else onstage. Make sure you tell him that you want the vocals up front and not the kick and snare. After all, what record have you ever heard where the kick is the lead instrument?

## THE GRAPHIC EQ IS NOT A TONE CONTROL

One of the most misused pieces of PA gear is the graphic equalizer. Almost every PA system now has a graphic equalizer (the one with sliders for individual frequencies) either built-in or connected to it. Unless you're not using microphones with the systems, it's best not to use the graphic as a system tone control. It's there primarily to combat feedback.

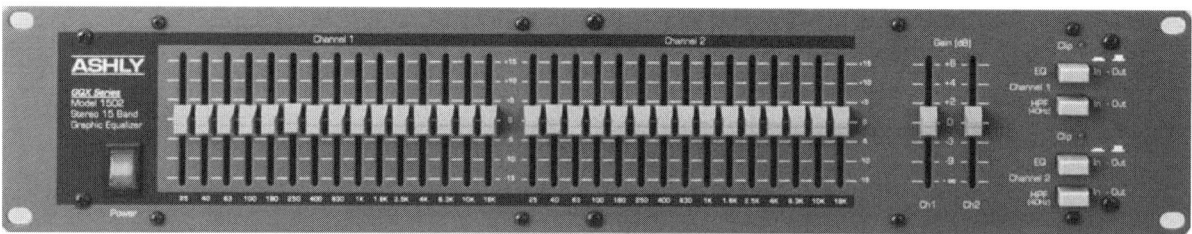

*Fig. 13.1. A graphic equalizer.*

## Why Is There Feedback?

Feedback is the ringing sound that occurs when sound coming out of a speaker re-enters a microphone and is re-amplified over and over. Every room has specific frequencies at which it resonates, and these are typically the first frequencies at which feedback will occur. This phenomenon is largely due to the lack of design and construction with acoustics in mind in venues where music is performed. This includes clubs, church sanctuaries, and even mega arenas where most large concerts occur (which are sometimes the worst acoustic spaces for music).

If you play one room exclusively (where you rehearse, for example), you're usually able to get your equipment to sound its best on a consistent basis. As soon as you gig in different venues, though, you'll probably have the frustrating experience of trying to get the required volume level while trying to control feedback. As a result, many people play Russian roulette with a graphic equalizer to try to get the most gain before feedback. Ironically, even if you do manage to control the feed and get enough level out of the PA, the audio might end up sounding sterile and lacking punch, because too much equalization has been used.

## Ringing Out the System

Fortunately, there is a way to use your graphic EQ to deal with this phenomenon and help get the best sound and most headroom from your equipment. It's called "ringing out the system" and while it's not a perfect solution, it's often the best fix in an even more imperfect audio environment. Here's how it works:

1. Make sure all of the mics are turned on and in the position they'll be used. You should have a mix set up with the approximate balances that you will eventually use.
2. If a mic input, graphic EQ, or power amp has a fixed-frequency "hi-pass" filter or "low-cut" filter (same thing), make sure that it's selected or engaged. This will eliminate low frequencies the ear can't hear but which are amplified nonetheless (you don't want to amplify the rumble of trucks outside on the street).
3. Slowly increase the gain of the sound system until you can just barely hear feedback. As it feeds back, lower the slider of the graphic EQ at the frequency the feedback is occurring until the feedback stops.
4. Slowly increase the gain of the sound system, until feedback occurs again. This time it will probably be at a

different frequency. As it feeds back, lower the slider of the graphic EQ at the frequency at which the feedback is occurring, until it stops.
5. Repeat the process (you might have to repeat four or five times) until you finally hear multiple frequencies feed back at the same time. At this point, you've reached the maximum headroom in the system before feedback. Back the gain down until the feedback stops, and then start your sound check, rehearsal, or show.

One problem with this method is that you have to find the frequency slider that controls the feedback you're hearing. This usually takes ear training to develop a feel for which frequencies correspond to which frequency EQ sliders. Another way is to use a spectrum analyzer (either an outboard device or a built-in function of a PA; see Fig. 13.2), which can be an invaluable tool for tracking down troublesome frequencies. This device helps show where the potential problems are, so you don't need to find them by trial and error. This will also help you avoid over-equalization where you eliminate vast swathes of frequencies in order to kill the problem.

*Fig. 13.2. A spectrum analyzer.*

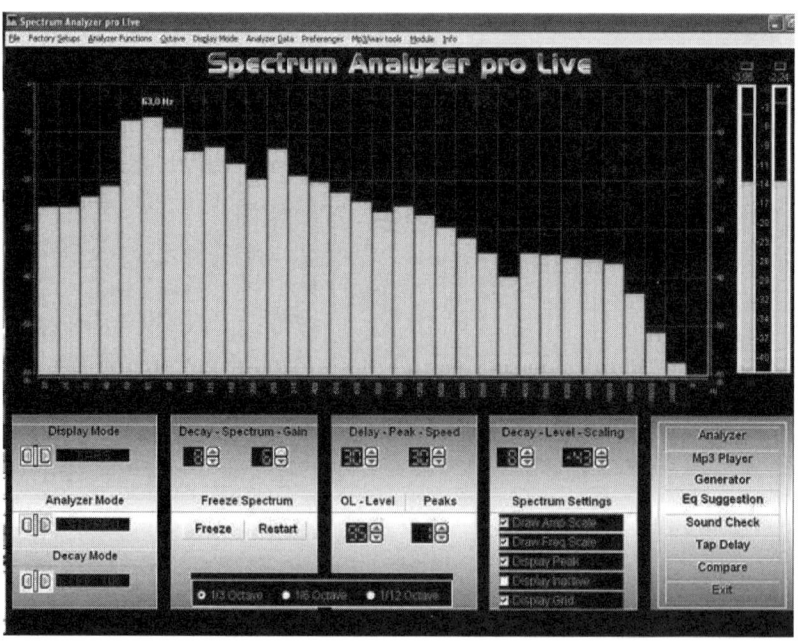

Another way to eliminate feedback is with an outboard device called a feedback eliminator (see Fig. 13.3). Feedback eliminators use digital processing to track the audio and watch for feedback. When feedback is sensed, a filter is automatically inserted at the proper frequency and adjusted to the right amount to help eliminate it. It's basically doing the same adjustments you do manually when you ring out the system, only thousands of times faster. While this can be really effective in some situations, a feedback eliminator can easily be fooled by things like intentional guitar feedback or long organ notes, and try to notch them out. You can end up with a sound system with no feedback, but also with no punch or intelligibility.

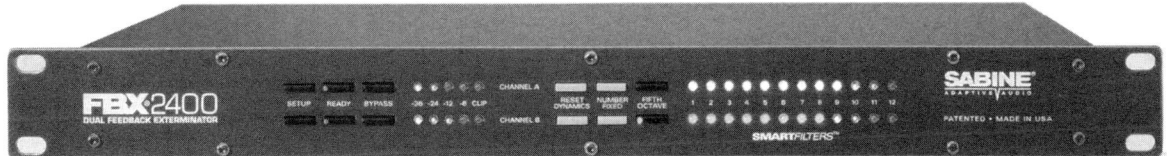

Fig. 13.3. A feedback eliminator.

Remember, no matter how much gear you have and how sophisticated it is, the limit of how loud you can get your system is mostly set by the acoustic environment, and not as much by the sound system.

## LET'S HEAR THOSE VOCALS

A few paragraphs back, we discussed how vocals were the most important component in a mix. One of the most important aspects of vocals is intelligibility, which is a fancy name for the ability to distinctly hear each lyric sung or word spoken. You can have a loud vocal, but if you can't pick out what the singer is saying, it still won't cut it. This is even more pronounced when speaking to the audience between songs. It's a total drag not to be able to pick up on what the person behind the mic is saying.

Bad intelligibility is usually the result of too much low end (low frequencies from about 120 Hz down) or too much lower midrange (in the 400 to 600 Hz area) EQ on the mic. Lower these a bit (start with the 400 to 600 Hz area first), and you should be able to suddenly pick out all the words. If that doesn't work, add a little in the 2000 Hz area, which is the part of the audio spectrum the ear hears best.

## MONITORS

Just about every performer is used to some kind of stage monitors, but it wasn't always that way. Believe it or not, back when I first started to play in the late '60s, monitors of any kind didn't exist. We had to turn the main PA cabinets in toward the band so that we could hear ourselves a little and hope that we didn't get feedback (there were no graphic EQs to help us control it back then either). While you still might have to do this if you don't have monitors, there are many types of affordable monitors, and they should be considered an integral part of your gear. Even if you play at venues that supply a sound system, bringing your own monitors can really help your comfort level onstage since they're always the same. That's what a lot of touring bands (such as Sting's) do. Let's take a look at what's available.

### Wedge Monitor

A wedge can be thought of as a regular speaker cabinet that's had its back cut off at an angle and laid on the floor (see Fig. 13.4). The angle has three benefits. First, the sound points up at the performer's head so he or she can hear more effectively. Second, properly placed floor monitors (at the base of the mic stand) play into the null of a directional vocal mic (the spot where it doesn't pick up very well), which increases the gain before feedback. And third, the low profile makes them unobtrusive so as not to block the view of the audience. Stage wedges come in various sizes with speakers ranging from 10-inch to dual 15s with a horn and beyond.

*Fig. 13.4. A typical wedge floor monitor.*

### Side-Fill

If you're playing on really big stages like in an arena, it's sometimes difficult to get a mix from the floor monitors that cover the stage. This usually isn't a problem if you stand or sit in one position during your set, but if you move around at all, you'll find you can't hear much of the band unless you're directly in front of a monitor.

That's why most large PA systems also include side-fills (see Fig. 13.5). These are basically the same type of full-range speakers used for the front-of-house sound system, only they point across the stage and contain a full mix of the band to provide the performers with a more enveloping and well-balanced sound. This allows all performers to hear a good rough mix of the whole band while still having individual mixes at their position on the stage via the wedge monitors. In the past few years, technology has made it possible to achieve a full-sounding mix at each position with relatively small wedge monitors, so side-fills are used less.

*Fig. 13.5. A band using side-fills.*

While the side-fills often have basically the same mix as the front-of-house speakers, sometimes they contain what's called a cross-stage or X-stage mix. True X-stage mixes separate the stage in half, with vocals and instruments from the center of the stage to the right mixed into the left X-stage system, and everything from center stage to the left mixed into the right X-stage system. This results in a more intimate soundfield on the stage, giving the musicians a feel similar to the one they had when they played on smaller stages. If a guitar player and bass player are standing next to each other, they can hear each other's backline amplifier and don't need more of these instruments blaring at them from a side-fill. However, they may not hear the piano player on the opposite side of the stage. The piano player can hear his or her amp or monitor, but may need to hear the bass player and a little guitar. Usually drums and lead vocals are mixed equally into both X-stage mixes.

While it might be tempting to use an extra PA speaker or side-fills as your only monitor, you won't get the same performance as you will with a well-designed wedge. Floor monitors properly placed at the base of the mic stand are playing into the null of the directional vocal mic, which increases the gain before feedback. If you forego the monitor wedges and try to depend strictly on side-fills, you'd probably get too much feedback when trying to get it loud enough to please everyone.

## Stand Mounted

As the title implies, these are much smaller, unobtrusive monitor cabinets that can be mounted on a mic stand and placed close to the performer's ear for better intelligibility and less overall sound pressure onstage. A good example of popular stand-mounted monitors are the Galaxy Hot Spot (see Fig. 13.6) and TC Electronic's VoiceSolo VSM-300, which is interesting in that it puts three channels of "more me" (more on this in the next section) and an overall mix input into a powered speaker. While these work well for acts with a rather quiet stage volume on small stages, they probably won't work if you're doing crank-it-up rock or anything with an aggressive stage level. The other problem is that they're quite directional, requiring you to stand or sit in just the right place to hear them.

*Fig. 13.6. Galaxy Hot Spots.*

## In-Ear Monitoring (IEM)

With artists used to getting the perfect mix in the studio when they make records, the idea of getting the same thing live onstage in wireless earbuds seems like a dream come true. And that's what makes in-ear monitoring (IEM) so attractive. It's like wearing headphones onstage, but without the bulky headpiece. Originally only used by top touring professionals because of the cost, in-ear monitors are now finding a home on stages of all sizes across the country, because many less expensive systems are now available.

There are three basic approaches to IEM, each offering a different level of control.

**The simple "more me" knob.** With this kind of system, you receive a total monitor mix from the house PA or monitor system, but you're able to add more of your vocal and/or instrument to the mix. Something like the Rolls PM50 combines a single mic input with a mono or stereo monitor feed. Shure's P2T is a wired or wireless mixer with two XLR/TRS combo inputs for mic or line signals (see Fig. 13.7). It's also available with a belt-pack receiver and ear buds as the PSM-200 system.

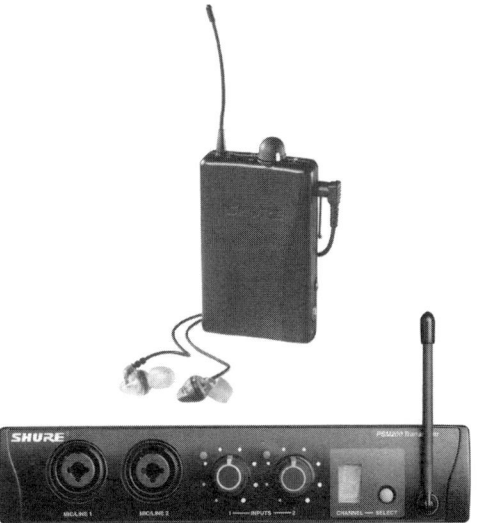

*Fig 13.7. Shure P2T personal wireless system.*

**The "me plus stems" approach.** This is where you control your own mix of stems. This means you'll have a separate mix of the drums (with maybe the kick separated), a mix of all the keyboards, a mix of the guitars, and a mix of the vocals. You then make your own personal mix. It's pretty easy to get a mix going when you only have to deal with one knob for bass, one for drums, one for vocals, one for your vocal, one for your instrument, and so forth. Hearback and Aviom are the largest manufacturers of these types of systems (see Fig. 13.8)

*Fig. 13.8. A Hearback personal monitor system.*

**The total personal mix.** This means you have your own unique mix tailored exactly to your needs. This setup offers maximum control, but requires a dedicated monitor console and operator because of the complexity involved.

Once you have a system in place, the next issue is how to get the audio from the mixer to your ears. Wireless belt-pack receivers are available from companies like Shure and Sennheiser, or you can plug headphones or earbuds right into personal mixers like the ones made by Rolls or Aviom. Make sure you put a limiter in the signal chain to protect your ears from volume spikes; otherwise you can cause some real ear damage. Pro earpieces come in generic or custom-molded versions from companies like Future Sonics (see Fig. 13.9), Sennheiser, Shure, M-Audio, Audio-Technica, Ultimate Ears, Sensaphonics, and Westone. If you're on a budget, nothing says you can't use earbuds intended for portable MP3 players like the iPod.

**Benefits of in-ear monitoring.** The benefits of using in-ear monitors are numerous: better quality sound, improved stereo imaging, less vocal strain, protection against hearing damage, portability, increased gain before feedback, and lowered onstage volume. Just one of those features would make IEMs a great purchase, but add all of them up and it's hard to choose floor monitors.

*Fig. 13.9. Future Sonics Atrio Series M5 earbuds.*

**Reduced stage volume equals a clean mix.** Believe it or not, IEM systems are best known for their ability to reduce that dreaded nemesis of soundmen everywhere—stage volume. When band members hear vocals or instruments through wedges and instrument amplifiers, they tend to turn up to hear themselves better, usually resulting in a loud stage. A loud stage causes a muddy house mix and forces the sound engineer to turn up the mains to compensate for stage levels.

**Simplicity of setup.** An IEM system can replace all the heavy speakers and amplifiers in a monitor system with a single rack of lightweight gear.

**Consistent sound quality.** Besides protecting your hearing against high sound levels, IEMs also offer improved and uniform sound quality and reduced feedback. You can bring a personal IEM system to every gig and rehearsal, and it will sound just like it did the last time you used it.

**Hands-on control.** If you use one of the self-monitoring systems like those offered by Aviom and Hear Technologies, you can control your own monitor mix onstage and mix it exactly to your liking. In smaller venues and in bands without the luxury of a separate monitor engineer and console, the soundman is freed from sending a number of separate cue mixes.

## The Disadvantages of IEMs

One problem with IEMs is that you can really hurt yourself if there's feedback or an audio spike from a mic being dropped. Some systems have built-in limiters to prevent ear damage, but the only way to be certain is to strap a really good limiter across the monitor feed from the house. That way you can always be certain you're protected should the worst happen.

Because of these potential problems, some soundmen and venues refuse to let you use IEMs for fear of being sued if hearing damage occurs. This is certainly an appropriate concern. If the soundman doesn't have any idea about a system you're bringing in, or has no ultimate control over your mix, he still may be liable if you hurt yourself. Once again, make sure you have a limiter patched into your system so a loud spike or a dose of feedback doesn't harm your hearing. If a soundman sees that you know how to use your IEMs and you're protected, he may feel protected too, and help you get a great monitor mix.

## WHAT'S IN YOUR MIX?

For bands not used to each member getting their own separate mix, it's not uncommon to be confused about what you need in your mix. Usually, you want things that guide you the most. Kick and snare for rhythm, the lead vocal, and a tonal center like a keyboard or rhythm guitar (unless what you play creates the tonal center), and any other instrument or vocal that you cue off of. Lead singers always want to hear lots of themselves and a little of the other vocals if they have to sing harmony, some kick and snare for rhythm, and either a guitar or keyboard for pitch. Drummers usually want their kick drum as loud as it can go, maybe the hi-hat, and some vocals. Players who sing backup usually want themselves and the lead vocal, some snare for rhythm cues, and a rhythm guitar or keyboard for pitch cues. One thing you don't want is the entire mix, since that can cause problems with feedback and intelligibility. If you're new to having a personal monitor mix, let the monitor engineer set up what he thinks you might need from his experience; then, go from there.

# CHAPTER 14

# Be a Professional

While this chapter is called "Be a Professional," it could just as easily have been called "Be a Diplomat," "Be a Compromiser," or, even, "Be a Nice Guy." It's about how to be in a band with other people who may or may not want to do and play things the way you do. Let's face it, a band is a family, and, like any family, it's going to have its differences. The only way a band can be successful is to resolve those differences before they get out of hand, and the easiest way is when everyone acts in a professional manner.

## WHAT IS A PROFESSIONAL?

In the context of this book a professional is someone who makes his living only by playing music. Whether that describes you or not, what you need is a professional's attitude in order to get ahead personally and with your band. Let's take a look at the qualities of a professional attitude.

A professional:

**Is always on time.** Time is money, and a pro is not only on time, but also early (as illustrated in many chapters of this book). If he's delayed and unable to arrive at the agreed-upon time, he calls ahead to inform everyone, and then gives his best estimate of when he'll arrive.

**Is always open to ideas.** Instead of arguing about the value of an idea, a pro says, "I haven't tried that before, but I'm really interested to hear what it sounds like." No idea is too crazy to at least consider. You never know when something that you initially thought was too far out is the perfect solution to a problem or is a great addition to a song.

*I always assume they may be going for something that maybe I'm not aware of. If they want to use a Radio Shack reverb on my bass, I'd probably say, "Great, I never tried that before. Let's do it."*—Paul Ill

*Try to keep an open mind and if someone has an idea in the room then always let that idea be heard. If it involves trying something different in the part you're playing, you can't get defensive about it. You have to just let it happen because that really goes a long way toward creating a good atmosphere in the room. When everybody drops their ego and just tries to serve the song, the best idea will rise to the surface and everybody will recognize it. It's human nature to want our ideas to be the best ones, but if you can be open to other's suggestions you can learn something and maybe do something that you wouldn't have thought of doing.*—Peter Thorn

**Is focused only on the music.** When a pro is at a rehearsal, gig, or recording session, he's there 100 percent in the moment and focused on giving the best performance he can. He's not thinking about his girlfriend, paying the bills, or the after-gig party. All his concentration is on the music.

*Make sure you can set everything up quickly and be zero hassle to anybody. You don't want to cause a problem to anybody, either technically or personally. Turn off your cell phone. Make it a point that everyone sees that you're turning off your phone or leaving it outside the studio so they all understand that you're not interested in phone calls while you're working. Make the session a priority. Don't bring reading material into the session with you. Don't be net surfing on your phone during a session.*—Paul Ill

**Is open to criticism or suggestions.** A pro doesn't take suggestions or criticism personally. He takes it in the spirit of making the music better. This is a hard one to uphold, especially when the criticism is coming from someone not as sensitive as you, but it's the right thing to do. If someone is being abusive, however, it's okay to say, "I don't agree with you, and unless you speak to me in a respectful manner, this conversation is over."

*Be as flexible as you can be. Don't be stubborn; trust the people you work with. If the engineer or producer has a suggestion, trust their advice.*—Brian MacLeod

**There's no "me" in "team."**

*You've got to really think of the band being more important than any individual in the band. There's no time or place for ego problems or for people who want to be noticed above the others; it's really about thinking about the songs and the music being bigger than any of the individuals.*—Brain Ray

**Presents his ideas in a respectful manner.** He doesn't say, "I should sing this because your singing sucks." He says, "Would you mind if I give it a try just to see how it comes out?"

**Takes responsibility for his mistakes.** A pro immediately owns up to a mistake, oversight, error, or blunder and says, "Sorry, it was my fault," and then accepts the consequences.

**Never parties on the job.** A pro is 100 percent focused on the music at hand. While a few beers might not constitute a party, they certainly don't help you play better during a rehearsal or gig if your mind isn't all there. There's plenty of time to party later, so save it until then.

**Treats his band mates with respect.** A pro treats his fellow musicians as equals and peers, and would never intentionally do or say anything to disrespect any of them.

**Treats his road crew, engineers, light man, and everyone working for the band with respect.** A pro understands that all of the people around him are working to make him sound and look better, and they deserve to be treated respectfully as well.

**Treats his audience with respect.** A pro understands he's there to entertain the audience and without them, he'd be playing at home in his bedroom.

If you assume a professional attitude by following the above points, you'll find that people respect you more, interpersonal tensions ease and band life gets a lot smoother.

## THE IMPORTANCE OF DIPLOMACY

One of the greatest talents needed in a team situation like a band is for the members to learn how to suggest things without offending others. Artists are usually very sensitive people and have thin skins by nature. You can be perfectly right about a particular issue, yet still be completely wrong in how you present it. The object is to help your band mates, not hurt them.

One who has a talent for choosing their words carefully can use it in a constructive manner, instead of using it to make cutting remarks that can be disrespectful and hurtful. If someone can't handle feedback and constructive criticism, the problem may well be the one who's delivering it, not the one receiving it.

To illustrate the point, there's an old story about a young man who was caught committing a burglary. When his time in court came, the evidence against him was overwhelming and the prosecutor had the case in the bag. All the defense attorney could do was to put the boy's mother on the stand in the hopes of gaining some sympathy, and maybe leniency, for his client. Sobbing to the jury, she went on and on about how hard she tried to be a good mother and how her son really was a good boy.

When the prosecuting attorney got his chance to cross-examine, he couldn't resist tearing her words apart and driving her pleas for mercy into the ground. His ego-driven need to destroy her claims left the poor woman a pathetic, blubbering mess. Out of sympathy for the mother, the jury found her son not guilty, despite all the evidence to the contrary.

The point is that one needs to know how to make a case, but it's equally important to know when to let it go. I'm sure everyone has worked with, or will at some time work with, a person who refuses any suggestion and won't back down, no matter what. The trick with a person like this is not to make him defensive or you'll never change his mind. Do it quietly enough, and the next time the subject comes up, he won't remember there being a difference of opinion about it, and might even think it was his own idea to begin with.

Set an example in how well you can accept ideas from others without taking offense, and you likely will find them accepting your ideas much more easily. Diplomacy is a discipline, and one well worth practicing.

# STEPS IN RESOLVING A CONFLICT

Being in any relationship requires compromise, and a band is no different from what you'd expect between family, friends, girlfriends, boyfriends, wives, husbands, bosses, and co-workers. There are times when you have to bend to keep the peace.

While compromise is easy for some people, others have a personality that would never allow it. Here are steps you can take to state your case effectively and resolve the conflict (unless the other person is so unreasonable that nothing will ever get through, in which case, jump down to "There's Always Somebody Else" in this chapter).

**Cool off first.** Conflicts can't be solved when emotions are running hot. Take some time to get away from the problem, and then brainstorm about what the problem is, what caused it and, most important, what the possible solutions are.

**Present accolades, support, and respect.** Acknowledge the person's accomplishments and talent first. Something like, "I want to start by saying the band has never been better since you joined, and the parts that you're singing are far better than I ever expected."

**Analysis of why the problem occurred.** When you give a clear explanation of why you think there's a problem or why it has occurred, you set the initial groundwork for solving it. If the other person knows exactly what your side of the story is, you might find that you're both on the same page, but on different sides of it.

**Take responsibility and use "I" messages.** If you're aware of having a part in a conflict, take responsibility and own up to it, but make sure everything is from your point of view. For instance, it's best to say, "I think you were really flat on that part," rather than "Everybody knows that you always sing that part flat," or worse, "You're singing sucks, man."

**Describe what I or we need, so the problem doesn't happen again.** This is the solution from your point of view. "We need you to be here ten minutes before rehearsal so you have time to set up. That way we can get our full rehearsal in, which we really need right now."

**Support their success.** Tell him you want him to win, because if he wins, so do you. "The better you sound, the better we all sound," or "Do you know how great we're going to sound once you get that part down? We're going to kill!"

## HOW TO KEEP A BAND TOGETHER

Some of the things band members do might seem small and petty yet cause enough bad vibes and resentment (some of which may go unspoken) to eventually contribute to a band's breakup. Here are a few items that will help keep everyone in your band happy.

- Everyone has an equal say in what the band plays or doesn't play (unless the band has a clear-cut leader). This usually applies more to cover bands.
- Everyone is on time for practice.
- All gigs are planned around everyone's work schedule.
- Everyone helps load and unload the equipment. When the guitars and amps are packed away, then everyone helps the drummer or keyboard player with his or her rig. Everyone is responsible for setup and teardown of the PA (if you have one), which includes rolling up cables, loading gear into the truck or van, and so on.

The key is to have mutual respect for one another. If you can find people who will follow the golden rules above, you should have a good foundation for a band that stays together long enough to become great.

Most of all, if you can make the music your top priority and keep it there, you'll be amazed at how quickly many trivialities and problems evaporate. My advice is to work with other players who share your priorities and sense of dedication since many interpersonal problems are generally due to a departure from the "music first" rule. Keep in mind that a personal friend won't always make the best musical collaborator. A personal relationship is often very different from the professional relationships we have with fellow players, and sometimes it's best to keep it separate.

# THERE'S ALWAYS SOMEBODY ELSE

One of the worst things that can happen to a band with unresolved differences with one member is to give in for fear of not finding someone to replace that member. Take it from the voice of experience, this means the eventual slow and painful death of the band, or it poisons the experience so much that you'll never have any fun, which is even worse. It's not even the fear of finding someone as good; it's a fear of the process, which can be long and painfully difficult.

Let me tell you that you're always better off to cut the ties to that member if you've exhausted all means of reason and compromise. There is someone out there who's even better than what you've had (you'll finally get along if nothing else). He or she just doesn't know it yet. Sometimes they may come from the most unexpected place. A player you may never have considered might be disenchanted with his current band and want to change. Someone new to the area may have just moved in. Someone with just the right amount of talent but no experience or visibility may be a great fit. They're out there, but you have to make the effort to look. And don't compromise. Make sure the new member is just perfect before you make a commitment to them.

Remember, there's nothing wrong with having a trial period of a few weeks of rehearsal or a few gigs to see if everybody is still in love with each other. In fact, it's the smart thing to do.

So where do you find the perfect replacement? Try the following:

- ▶ Word of mouth—tell every band you know that you're looking for someone
- ▶ Tell every musician you know that you're on the lookout
- ▶ Put a sign in the all the local music stores
- ▶ Put a sign in all the local rehearsal studios
- ▶ Put a sign in all the local recording studios (if they'll let you)
- ▶ Post on any local Internet billboards or lists
- ▶ Post on your local Craigslist (if there is one)

Find another player to work with or at least one who will try to deal with problems head-on. These are your choices. As a psych friend told me: it's possible to change people a little bit one way or the other. But if you're going to affiliate with them over a period of time, expect that it is as good now as it is ever likely to get. If you approach these kinds of relationships with this outlook, chances are you won't be disappointed if the other person isn't making enough progress under the circumstances.

## WHO'S THE LEADER?

Although most bands start as democracies where everyone has an equal say (at least on the surface), bands work better if there is a leader with a strong focus. Even in a totally democratic band there are one or two members who naturally assume more responsibility than the rest, but the problem is that everyone in the band wants to feel like they're the most special member, even if they know they're not. Everyone should feel like they're contributing, even if there's a single person leading the charge. It takes real leadership to pull this off.

If you're building a band, you have to be the leader and have a focus on what you want to play and where you want the band to go. You have to be upfront with your band mates about what you expect from them, how much you want to gig, if or how they'll get paid, how much you'd like to rehearse, and all other band issues. If you are not as experienced as some of the other members, this may weaken your leadership if you're unsure of yourself and your band's mission, so don't be afraid to rely on them for advice.

In any creative enterprise you want as many ideas as possible, but everyone needs to understand that not all of them can be used. While some individuals may consistently have more and better ideas, everyone should be allowed to contribute. (Even the Beatles let Ringo sing a song every now and then, and it didn't hurt them a bit, even if he didn't sing as well as John, Paul, or George.) Above all, make sure the music is fun for everyone playing, because the audience will definitely pick up on it if it isn't. Every player should have fun doing what they're doing, and not be stewing about a crude and careless remark made by someone else.

Remember, the talent in leadership lies in getting people to want to do what you suggest, not by forcing them to bend to your will because you have the sharpest tongue.

If you're in a band with a clearly defined leader (it's his or her band), you must accept your role as a sideman. If this makes you unhappy and isn't the kind of band situation you ultimately want to be a part of, consider it background for the future and gain whatever experience you can from it until you find something better. Unless your personality and talent are such that you'll always be the leader, you'll find *this* an invaluable lesson.

Finally, you all have to realize that you're in the band together, regardless of who the leader is. Remember that all boats rise with the tide. As one member goes, you all go, so you might as well do it together.

# CHAPTER 15

# Your Show

Another easily overlooked item about your music is the show. It's not enough to be a good band anymore; you've got to have your show down, too. Here are a number of items you must be aware of in order to make your show as good as it can be. Once again, it doesn't matter what kind of band you are or what kind of music you play; these items are generic and if you follow my advice, I guarantee you will be better received by your audience.

## IT'S MORE THAN A COLLECTION OF SONGS

What exactly is a show? It's much more than just a collection of songs. While the world is full of performers who seemingly have no stage show, often there's more going on than meets the eye.

Everyone can name a great performer who just stands there and plays and gets rave reviews, and while that can be you too, today's audiences are a lot more sophisticated and require a certain level of professionalism from a performer, even with a minimal show. Let's look at some typical shows and spot the differences between them.

### An Amateur Show
In an amateur show you'll typically find the following traits:

- ▶ The band doesn't know what song to play next
- ▶ The band tunes up in-between songs

- The band has mindless banter with audience
- The band has inside-jokes that only they or a few people around them understand
- The band takes too much time between songs
- The band keeps the audience waiting while changing guitars, clothes, etc.
- The band doesn't acknowledge the audience, or worse, disrespects them

## A Tight, Professional Show

Likewise, in a tight, professional show you'll typically find the following traits:

- The band has a set list and knows exactly what they'll be playing and how much time it will take
- The band knows exactly what will happen between songs
- The band knows exactly when, where, and how the audience will be addressed
- The band takes as little time as possible between songs, or has something predetermined to entertain in those spaces
- The band plays to the room

## A Big Production Show

A big production observes all of the above and has the entire show planned.

- The band designs the set for maximum audience impact
- The band works out sound and music cues beforehand
- The band works out lighting cues beforehand
- The band works out wardrobe, guitar changes, and other details beforehand

## Your Set List

As I said in Chapter 8, dynamics apply to a set or show. Be sure that the show builds in intensity and peaks at the right time. It might start off with a couple of songs that are a 7 or 8 in intensity with a 10 being the most intense, back off to a ballad or something acoustic in the middle of the set that's a 3 or 4, then end the set with an 8 or 10. Once again, tension and release at work.

Let's look at a typical set list for a 45-minute set or show.

Song 1. Intensity level 8
Song 2. Intensity level 8

Singer speaks to audience, guitarist changes guitars

Song 3. Intensity level 7
Song 4. Intensity level 6 (alternative Song 4A. Intensity level 6)

Singer speaks to audience, sets up next song, guitarist changes guitars, drummer on percussion

Song 5. Intensity level 5
Song 6. Intensity level 7 (guitarist changes guitars, drummer back to drums during intro)

Singer speaks to audience, keyboard player sets up backing tracks

Song 7. Intensity level 8 (alternative Song 7A. Intensity level 8)
Song 8. Intensity level 10
Encore. Intensity level 10

As you can see, the songs are set up so all changes are smooth and there's no extra time taken between them. Alternative songs (called "audibles," just like in football) are predetermined and everyone knows what's going to happen in the set. If you plan your show or set and practice it at rehearsal until it is smooth, you'll be surprised at how professional you will sound.

Another thing: the old showbiz adage of "always leave them wanting more" really works. You're a lot better off leaving too early than too late; sometimes a single encore song (or none at all) is best.

## THE BIG ENDING

The endings to your songs can make a big difference in how your songs are perceived. As a guitar player I used to work with once told me, "The bigger the ending, the bigger the applause." I thought he was crazy, but, sure enough, he was right. The bigger, the more bombastic you can make an ending, the more the crowd seems to love it.

What's a big ending? It's when you hold it out with strumming and drum fills, flashing lights, pyro—whatever you can add. For an example, watch almost any concert video of your favorite artist. A big ending might not be best for every song, but it'll work for most of them that you play live.

## PLAYING WITH BACKING TRACKS

Your band may decide that it will sound better if it uses backing tracks to fill in the parts that can't be reproduced onstage. Whether it's "cheating" or not, I'll leave you to decide. Many performers use totally canned backing, and the audience seems to think that's okay. In fact, most major label releases require you to do special TV mixes that have everything but the lead vocal on it so a band can look like it's performing live on television. Only you can decide if this will work for your band. Keep in mind many of the things that make a band great (like dynamics for instance) will probably take a hit if you use backing tracks, but that shouldn't prohibit you from going in that direction if you're sure it will help the band.

Until recently, backing tracks came from a stack of MIDI modules, which then evolved to DAT tape players, which then evolved to Minidisc and CD players, and now come from either iPods or computer-based MP3 players, or even full-on computer-based DAW playback. Whichever way you go, the mechanics of using backing tracks are the same.

▶ If you're using a stereo MP3 player like an iPod, one side of the stereo signal contains a click track for the drummer to follow and the other side contains the backing track that are fed to the house PA system and the monitor system. It's important that all the members of the band hear the backing tracks so they can play in time with them. If it's only the drummer who hears the track, the song might start sounding stiff, or the band could start to run away with the tempo. You should treat the backing track as if it's another member of the band!

▶ Another way is to use an actual DAW like Pro Tools that feeds tracks from a laptop with a high-quality USB or Firewire audio interface (don't bother with the poor-sounding headphone jack on the computer). This way you can have all the songs pre-set on one timeline to make them easy to call up between songs, and you can give the soundman multiple tracks to help the mix balance (if you trust him to do that).

Whichever method you use, make sure that you either have a backup or a plan B in case the computer dies, you can't find the track, or the MP3 player freezes. It's embarrassing to be waiting onstage with nothing to say while waiting for the computer to boot up.

# SOUND

While we've talked about the PA system itself in Chapter 14, the audio aspect of your show (besides the hardware involved) is terribly important. The trouble is that the possibilities are often overlooked with the system on autopilot from show start to show finish.

If you have a house soundman, have him help you by giving him detailed set lists beforehand with desired audio cues. Believe me, he'll enjoy having something else to do besides babysitting the faders.

Example: "Kiss on my Lips"—Add long (you could get specific and say 4.0 sec) Hall Reverb on lead vox at the end of 2nd chorus. Add 350 ms delay to guitar solo.

# STAGE LIGHTING

Usually everyone in the band is so concerned about the music, they completely forget about the show (which is understandable and exactly the right priority), but one thing that can take your show to a new level without a great deal of effort and expense is lighting. All it takes is some forethought.

Let's cover some different scenarios:

- ▶ No lights at the venue
- ▶ Use the house lights
- ▶ Use the house lights but have a few of your own to augment what's there
- ▶ Use your own lighting rig and control it from the stage
- ▶ Use your own lighting rig and have a dedicated lighting person

### Get Some Lights

If you want to be seen you must be lit! Lighting draws attention to the action and enhances the mood, so even a simple lighting kit is a great investment and assures that if a venue doesn't have lighting (like at a party for instance) you won't be in the dark. If you play at a place that has some lighting, then your lights can be used to augment what's there (by focusing on a band member or on a dark spot of the stage) so you look even better.

It used to be difficult to buy professional lighting unless you were a pro and knew exactly where to look for it. Nowadays, finding a lighting package at a reasonable price is easier because most music stores either carry some lighting or can order it for you. Many manufacturers have systems available for as little as $400 (although most of the better systems start at about $1,000), so for about the price of a decent amplifier, you can really raise your game, show-wise (see Fig. 15.1).

*Fig. 15.1. A basic inexpensive lighting package.*

Try to get at least two lights for each side of the stage (four is better), but remember that the most common professional stage rig for concerts is a multi-color front wash and a multi-color back wash.

Here are a few things to think about when buying a lighting package:

**Hardware.** Make' sure your system has all the mounting hardware such as clamps, stands, and trusses included (bulbs too). Lighting doesn't do you any good if you show up to a gig and can't mount it anywhere. In fact, make sure you have a lighting stand available, no matter what.

**Go with LEDs.** If possible, buy the new LED lighting technology for its advantages over traditional tungsten-halogen stage lights (see Fig. 15.2). Not only is it a lot cooler, but you never have to replace expensive bulbs. Another thing is that it takes a long time for a traditional tungsten-halogen fixture to cool down enough to handle, which delays your pack-up. The LED's low weight is great on the back, plus they don't have any latency for flashing light effects and don't need expensive dimmer packages. The downside: they're not good at lighting anything more than ten or so feet away, and their color isn't exactly what traditional lighting people are used too, but those things probably won't affect you too much. In my opinion, the advantages outweigh the disadvantages by a long shot. LEDs are a little more expensive, but worth it.

*Fig. 15.2. A typical LED lighting fixture.*

**500 watts is enough.** Normal tungsten-halogen (non-LED) stage lights are really hot. I mean really hot! Don't get more wattage than you really need or you'll cook onstage (and I don't mean musically). Anything more than 500-watt fixtures can actually be too bright onstage, eliminating all shadows completely. The contrast between light and dark is what gives a stage depth and keeps it interesting. One-thousand-watt par cans are meant for huge stages where the lights are mounted far away on a truss. Five hundred watts per fixture is usually plenty for most venues. By the time you start playing large venues, you'll only have to worry about the creative aspects of the lighting because you'll have a real lighting company to do it for you.

**Fog is a great addition.** Nothing makes lights—and, therefore, the band—look better than smoke or fog. You can now buy a baby fog machine for as little as $100 (it only works for small stages though) and it should be considered an essential part of your lighting kit (see Fig. 15.3). The basic difference between consumer and high-end professional models is that consumer and semi-professional models usually cannot sustain a continuous output of fog. They will usually generate fog for a short period, and then need to pause to reheat before they can make fog again. More expensive models can generate fog continuously without the reheat cycle in between, but they cost much more than consumer or even semi-professional models.

A word of caution: try not to mix fog fluid and machines from different manufacturers. Fog machine manufacturers design their fog fluid to be compatible with their fog machines. If a machine is calibrated at too low a temperature for a given fluid, the result can be wet fog that can leave a sticky residue if running for long periods of time. If the temperature is too high, the fluid can burn, thus changing its chemical composition and creating harmful by-products.

*Fig. 15.3. A typical fog machine.*

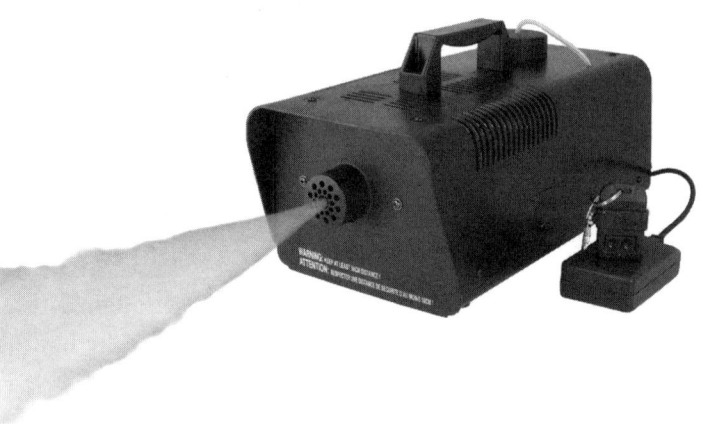

For these reasons, some club owners are justifiably reluctant to allow the use of a fog machine. A way around this is to light stick incense for a while. It's not as good, but you'll get some temporary smoke and it'll smell nice too. Just be sure your incense isn't stationed below any smoke detectors!

**AC extension cords and outlet boxes.** A couple of items always overlooked are additional AC extension cords and multiple outlet boxes. Don't skimp on these; make sure you get something heavy enough for this kind of use, preferably 14-gauge with 3-prong connectors. Don't forget the multiple outlet boxes too. You'll need at least one for each side of the stage just for the lights.

**Lighting gels.** If you do nothing else, buy some colored gels (see Fig. 15.4). Even if you don't have any lights, they can really help when you go into a club that has its own lighting package. Gels can wear out over long periods of use and most house gels are faded or burnt. Putting your own gels in can make you look a thousand times better than any of the other bands playing there. If your lighting rig uses traditional tungsten-halogen lamps, then the light that comes out is white and you can only change it with a gel, so you'll need them anyway, but the new LED lights are usually capable of multiple colors because they use an assortment of red, green, and blue LEDs. That being said, the colors from an LED light are usually not as bright as colors from traditional lights because they're not using all of the LEDs available (except for when white is the desired output).

*Fig. 15.4. Lighting gels.*

Gels are fairly inexpensive (around $2 per pre-cut sheet) so it shouldn't be too much of a financial hardship to pick some up. The two main manufacturers are Lee and Rosco and they both have swatch books showing samples of the vast color choices and assortments for theatrical lighting. Check out www.leefilters.com and www.roscolabs.com.

**What's your color?** If you think about your band, your songs, and your show, you'll realize right away that certain colors suit certain types of songs better than others. Quiet, introspective acoustic guitar songs in a minor key might work best in blue or lavender. If you're a booty-shaking funk band, hot reds and ambers might fit you best. Brutal nu-metal? Then try reds, greens, and cold whites. The idea is to enhance your show by choosing the colors that best fit your music.

**Stage (not DJ) lights.** You might be tempted to buy DJ lighting but DJ lights are mostly for effects and can be over-used. That's not to say that strobe lights and mirror balls won't work as your set reaches a climax, but until you get the basics down, it's best to stay with the basic theatrical spots and floods. That being said, some simple white moonflower lights (see Fig. 15.5) can really enhance certain spots in the show (conceal an array of three or four behind the drummer and maybe a couple off to the side of the stage). With a little fog, these lights provide a massive effect for the money.

Fig. 15.5. A moonflower stage light.

It's easy to go into more detail about buying stage lighting, but it's not necessary here. There are plenty of lighting books available and lots of information on the Internet. Do a Google search for "stage lighting" and you'll find a ton of dealers and manufacturers. Some of the manufacturers to be aware of are Chauvet, Altman, Elation, Strand, and American DJ.

**Lights at the venue.** If you don't want to be bothered with lighting, you're stuck with whatever the venue has to offer. One of your first questions to the powers-that-be should always be, "What kind of lighting is available?" Ask the promoter, venue manager, or soundman—whoever you think is the right person—if it's possible to ensure that all the stage lights are working for your show. The usual reason they don't work is because that person usually can't be bothered to replace the blown lamps and/or fuses. Ask them in plenty of time too; they may need to order or pick up spares from their supplier. Five o'clock on the afternoon of your gig is going to be too late!

On the day of the gig, give yourself a fighting chance in the lighting department. Either allow more time in your schedule to sort out the lights, or better still, sucker a friend into doing it for you with the promise of a place on the guest list or a few beers. If your friend knows your songs and has a vague sense of rhythm too, you're onto a winner (unless you're a jazz band, in which case it doesn't matter). Many of the world's top lighting designers started their careers by helping out a friend's band. Put your new gels into the lights and focus them (get them pointing in the right directions to light up the band). Light the band from the front so the audience can see your face, and use back, side, and floor lighting for mood. Ninety-nine percent of the time, stage lights are paired up symmetrically (one stage left and another stage right), so you'll want to put the same gel color in both lights of each pair.

> **Be very careful** when positioning lights, because bad things can happen, such as getting hit with a jolt of electricity, getting burned by hot metal, dropping hardware on peoples' heads, or falling off stands while reaching for the lights. Take care! Also, you'll be thankful for a pair of heavy duty gloves to keep you from getting burned, but be aware that they won't protect you from electrocution!

Try, if at all possible, to sort out the lights before there's any band gear (or musicians) onstage; it eliminates the possibility of dropping things on people's heads and it's just so much easier to move the ladder around. And remember, beer crates, barstools or flight cases (especially if they're on wheels!) are not things to use to reach the lights. I learned this the hard way by tumbling off a large flight case and having it fall on my ankle, resulting in a severe cut and a trip to the ER!

It's important to pay attention to what the venue people tell you about the lights. It's not uncommon to turn on all the lights at once in a small venue and blow a fuse, plunging the whole room into darkness. Murphy's Law says that the fuse box will be in a locked closet somewhere, significantly delaying your setup and starting off on the wrong foot with the venue! Turning on all the lights at once usually looks like crap, too.

Give your light man friend a set list for the show with indications of what you think might be good. Something like, "First song: up tempo, lots of flashing red" or "the big ballad, mostly blue, then white for guitar solo." If your brand new light man has a sense of rhythm, he'll soon be swinging along with the band, but tell him that continuously flashing lights soon gets on everybody's nerves and looks like the visual equivalent of mud. Try changing the color only once every bar or so in a rock tune, and for one song find a nice look and hold it all the way through (the big ballad is always good for this). That way, when the band kicks in with another rocker and the lights do the same, it'll be even more effective.

At the end of the night, don't forget to take your gels out of the lights and put the house gels back in.

## THE STAGE PLOT

One thing you should always have when playing a venue with a house sound and/or light man, is a stage plot (see Figs. 15.6a and b). A stage plot is a diagram of where everyone stands onstage, where the amps are set, and where the various input needs are. This will not only make everything go a lot faster, but if you have any special needs (an extra direct box for instance) the soundman or light man can actually be prepared if they get the info early enough (like a few days before the gig).

Some things that a plot should show are:

- ▶ Where everyone stands onstage
- ▶ Which players require vocal mics
- ▶ Where the drums are set
- ▶ Where the keyboards live
- ▶ Where the amplifiers are set
- ▶ Anything else that requires an input that's not apparent (a computer for backing tracks for instance)

A simple lighting plot should say:

- ▶ Which players require spotlights
- ▶ The colors desired
- ▶ Any special effects required
- ▶ Any special effects that you brought

*Fig. 15.6a A sample stage plot.*

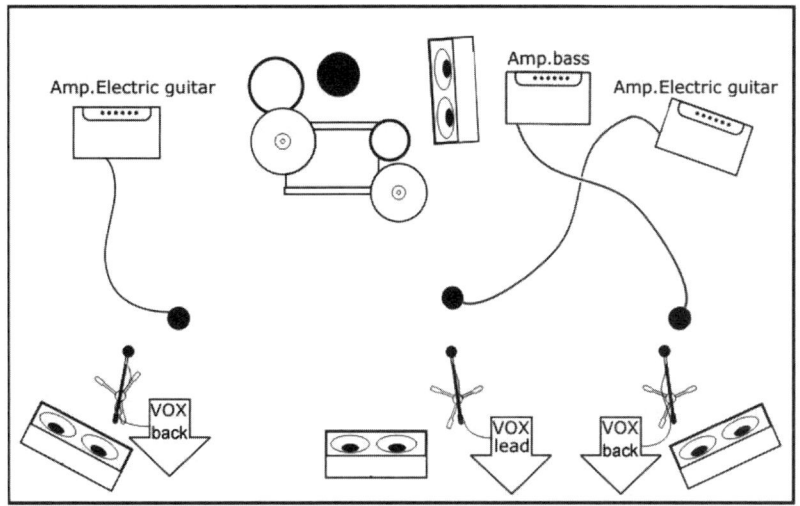

Stage Plot shows vocal mics, backline placement, and monitors required.

*Fig. 15.6b Another sample stage plot.*

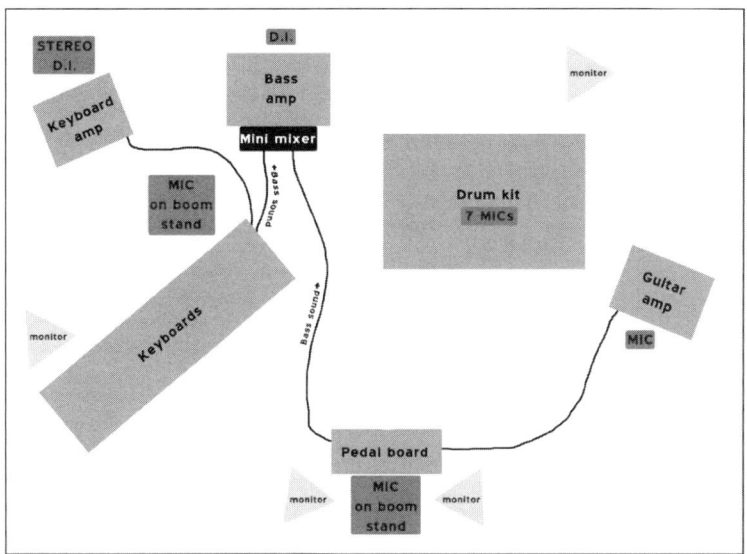

Stage Plot shows backline, vocal mic, and monitor placement, DI's required, and mics required on drums.

## Setting Up on a Large Stage

While on this subject, I have seen many small, local bands perform on a large stage for the first time. They don't have an elaborate monitor system, but they spread out anyway. This can be a big

Your Show    **187**

mistake because now they don't have the intimacy of the small stage that they're used to and they lose their tightness. If you do this, don't be surprised if an argument breaks out between the bass player and drummer about rushing and dragging the beat. Until you're used to playing on big stages with large monitor systems, stay with what you're used to and setup somewhat close to one another.

# CHAPTER 16

# The Importance of Video

Video is an essential element in a great band's arsenal of tools, but not for what you might think. There are plenty of books out there that will show you how to make a music video, publish it on YouTube, and distribute it around the Internet, so I'm not going to bother going into that (not much anyway). In fact, we're going to discuss using video as a learning tool, because it just may be the best one there is.

## VIDEO AS A LEARNING TOOL

Just like audio recording yourself as much as possible as discussed in Chapter 12, video recording your gigs should be a standard procedure. Why? It's like looking in a mirror. You're able to step back, free from the distractions of playing, singing, and putting on a show, and actually see yourself the way the audience sees you. But be cautioned; sometimes it won't look pretty, especially in the beginning.

It's really important that a new band video at least its first few gigs because you never get a feeling for what you're really doing right or wrong until after the fact. If you're playing regularly (like every week), shooting a gig once every couple of months is a good idea as well. I recommend that the whole band get together to watch so that you don't have to go back later to a band member to explain any perceived imperfections if they didn't watch with you. Also, by watching together you can discuss any areas in your playing or show that pop up, as well as discuss new show ideas that you'll inevitably get as you watch. Some people just can't stand watching themselves (even some television and movie stars) and will resist, but think of it more as a learning experience than as a fashion statement. If you always hate how you look or play but can improve your performance to the point where you at least find it tolerable, then imagine the great reaction the audience will have as a result.

## MAKING A GREAT LIVE VIDEO

There are basically two things that you need to make a great live video (assuming that you play great and put on a great show): great audio and a tripod. Forget about camera quality, resolution, format, or any kind of specs. If your video sounds bad or is shaking like crazy, it's just a bad video, although there are a few exceptions that we'll touch on in a minute. Let's look at the audio first.

Keep in mind that this product is not for distribution. It's never to be used on YouTube, your Website, to show your friends, or to try to get gigs. If you put something out that can be potentially distributed around the world, you want it to be great. This is simply a recording only for internal band use so everyone can see and hear their mistakes and find out what they can do better.

### Audio is 50 Percent of the Final Product

Despite what anyone tells you, audio is always looked down upon as the poor stepchild of picture by video people, mostly because they don't understand it. That being said, if the sound is bad then the picture always seems worse than it really is, so it's really important to pay close attention to the audio when making a video.

Here are some rules of thumb regarding audio for video:

> Bad audio + good picture = bad video
>
> Good audio + bad picture = bad video
>
> Good audio + good picture = maybe a good video
> (it still depends on how you played and looked
> and how it was edited)

So you see that the only way you stand a chance to get something decent is to make totally sure that the audio is at least the same quality as your picture.

## Audio Recording Tips for Video

There are a couple of things that you can do to make sure that the audio quality is a lot better than what you can get with just the mic on the camera.

**Use an external mic.** You probably have some extra mics laying around already, or at least you can borrow a couple, so let's put them to use. The problem is that most consumer cameras have mini-jack mic inputs that won't readily interface to an XLR or phone plug. No problem; buy an adapter (see Fig. 16.1). They're cheap and just about any mic you choose is going to be better than the $2 on-board camera mic. It will make a world of difference.

Another possibility is to use a feed from the mixing board, or a combination of board feed and microphone that you can balance later. Either way, refer to Chapter 12, "Record Yourself," and just treat the camera as if it were an audio-only recorder.

**Turn off the limiter.** Most cameras have a built-in audio limiter to help keep audio overload to a minimum. While this might work okay when shooting those nice vacation movies, it's horrible for band use, squashing and twisting your audio into a heap of crap even on the most expensive professional cameras. In all but the cheapest cameras, you can defeat the limiter by diving into the software menus and finding the Defeat selection in the audio section. You'll hear the benefits of this action immediately.

**Turn the input level down.** Just about any band will easily overload the audio inputs of a camera since they're usually designed for capturing the noise of a family outing rather than the level of any number of instruments playing. If there's a level control knob on the camera, turn it as low as it will go without turning it off. If it's in a software menu, do the same. If you're still overloading the input (the overload indicators are flickering red), you'll have to get an attenuator pad to lower the microphone's output (see Fig. 16.2), but these are pretty inexpensive (less than $20) and can come in handy for some everyday audio purposes as well. Remember, it's a lot better to have audio where the level is too low than too high.

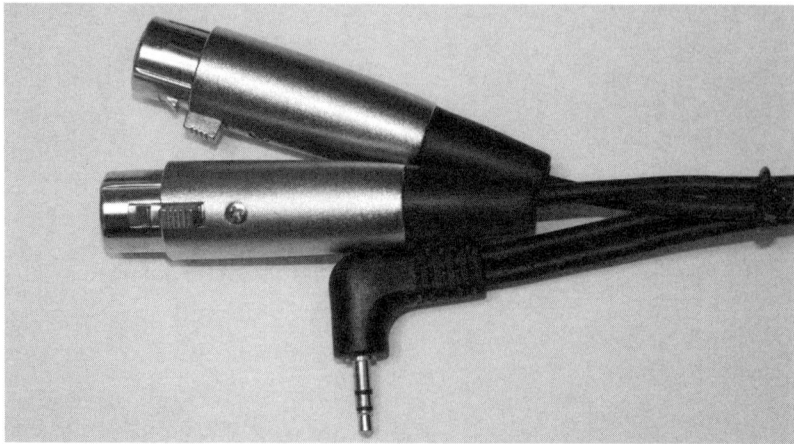

Fig. 16.1. Mini-to-XLR adapter.

Fig. 16.2. In-line microphone attenuator.

### Get a Tripod

If you're shooting a gig to just see how you're doing or shooting a music video, you'll need a tripod for at least some of the things you shoot. If you're shooting a gig, get a tripod and set it up as high as it will go, so you won't see audience heads and people passing in front. A nice, stable image will make viewing a lot easier later.

If you're shooting something for a music video, hand-held shots can look exciting and hip, but you'll need at least some tripod shots for things like B-roll, establishing shots and anything where you need more than a couple of seconds of a steady shot. Although tripods can run as high as a couple of thousand dollars, even a $25 cheapy is better than none at all. As with most everything, the more you spend the better it will be, in that it will last a whole lot longer, be sturdier, and be lighter, but anything is better that nothing.

## IF YOU'RE MAKING A MUSIC VIDEO

Okay, you really need that music video after you decide that either your live show is really strong and compelling, or you can't be bothered with a typical MTV abstract video. Here are some things to think about that will help take everything up a notch.

### Get Establishing Shots

An establishing shot is something like a marquee with your name on it outside the venue, the venue exterior and sign, a flyer or newspaper advertisement with your name in it—anything to establish the time and the place of the event. Maybe you don't want anyone to know the time or place of the event. That's okay; shoot it anyway. Who knows when that footage might be a valuable addition to a documentary or a "Behind the Music" special about the band when you get famous! It'll also have great nostalgia value many years from now. I can't tell you the number of times that I've racked my brains about some club or concert hall that I played in 20 years ago.

### B-Roll is So Important

B-roll is cutaway shots that are used to cover up an edit of an interview, audio narration, or a picture edit that might jump or look funny. A close up of a guitar pick, pictures on the wall, an empty stage or a stage with just your gear on it, a close up of the kick drum head with your name on it, a pan across an amp head, hands on a keyboard; these are all examples of B-roll. You can never have enough B-roll so shoot everything you can think of. In the hands of a good editor it will all be used somewhere.

### Shoot More Than One Take

More than one take allows for multiple camera angles if you only have one camera, and if you have multiple cameras then it allows for more interesting angles that a good editor can always use. If you have the chops, you can even cut between several uneven takes to make one good one.

### Shoot A Lot More Than You Need

While I don't suggest that you shoot at the ratio of a motion picture where they shoot at least ten minutes for every one minute they end up using, the more you shoot, the more good footage you'll have to choose from and the more easily you'll be able to cover up that funny audio or video edit. While I can't tell you the perfect shooting ratio, too much will either cost you extra money in post-production (which is okay if you can afford it) or burn out your editor if he or she is doing it for free. It's best to ask exactly how much footage your editor would like and if they want any specific shots before you shoot.

### Don't Mix Formats

Try not to mix cameras with different formats, resolutions, CODECs, frame rates, and so on. as it will really make things a lot more difficult for the editor later. For instance, don't mix a camera that shoots DV with one that shoots HDV unless you have them both on the DV setting. Don't mix an HDV camera with one that shoots ACHDV, and especially don't mix a DV camera with something like an old Hi-8. That's big trouble. You're usually a lot better off using a single camera and shooting multiple takes than using two dissimilar cameras.

## SOME SPECIAL DVDS TO CHECK OUT

Since we're talking about videos, here are a few from some successful artists that can be used to illustrate some of the points of the book. These DVDs aren't built around abstract music videos (are they really effective or pertinent anymore?), but more around the band's stage shows with general background info.

**Talking Heads, *Stop Making Sense*.** Want a visual illustration on how to pull off what Chapter 15 is talking about on how to put on a great show? This film shows how a little new-wave band with some good songs put on a show that was so unforgettable that it was immortalized on a DVD even before artist DVDs were popular. If you only check out one of these DVDs, this is the one.

**Led Zeppelin, *Led Zeppelin*** (not *The Song Remains the Same*). Want to know how to play *big*? Take a look at this DVD and see how three great musicians and a singer can sound so incredibly huge. Regardless of whether you like the band or the music, this is one of those DVDs where you plan to watch for five minutes and you look up and five hours have gone by.

***Standing in the Shadows of Motown*.** From a strictly historical perspective, everyone who's ever tried to play in a band should see this movie, as it's a treasure trove of information and a really fun watch. It's also an excellent example of the deepest grooves and back-of-the-beat playing. From the point of view of this book, it shows you how it used to be possible to cut three number-one songs in three hours. Motown internally developed fabulous songs, fabulous producers, fabulous world-class musicians, and fabulous artists. Don't have those things? Welcome to the club, even Motown only had it all for a couple of years. After that, they were back to working long and hard like the rest of us human musicians.

**Tom Dowd, *The Language of Music*.** This movie profiles the life and what has become the legendary work of a real music pioneer, producer/engineer Tom Dowd. Dowd worked for Atlantic Records during its heyday and collaborated with artists like Aretha Franklin, Ray Charles, Eric Clapton, Cream, Otis Redding, John Coltrane, The Allman Brothers Band, Rod Stewart, Lynyrd Skynyrd and many, many more (it also includes interviews with many of those artists). To understand how recording used to work and how it has evolved through the years, and for some great history on the music business (more of the music than the business), you won't go wrong giving this DVD a watch.

***Woodstock*.** This was the concert and movie that really started it all in terms of music as a big money business. While there are some really great performances back in an era when the industry was young and unsophisticated in so many ways (like money and audio gear), the best part of this film is the editing and that's why I cite it here. Note the camera angles, mostly from below the artists to make them look bigger than life. Note the use of split screens to keep viewer attention high. Note how long a camera shot stays on the artist to draw the viewer into the performance. In these days of ultra-quick-cut, MTV-style editing, *Woodstock* is the antithesis, in that it allows the performance to develop in a way that quick cuts never could. It should be noted that this was the first true "festival" attended by hundreds of thousands of people, and sound systems were still in the dark ages, so the bands played without a monitor mix (they listened to the same mix as the audience). The sound was also recorded on only seven tracks of an 8-track recorder (the $8^{th}$ track was for sync to the picture). If you want to learn how to make your live footage really compelling, study this DVD.

**Any Rolling Stones DVD.** They call the Stones the World's Greatest Rock 'n' Roll Band, but I think that applies only to their songwriting and longevity, since their performances consistently have been a step above garage band. Watch any

Stones concert DVD (I'm partial to the latest one, *Shine a Light*) to see what *not* to do to sound great. They violate all the rules, yet they're the Stones and have those great, great songs. Don't think that just because the Stones can get away with sloppy playing that you can, though. You can't because you're not them. Don't even think about it.

## THE EPK

I'll mention the Electronic Press Kit (EPK) here because having one was once the hip thing to do. Everyone's heard of a hard-copy press kit: it has some reviews on the band, some sample music, individual bios, and band background in a little binder that you give to press people, agents, or club owners so they can familiarize themselves with the band. It became hip starting in the early '90s for bands to have an electronic version of the hard copy press kit, with video tapes (these were the old days after all) of shows and music videos, clips of interviews and audio sound bites for radio. This was all well and good if you where a band with a following that the press actually wanted to cover. If you're a new band that no one's ever heard of and has no story, why bother?

Today it's popular to do an online version of the EPK, again with clips from gigs, interviews with the entire band and individual players, MP3s of your songs, lots of still photos, and audio sound bites. My advice: making a great EPK is somewhat of an art form and really takes someone who knows how to produce one to make you look great. Not only does the production have to be of a really high quality, but the band also has to have something to say, a great back story, or at least be made to sound and look interesting enough to even have an EPK in the first place. You're a lot better off not spending the time and energy it takes to really pull this off. Spend the time on making great music instead. Everything you do has to be great to make you come off as great. Leave the EPK to the pros when the press is actually asking for your time.

# CHAPTER 17

# To Summarize

So now that you've read the first two parts of the book and have some fresh ideas about how to improve your band's sound, let's summarize the advice and tips that we've looked at so far.

**Your Playing**
Don't use gear just because X does it.
Know your limitations—just play what you play well.
Use great-sounding gear that fits.
Play in tune and on time.
Less is more.

**For Drummers**
Simple is best.
Keep your fills even (don't rush or be lazy).
Play dynamically.
Keep your drums in tune.

**When Recording**
Arrive early.
Turn off your cell phone.
Make sure you're in tune.
New strings, tubes, reeds, and drumheads help the sound.
Bring all your gear to the session.

Bring extra strings, picks, tubes, cables, heads, reeds, cables, and batteries.
Know your parts before you arrive.
Have your amp tuned up.
Make sure your cables are good.
Make any charts, notes, or cheat sheets beforehand.
Bring a utility kit.

**For Vocals**
Remember the 3 Ps—Pitch, Passion, Pocket.
You've got to hear yourself to stay in tune.
Avoid alcohol, dairy products, tea, coffee, and cola before a gig.
Change the key if necessary.
Take care of yourself.
Take some lessons.
Mic technique is important.
Rehearse harmonies without the band first.
Phrasing is everything—concentrate on attacks and releases.
Pay attention to background vocals.

**If you Get a Sore Throat**
Rest.
Drink lots of water.
Use your voice as little as possible.
Avoid alcohol, dairy products, tea, coffee, and cola before a gig.
Try some fresh lemon and honey in warm water.

**The Band**
Dynamics are key. When you play loudly, play as loudly as you can. When you play softly, play as softly as you can.
Don't confuse volume level with intensity.
Play together—listen to each other.
Timing is everything. Concentrate on:
- Starts and stops
- Accents
- The groove and the pocket
- Attacks and releases
- Builds
- Turnarounds

Play everything clean and crisp.
"How are you playing it?"
Faster does not create more excitement.

Calm down on the gig.
Play big, not loud.
You don't have to be just like the record, just sound good.
Play in tune!

**The Song**
Arrangements are key.
Make sure each instrument has its own sonic space.
Make guitars sound different—different registers, different rhythms, different lines.
Limit the number of elements.
Make sure everything is in its own frequency range.

**Rehearsals**
Have an agenda.
Know your parts before you get there.
It's the little things that count (dynamics, turnarounds, builds, attacks and releases).
Practice in the round.
Don't rehearse a song to death.
Rehearse your show.

**Onstage**
Play dynamically.
Play big instead of loud.
Have an even frequency balance.
Stay out of volume wars.

**Your Sound System**
Vocals take priority.
Ring out the system for more gain before feedback.

**Be a Pro**
Always be on time.
Always be open to ideas.
Be focused only on the music while you're playing.
Be open to criticism.
Take responsibility for your mistakes.
Present your ideas in a respectful manner.
Never party at a rehearsal, gig, or recording session.
Treat your band mates, crew, and audience with respect.

**Record Yourself**
Record your gigs and rehearsals.
There's no such thing as a demo.
Go to a real studio to cut basics.
Hire a pro if you can.
Bring all your gear to record.
Don't expect to sound great the first time.
Be prepared to work hard.
It's not a party.
Don't call your original songs "originals."

**The Show**
It's more than a collection of songs.
Have a set list.
Have a stage plot.
Know exactly what will happen in between songs.
Know exactly when, where, and how the audience will be addressed.
Plan as much of the show as you can.
Plan the dynamics of the set for maximum audience impact.
Work out the sound and music cues in rehearsal beforehand.
Work out lighting cues beforehand.
Work out wardrobe, guitar changes, etc. beforehand.

**Video**
Shoot your gigs.
Use an external mic.
Turn the input level down.
Turn off the internal limiter.
Get a tripod.
Shoot establishing shots.
Shoot as much B-roll as you can.
Shoot more than you need.
Don't mix different formats from different model cameras.

# Part Three

## The Interviews

# CHAPTER 18

# The Interviews

## CHRIS BOARDMAN

Chris Boardman's career path was a lot different from most musicians', because he had enough talent to jump to the big time at a time in his life when most players were still learning their craft. And while this book admittedly leans toward rock bands (even though the information works across any genre), Chris's experience in another side of the music world illustrates a theme carried through the book and the interviews: that hard work, perseverance, and a professional attitude are just as important as raw talent (maybe even more so). After many years in the music business in a variety of genres, Chris has some observations and advice that are well worth noting. You can find more information about Chris, including his wide range of credits, at chrisboardmanmusic.com.

*Can you give me some of your background?*
I started playing piano when I was four years old, auditioned for Julliard when I was eleven (got accepted but didn't go), quit playing for a few years, got interested in rock when The Doors became popular, then discovered jazz. I started gigging when I was fourteen, eventually moved to California to go to Cal State Northridge, wrote my first arrangement for a TV show when I was twenty, left college to be Mitzi Gaynor's musical director when I was 22 in 1976. (Author's note: Mitzi Gaynor was a star of Broadway and film musicals in the '50s who went on to become one of Las Vegas'

top attractions for several decades.) I traveled on the road with her doing small Broadway-like shows, then went to work for Tom Jones as his musical director, and then went on tour with Seals and Crofts for about three years. As a player, I did the *Fridays* television show (which gave comics and television stars Michael Richards and Larry David their start), then I quit playing and just went into orchestrating and arranging, but eventually started a band called Wishful Thinking with Tim Weston and David Garibaldi in about 1983. It was a contemporary jazz group and we did three records with the last one making it to the Top 10 in *Billboard*. I left that and did a solo album, then retired from playing to just do the film thing.

On the writing side of things, I did my first network variety show in 1974 at twenty years old. In late '77, I worked on *The Wiz* with Quincy Jones. Then my mentor Billy Byers launched me into his work circle, so from 1977 to about 1990 I probably worked on 50 network variety specials. In 1984, I started doing film as an orchestrator. I did *The Color Purple* in 1986 and got an Academy Award nomination. I orchestrated *Silverado* that same year, then went on to conduct, arrange, orchestrate, and compose over 120 films for television and movies over the last twenty years. I worked with a lot of great people from Quincy to Steven Spielberg to Michael Kamen to James Newton Howard, so it's been a good ride.

In the '80s, I was getting all this notoriety from Wishful Thinking, and the people who knew me as a jazz keyboard player had no idea that I was winning Emmy awards as an arranger (I was nominated 13 times in 14 years). I was proud of the fact that of the first three scores I did, I was nominated on two of the three. Then I decided I needed to make a living (laughs) and raise my son, so I paid a little more attention to that.

*What were your defining moments both as a player and writer?*
Two come to mind. One was during my education with Billy Byers, which consisted of going out to his house in Malibu on Sunday's and listening to records. I distinctly remember the light bulb going on while listening to "The Shadow of Your Smile" from Johnny Mandel's score to *The Sandpiper*. I was blown over by the sophistication yet the accessibility of it.

As a player, I was always focused on being a writer and playing was just an afterthought, but the defining moment for me as a player was when I bought a Prophet V (the first polyphonic and programmable synthesizer). I was one of the first guys in Hollywood to actually plunk down $4,500 in 1978. That pushed me into the world of being an early adopter.

*Where did you move to Hollywood from?*
I was raised here in Los Angeles but when I was 13 we moved to Ogden, Utah because my dad was a jet engine designer and he got transferred. I wasn't ready to leave home after high school so I stayed around Utah and did a couple years of junior college. At that time I was working in one of the busiest casual bands in the area. The funny thing is that they were all my high school counselors who were in their 40s and 50s and I was like 17. They never rehearsed and they played every request because they'd been doing it for so long that they knew all the tunes, but I didn't know any of them. It was trumpet, bass, drums, and piano. The trumpet player would tell me what key it was in, count it off, then stand next to me and hum the tune in my ear so I would have to make the changes on the bandstand. They loved to watch me scuffle.

After a couple of years of that I realized it was a dead end for me. I was playing with a high school music teacher from a small town who was just miserable because he didn't have the courage to fail, and so he stayed as a small town music teacher and led a life of "what if?" At the opposite end of the spectrum, all my peers would say, "I wonder if I'm good enough to make it in Hollywood or New York," but they didn't have the courage to try it. After living in that environment, I realized that I would much rather go and give it a shot and maybe fall flat on my ass and say, "Gosh, that didn't work," than be one of those guys who were riddled with self-doubt. To use a baseball analogy, a pitcher knows that if he doesn't get the guys out, he's out of the game but he can walk away with a clear conscience. Art is a little different because there is no defining line like that; you have to find it within yourself. So I made a big commitment to myself at about 18 where I said, "Coulda, shoulda, woulda is not going to be a part of my vocabulary." As you well know, it's better to fall down and learn from your perceived failures than not have the courage to give it a shot.

*Did you know anyone when you moved back to Hollywood?*
Actually I didn't. I had been gone six or seven years and everyone I knew from before had grown up. The only person I knew was Billy. I had met him at a clinic in Las Vegas. I was terrified and thank God Billy opened his arms. He would have a Sunday open house and I'd go hang out with him, then I started hanging out on his sessions just trying to soak up as much as I could.

I asked him how to get a job and he said, "Stay home and get good and people will find out about you." I never understood that and it didn't make any sense to me at the time, but now in hindsight it's probably some of the best advice I could've gotten.

*So is that what you did?*
Yeah. Then, he got me a job with Mitzi Gaynor as her musical director. I had never seen a nightclub act, let alone conducted a band before, so my only real defense was to be as good as I could possibly be for the job at hand. I figured if I could do that much, then I'd be cool and get through it. That's stuck with me all these years. In everything I do, I try to be as good as I can possibly be at it. I fail a lot because not everything works out the way I would like it to work out, but I still learn a lot in the process. Quincy Jones is fond of saying, "Your self-worth is not determined by what others think of you." If you accept failure as a learning process then there is no limit to what you can achieve.

*You went from Mitzi Gaynor to Tom Jones. How did that happen?*
I learned about the cruel aspect of show business from Tom Jones. His musical director (Johnny Spence, who was with Tom from the beginning) hired me to replace him because he wanted to stay home to spend more time with his family. I had to leave Mitzi's gig and I didn't have any time to rehearse or prep. They sent me a tape of the show and the piano/conductor parts. After doing a dance show with tempo changes where you really have to be a conductor, conducting a singer's show is a piece of cake. Everyone in the band knows all the material so it's really hard to screw up (laughs). I went out and conducted the second show I saw. I was twenty-three years old and I intimidated the shit out of everybody, so I was not welcomed by the entourage. Musically I had it together, but emotionally and life experience-wise I was a little too young to be in that type of pressure cooker with a bunch of wacky people.

Johnny ended up dying of a heart attack ten days after I started, so the wheels came off the tour. This was in the summertime and I felt obligated to at least get to December when the tour was over, but Johnny was the glue that kept the organization operating, so I was like a corporate orphan. I had no support from anybody and everyone else on the tour was so lost without Johnny that I bore the brunt of all their discontent. I lasted for about three months, then developed an ulcer and had to leave the tour because I was bleeding internally.

I'll never forget, I was in the hospital with an IV in one arm and blood going in the other in Terre Haute, Indiana when the manager called and said, "Well, you gonna make the show tonight?" I said, "Gee, I don't think so." And he said, "Alright, see you later," and they just left me there. Had it not been for one of the background singers, my luggage would've been left in the hotel. I had never failed at anything up until then, so emotionally that was a tough time, but it was a good learning experience.

*How did you rebound from that?*
It took me about six months to get my health and mind together. I had met a young sax player on the Mitzi tour (Scott Page, who went on to play with Pink Floyd, Supertramp, and Toto). We became friends and started to do club dates together. We played a regular gig in Toluca Lake, an L.A. suburb, on Sunday, Monday, and Tuesdays. During that era there was so much going on. Everyone was working and there were all kind of road gigs, film, and record dates. It was a pretty crazy time, so there were a lot of musicians around and they all would come and sit in and hang out, so I just focused on that for a while instead of going back into the world of show business. About a year later we auditioned as a band for Seals and Crofts (of "Summer Breeze" fame) and got the gig. I had to make the choice between going on the road as an assistant conductor for Sammy Davis Jr. or going on the road with Seals and Crofts, but I figured I'd be better off playing music of my generation for a while instead of going down that Broadway route again.

*What did you learn from Seals and Crofts? It was completely different than what you were doing before.*
First of all, everything that I had been exposed to was about notation and reading in the TV and production world, so the most significant thing I learned was that you don't have to read music to make music if you have music in your heart and soul. It's just that some people train and some people don't. I'd look at Jimmy Seals and the poor guy was so frustrated. He had the whole thing in his head and knew exactly what he wanted but he had no idea how to express himself.

One of the best things I learned from the Mitzi Gaynor experience was how to be a professional. Your life could be in complete turmoil for 22 ½ hours a day, but once the clock hit 8:00 p.m. to whenever the show was over, you had to do the job with a smile on your face (and you'd be grateful that you had the job as well). It doesn't matter what's going on with the rest of your life when you're on stage.

*Did you record with Seals and Crofts?*
No, I didn't. I did a couple of sessions but nothing came of it. I desperately wanted to record with them, but at the time there was a big dividing line between the road musicians and the recording musicians. Session work was the cream of the crop for a player.

It's funny how Hollywood works. If someone has a hit record, then everybody wants to hire the people who worked on it as more of a business decision. It doesn't have anything to do with musicality, but it has everything to do with the people writing the checks being comfortable with whom they're paying.

*What do you see that's common with all really good musicians you've worked with?*
Humility. All the great ones are humble and hard workers. It's always about self-improvement. The music business is brutal. Either you play it right or you don't, and if you don't, you don't get called back. When I was twenty years old, I was working with people who were in their fifties who had been doing sessions and gigging for thirty years or more. I looked at their attitude and it always was, "I want to be better, I don't want to just get by." The people who I've seen survive in this business are the ones who have that burning passion to pursue it as an art form. It's not about the notoriety or the fame that goes along with it. In today's world, you can't merely be good; you have to be great to stand out.

*Do you have any advice for someone just starting out?*
I'll paraphrase something that Bob Ezrin (producer of Pink Floyd, Alice Cooper, Peter Gabriel, and Kiss, among others) said, which was, "The first thing I ask a new artist is, 'Will you die if you don't do this?' Any answer other than yes and you should go do something else. The next thing is to go practice your craft until you get good at what you do, then share it with as many people as possible and enlist your fans to help you." That's about a succinct a way of how to develop a career path as I've ever heard.

I tell people all the time, especially about being a composer or arranger, "I can't tell you the number of Sunday afternoons that I spent hunching over a score pad scribbling away while everybody else in the world is out enjoying a bright sunny day." That's my choice, but you need that kind of commitment level. I'm a living testament from my experience with Tom Jones to the fact that the business will eat you up, so you have to have the passion to counterbalance it. I have met a huge number of doctors who are incredible musicians, but they just didn't have the same passion, for example.

I was in artist development for a while and my goal was first and foremost to help make better people on a personal level, mostly because all of us have something to say and the burning need to get out there and express it. But it comes down to trying to understand who you are in the world and why you have such a burning desire to put yourself through this. So if music gets you to a place of peace in your life and you enjoy doing it, then that's a great thing. But the moment it stops being fun and you lose that passion and joy, it's time to go and do something else.

*Do you have any advice for someone just starting to record?*
Listen to great records and try to emulate them, and talk to people and ask questions. What a lot of young people don't realize is that if you have a genuine interest, an expert will be happy to talk to you more times than not. Now if you're a jerk and you intrude or you're disrespectful or after their job, that's a different issue, but if you really want to be good at your craft, find somebody who does it and learn from them.

*If you could go back and give some advice to the earliest bands you played with in high school, what would you tell them?*
Listen to a lot of different kinds of music because you'll bring something of what you listen to into everything you do and it will make you different from the other guy. The other thing is to find out who you are—to find your voice so you can express that through your music. That's what will differentiate you from everyone else.

## FRANK FITZPATRICK

Growing up in the middle of the Detroit music scene helped shape the background that eventually made Frank Fitzpatrick one of Hollywood's most sought-after composers and music supervisors. Frank's credits are many, having created the soundtracks for over two dozen feature films (including *Scary Movie 3, Queen of the Damned, Friday,* and *In Too Deep*) and scores and themes for several television shows including the renowned *Larry Sanders Show*.

Frank has written and produced songs for gold and platinum artists including Jill Scott, Fat Joe, Dave Hollister, K-Ci & JoJo, Brownstone, Lina, Carl Anderson, Ice Cube, Akil (of Jurassic 5), Jazz (of Dru Hill), and The London Symphony. He also wrote the opening song for the *High School Musical* tour, and the "Angeli" theme for the Victoria's Secret advertising campaign. Listed in *Variety* as one of the "Top Music Supervisors of the Decade," Frank has contributed to the sale of over six million soundtrack albums, including the multi-platinum original *Friday*.

At the core of Frank's success is his attention to the groove, making sure that the pocket is so deep that the listener can't help but dance along. Since both making music and helping others is at the center of his being, Frank was eager to share his insights on finding the groove and getting the best out of musicians, regardless of their skills.

*Tell me about some of the early bands you played in. What kind of music were you doing?*
I never played as a sideman with any famous bands and I never created a band that became famous (laughs). Because of my Detroit background, everything I play is pretty soulful so I always played in funk and R&B bands, and sometimes maybe crossover into Southern rock. Then I had a jazz trio when I was in music school and put together combo dates for parties and events—that kind of stuff.

After I moved to L.A., I only played on records that I was producing or maybe I'd sit in with a reggae band that I might've been producing or something like that. It was always about rhythm and pocket for me. I've always been very anal about rhythm, great grooves, and paying a lot of attention to pocket.

*That's just what I want to hear about.*
All that comes from being a player but a lot of it comes from the producing side. It's about two things: in terms of the band, it's about the energy and the vibe and feel. You just have to go back and listen to the great rhythm sections that cut countless hit records—the guys in Memphis at Stax, the *Funk Brothers* at Motown, the *Wrecking Crew* in L.A.—and you'll find that it's not about a great guitar solo and it's not about anything flashy; it's about solid playing and phenomenal grooves. It's not a head thing, it's a body thing.

The other thing is the truth of the artist, which is the ability to deliver a great song. It's just like what Don Was did with Bonnie Raitt on her big breakthrough album *Nick of Time*. Even with the best of L.A.'s studio players in the studio band, every song still had to carry its weight just with Bonnie and an acoustic guitar. If it didn't hold up like that, then there's no point in putting production behind it.

*Is that what "the truth" means to you?*
That, and the performance of the artist. You're telling a story that's real to you. Do you believe in what you're singing about? You have to convey it from a place other than your memory of a bunch of words and chord changes.

How do you put a band together to get that great groove? Where do you start?

The groove can start from any element. You can build a groove off something like a rhythm guitar and build around it, but ultimately it comes down to the bass and drums being locked right there with it. It doesn't mean that it's square and machined out, it just means that there's some basic factor in the track that has this irresistible feel to it and everybody in the band adheres to it.

Quincy (producer Quincy Jones) used to say that some singers have it in the pocket of their voice. Supposedly Michael Jackson has such an amazing pocket that he could sing a line and you could build a groove around it. So it can come from any source, but everyone in the band has to be aware of what it is, hear it, and feel it.

*Can the groove come from the writing?*
The groove really comes out of the playing; the writing is more the truth of the song. With a younger band, it's figuring out what's not working a lot of times. What I'll usually do is break out elements and see who's not hanging with the rest of the band. You can break it down to what elements feel great by pulling everybody out one at a time. A lot of time I'll just go back to bass and drums and start adding things from there. As soon as I add something that messes with the groove, I know what's wrong. It could go the other way around though, in that maybe the bass or drums aren't locked.

*How often do you work with bands that aren't session players?*
Off and on. Almost any time you work with a band, you come across guys who can get away with stuff onstage that doesn't work in the studio. It's usually looser playing. You can get away with a lot of stuff in performance, thanks to the excitement of the evening.

What's the one thing that you see from great session players that you don't see from a band?

You don't have to tell them what you need; they just automatically go there. When you have to explain to someone how to make something feel better, it becomes a hard place to have it come from if you have to wrap your head around it first. As soon as you have to think about it, you're going to miss part of it anyway. But you can get there, you just have to listen and practice and always pay attention to it.

For example, if I have Chad Wackerman on drums, I can tell him to lay back one more hair on the beat and he'll know what I mean, where with younger players there's only ahead of the beat, behind the beat, and on the beat. For advanced players there are a hundred variations of all of those places. Most young players hate to do what classical players grow up learning and that's practicing to a metronome, mostly because it sounds so rigid, but you have to develop your internal clock first. You can really learn a lot by just playing to some sort of a clock and recording yourself because you really have to be a pretty advanced player to hear what you're playing while you're playing it.

*If you were able to go back to those early bands you played in, what advice would you give yourself?*
Play with a lot more people and practice like a mother as much as possible early on, because you just don't get the opportunity to do it later. It's really hard to play catch-up, because there are too many guys who have done the early work or just naturally have "it" to begin with. If you move to L.A., chances are you're already so behind the curve in that it's really hard to play catch-up because it's a full time gig just to stay afloat. The other thing is to try to play with people who are better than you. It's just like tennis. Your game will improve immensely if you play with someone who's twice as good as you.

*If you could go back, what advice would you give your old bands to make them better?*
The band is only as good as the elements that make it up, so each one has to be willing to take responsibility for their part in it. I would have each person in the band make a commitment to raising their level of performance to contribute to the band. I would do the same thing with the songs. Strip them down and make the band perform them with nothing going on and make sure that everybody still loves them. People get lost in the wall of their own sound sometimes, but if you don't break things down and create space in the arrangements, you never really know what's going on. You're just covering it up with noise.

*What was your defining moment in music when the light went on and you went "Oh, I get it now"?*
As a writer, it was when I began listening to things I did a couple of years earlier. When we're making records, we get into all the things in production that sound so cool, but you can't tell if they hold the test of time until you've had a chance to look back from a distance.

As a guitar player, I agree with you that you should learn every song first on acoustic guitar by yourself; then anything else you do is going to sound great when you have all the extra toys around you. The lesson I got in composing was not to create beyond your resources. You want to strip everything down to the essence first. There are a lot of guys who can play like Steve Vai, but you don't always have to go there to be great. Bob Marley never did and neither did Curtis Mayfield. They just did what they did with a lot of conviction, heart, and feel, and that ultimately means a lot more than any of that other stuff.

## PAUL ILL

A little bit of a disclosure here: Paul is one of my oldest and dearest friends, and we've played in many bands together through the years. In every band, he was always the best musician with the most musical ideas, attributes that have taken him very far in the industry jungle known as Hollywood. Paul has since become one of the most in-demand bass players in Los Angeles, doing sessions for such diverse artists as Courtney Love, James Blunt, Tina Turner, Bill Ward (of Black Sabbath), Christina Aguilera, Pink, Alicia Keys, and Daniel Powter.

*What gear do you use for playing live?*
I play live under varying and diverse conditions so it depends on the environment I'm going into. I will always bring a Fender P-bass with LaBella flatwound strings everywhere I go. I will usually add one bass to that because I never like to go to a gig with only a single bass in case there's a technical difficulty with that instrument. Most of my instruments are vintage, so when the weather changes, my instruments can change noticeably fast. Usually what will happen is the neck will shift and one string will have less volume than the other strings, markedly so to where it takes you out of the moment.

So I'll always bring a P-bass with flatwound strings and then I'll usually add a second Fender to that and it usually has flatwound strings too. Sometimes just to mix things up, I'll bring a bass with roundwound strings. They're usually P-basses (Fender Precision) and Jazz basses. I'm very blessed to have three Ps that are vintage and three Js (Jazz bass) that are either custom shop or vintage so I'm very fortunate to have a quiver of great sounding instruments to pick from.

Amplification-wise, it also depends on the situation. I've been fiercely loyal to Ampeg for a long time, although there were a couple of years where I was using a Line6 Bass Pod Pro or the bean Pod in front of everything. I was in some touring situations where it just made more sense to travel with a Bass Pod and a power amp than a vintage SVT because an SVT is like having a late '60s hot rod. The maintenance required is significant and you've got to have people who know what they're doing to work on them.

Most times I will take an Ampeg SVT head with a specific cabinet, or a 1971 Ampeg B-15 to a gig. It all depends on the size of the room, who the drummer is, the size of the drum set, and the type of amps the guitar players will be using. If the guitar players are using combo amps, I have a variety of speaker cabinets that I'll match to what they're using. I have an old EVM 115B woofer from the early '80s in an Eden cabinet, and then I have a ported 4×10 Eden cabinet, a 2×10 SWR, and a 6×10 SWR.

For quite some time I was using two matched SVTs with matched cabinets in dual mono. One rig was just for an effected sound. I had this really big pedal board with a volume pedal after it so I could blend the effects in the clean amp sound. I'm not a fan of bi-amped bass amplification. I have friends who have incredibly sophisticated rigs that give a spectacular sound, but it's not for me. I've settled on one amp and flatwound strings for my sound.

*What do you take with you to the studio?*
I over-kill. I bring so much more stuff than we'll use because that's part of the charm of hiring me. It's part of the "oooh, aahh" factor, and also it's to be of service to the muse and the spirit of the session. If you're not sure what you're going to be doing or where the music is going to go, that one extra piece that you bring can make the difference. I'll bring as many basses as I can fit in my car for that day with a B-15. Very rarely does someone ask me for the SVT and a big cabinet.

I'll tend to bring a P-bass with flatwounds, a Jazz bass with flatwounds or roundwounds, a Hofner President (which is the Cadillac of the Beatle basses), an old Kay "Jimmy Reed" bass, maybe some weird esoteric bass like a Fender Coronado, or maybe a baritone guitar or a Nord synthesizer. Then I'll grab a bunch of effects like a Bass Brassmaster, an envelope filter, or something weird like a synth-emulator pedal that the studio most likely won't own.

I also bring a vast selection of picks: felt picks, soft picks, and picks of varying thicknesses to get a different tone. I'll demonstrate what each one sounds like at different pickup positions so they can see if it fits the song. I used to always play with my fingers but in the last five years I've changed to about 65/35, depending upon the record. On the Christina Aguilera record I did, one of the songs was a Hofner Beatle bass with a felt pick, which you'd never expect on a record like that.

*Is your number-one bass the same for live and recording?*
No, my number-one bass for recording is my 1966 P-bass, which blows everything away in the studio, but live it's a bit unwieldy to play because it has a wide old Fender neck.

*Do you tailor what you bring to the session, or do you bring the same stuff for each one?*
No, I'll intuit what's needed. Like I said, I'll bring a P-bass and then something that's going to sound markedly different. I'll also try to bring something in between like a Rick with flatwounds. In talking to the person, you get a feel for what you're getting into idiomatically. If they're doing a Lucinda Williams or T-Bone Burnett Americana kind of thing I might think, "That's more for my Kay than for the Hofner."

I also believe in the intuitive thing of doing what's right in front of you. What I mean by that is if you've just bought a new guitar, whether it's a $120 acoustic guitar to play in your living room or a very expensive vintage collectable instrument, bring it with you even if they don't ask for it, because it was put into your hands for a reason. It might find an application that day.

*What's the defining moment for a bass player?*
I've always said that "Les Izmore" (less is more) is my favorite bass player. I think the defining moment for any bass player is when they play with a really good drummer. I've been so blessed to play with so many great ones, from Matt Abts (of Government Mule), or Brian MacLeod, or Kelly Scott, Nathan Wetherington, Ronnie Ciago (all in-demand session drummers), or Bill Ward (from Black Sabbath).

You've got to understand the function of the bass. How many bass players have ever been able to capture an audience for more than about two minutes by themselves? Jaco could do it. Stanley Clark could do it for a minute, but it's basically athletic. They weren't snake charming people with a song. Most bass players require an ensemble to make an impression upon people where they walk away saying, "That bass player is amazing." Like Pino Palladino with Jeff Beck where you walk away saying, "God, Pino was so great!"

A defining moment for most bass players comes when they really hit a groove with a drummer and they go, "This is what's been lacking." Not that they've been playing with marginal drummers up until then, they just haven't found that magical mesh.

*What was your defining moment as a player?*
Playing at the private Willie Dixon memorial right before his funeral. I brought a P-bass with flatwounds and plugged into whatever was there and went, "Yeah, you don't really need anything else to sound good." At the time I was playing with Reeves Gabrels with a sophisticated rig with a huge pedal board and MIDI-step pedals, which is beautiful because your pallet is really broad, but playing Willie's songs with his family with just a simple setup was a defining moment.

*Who was your biggest influence?*
James Jamerson, John Paul Jones, Jerry Jermont (the Atlantic Records studio bass player), Leland Sklar, and Will Lee. Jack Bruce in Cream was another big influence. The post-modern influence was Doug Wimbush. His use of sounds and timbre and groove changed the way I perceive bass.

*Were the other guys an influence because of their ability to groove?*
Yeah, but more because they served the song. They never leave their fingerprints on anything but it's always them just the same. Tony Levin's the same way. It's the way they're always thinking, "What can I do to make this song more appealing to the listener?" It's not really about their chops or facility; it's more about the choices they make sound-wise and note-wise.

*Do you have any studio tips or tricks?*
Make sure that your gear is comfortable to you. Make sure everything's working, the cables aren't crackling, your basses are in tune and intonated, your tuner is working, and your amp sounds good. Make sure that you can set everything up quickly and be zero hassle to anybody, either technically or personally. Turn off your cell phone. Make it a point that everyone sees that you're turning off your phone or leaving it outside the studio so they all understand that you're not interested in phone calls while you're working. Make the session a priority. Don't bring reading material into the session with you. Don't be net surfing on your phone during a session.

Play as often as you can. Play along with records and with musicians that will educate you either spiritually, or socially, or musically. Don't make it all about your physical chops because there are always going to be a lot of people who can play better than you. In my case, other people bring their thing to a session and I bring mine. That's also important. Find your thing. Find what you bring to the music.

*What's your thing?*
My antennae are pretty shinny. I'm able to pick up on the feeling in the room and what other people (the other musicians, the producer, the artist) are doing musically, and then contribute to the ambience in the room in a way where they want me to come back. Also, I tend to approach every session, whether it's in somebody's little cramped studio with Pro Tools LE or if it's in a multimillion dollar facility, the same as if I were at Abbey Road with the Beatles. They're all equally important. I'm as enthusiastic or excited about coming over to somebody's house for $50 as I am for a triple-scale record date. To me it's all the same and I think people sense that enthusiasm and excitement.

*Do you have any tips for laying in with the drummer?*
I've had the honor of playing quite often with James Gadson (the great Motown session drummer). One of the things I did during the first gig I played with him was to face him instead of facing the audience. I took off my shoes and slid my left foot underneath his bass drum and really began to understand the dynamics of his foot so that not only did my attacks match his foot, I learned the differences in his dynamic level as well. I learned how to translate that into my right hand. We bonded pretty quickly when he saw my willingness to become a student of his right foot, but to me it was like playing with Yoda. He's James Gadson, after all.

So putting your foot up against the bass drum is one trick. The other is to set up so that you can see all of the drummer's appendages, so that you watch his feet and hands as well as listen. It's a visual idiom sometimes. Watch his body. Watch his face. When he grimaces, maybe you can lean into a note with your body. It's choreography almost, but it makes a difference.

*Are there any mics or direct boxes that people use on you that you like?*
I really like anything that came from the Abbey Road sensibility like the Telefunken VT22 preamps. It's pretty obvious why those records sound so good so I tend to favor that kind of vintage thing. I really like LA-2As a lot. For my basses, that seems to be pretty magic.

I tend to defer to the engineer or producer most of the time because that's their domain and responsibility. I try to be of service to them without patronizing them, even if I think they're doing something unorthodox. I always assume that they may be going for something that maybe I'm not aware of. It's like if they'd want to use a Radio Shack reverb on my bass, I'd probably say, "Great, I never tried that before. Let's do it."

*What do you need in your phone mix?*
Ideally you have your own control of it, which is the way it usually goes these days. The engineer/producer usually creates a really good stereo mix that you can access in order to hear what they're hearing so everyone has a common context. You just add a bit more or less of whatever you need. I generally favor drums and turn myself down. I want kick and snare obviously. I want to hear the singer a little bit but not as much as other players usually do. I want to be able to hear a little bit of everything because the bass player's job is to drive the bus. I have to know who's on the bus and keep the students happy! I like to hear the click as well so I can hear when the drummer pushes and pulls so I can push and pull with him. It also helps to be able to dialog with people if you know that when you get to the bridge someone's rushing, or you're rushing. I also frequently compare headphone mixes with the other players, if I'm comfortable with them, just to see what they're hearing.

I've found that it's not only what I hear but what headphones that we're using as well. A new discovery for me is the new Beyer Dynamic phones (DT-800s), which I like a lot. The Audio Technica M-40s also seem to be friendly to my hearing.

The other thing I do with my headphones is pan the individual players to match where they are in the room. If the electric guitar is to my left, I put it to my left in the phones. That way when I'm talking to them, it corresponds.

*How about onstage tricks?*
Remember why you're there as a bass player. You're there to support the singer. If it's a song-oriented band, your job is to make sure that the singer has a great gig. That's first and foremost. Make sure that the songs are served, but you have to know how to focus yourself as to when to pull out the stops and when to be a forceful presence if that's required. It's every musician's job to serve the song, but for bass players in particular, everyone is depending upon you to play the right notes and the right rhythm. You've got to drive the bus, so you have to be present in the moment for that at all times.

The other thing is situational awareness onstage. Know if the drummer's having problems with his monitors and struggling, you should be aware so you can help him or cover for him if he needs it.

Also remember that it's a gift and honor to be there. It's a very valuable experience every time you play. You have to nurture that experience so you can make something really cool. Make your gig at the coffeehouse or bar as important as if you're playing Madison Square Garden in your own mind. Make every gig fun and exciting, even if it's the same five nights a week in the same venue. Change it up. Make it fun and exciting for you because that means it'll be fun and exciting for the audience. That might mean changing your set, doing acoustic versions of songs, letting someone else do the vocals on a song. Have someone sit out for a song, or play percussion. Don't trick yourself into thinking that it's mundane just because you do it all the time because it's not. It's magic every night.

*What's the worst gig you ever played?*
The worst circumstances I've ever been in was working with an artist who thought he was justified in treating people badly because of their degree of achievement in the marketplace. It was the worst feeling in the room that I've had in the past five years. Just because someone had achieved a fair amount of record sales at some point in his career doesn't mean he or she can treat people badly. That was the worst gig on a psychological level.

The worst gig I've played live was when the group I was in was about to grasp the brass ring, when one of the band members made a "lifestyle choice" that rendered him unable to play. He drank a lot of alcohol to cope with some stress placed on him, flew into a rage before we went onstage, and we couldn't play as a result and it killed a deal that would have changed our fortunes. That was probably the most demoralized and depressed I've ever been.

*What's the best gig you ever did?*
For me the best gigs are the ones that make me feel good. They're not really the ones with the biggest crowds or lots of bells and whistles. Playing with James Gadson in a small restaurant in Beverly Hills can be sanctifying. The Willie Dixon memorial was the most memorable as was playing in front of 450,000 people in Italy with Juliette Lewis for a May Day festival. Another great day was when I was 19 years old jamming in a ramshackle house in the jungle near Cocoa Beach (Florida) with four friends. We were trying to play like "Bitch's Brew" and when we recorded it and played it back, we realized that we were capable of playing improvisational music like the big guys. That was exciting.

*How about the best recording session?*
I would say playing with Tina Turner live in the studio was pretty spectacular. That was pretty magnificent for a white kid from the suburbs. Doing preproduction with Tom Dowd for Merrit Morgan's record was amazingly enlightening. My first real session with Jack Douglas for Aerosmith's *Rock in a Hard Place* was a defining

moment. It was special because it was my first official session. On every record I do with Linda Perry (songwriter and producer), whether it's for Christina Aguilera or Courtney Love, we hit a stride where the magic is unbelievably cool for everybody. Playing with Alicia Keys was great. I've had quite a few.

*What do you hate about playing bass?*
The fact that I don't do it enough. Another thing I hate is the assumptions people make about bass players. Unless you're a lead singer or writer like Paul McCartney or Nikki Six or Roger Waters, it's very hard to be perceived as important. It seems that a lot of people don't view you as a contributor unless you have a guitar or keyboard in your hands.

Onstage, bass players tend to be the ugly sister. You get the least amount of room and they think you don't need a monitor. There's a lot of bass player jokes about this, but it's not so in black music. You don't think of Bootsy (Collins) that way. You don't think of Larry Graham that way. They get equal billing with the guitar players. I'm talking from a white pop point of view.

Also because of the nature of the instrument, we develop a different skill set. Generally, most keyboard players and even guitar players are better transcribers because of the nature of the instrument. Bass players tend not to have as deep a harmonic sophistication, although someone like Charlie Mingus disproves that.

*What do you look for in an instrument?*
If it's a Fender, I make sure there are no dead notes on the G string. That's the first thing I look for. Also, the character of the instrument. St. Leo (referring to Fender Musical Instrument founder Leo Fender) was a furniture maker first so there are some inherent flaws in the old Fender basses that I like but I don't like the compromises you have to make to eliminate them from the design. I'm a bit of a purest. I'd rather have the flaws of a vintage instrument than have a modern instrument that's perfect with no dead spots. I'd rather have the dead spots, unless they're just horrendous. Usually the dead spot on a Fender bass is between B and E on the G string. Sometimes it can be more than one note, although usually it's just one note. Cellos have the same problem and it's called a "wolf tone."

Then I look for the obvious. Does it sound good? Does it feel good? How's the comfort, playability, and general vibe? It could be a $99 imported instrument hanging in a little suburban music store, but it just might be magic. Give it a chance.

# BRIAN MACLEOD

Brian MacLeod has been one of the most in-demand session drummers in L.A. for quite some time now and with good reason. Brian has the ability to make tracks feel not just pretty good, but awesomely great. Although he has plenty of chops, just listen to the groove in Sheryl Crow's breakthrough hit "All I Want to Do" and you'll hear exactly what Brian is known for. And if you're a fan of the television shows *The Office* or *Dirty Sexy Money*, that's him playing on the theme song. Add credits like Christina Aguilera, Madonna, Chris Isaac, John Hiatt, Tears for Fears, Jewel, and many more, and you get an idea of just why the Brian MacLeod touch is so sought after.

But there's more to Brian than just drumming. As a member of and player on The Tuesday Night Music Club, which shot Sheryl Crow to fame, he's been Crow's frequent songwriting collaborator in the years hence, helping pen (among many other songs) the ever popular "Every Day is a Winding Road," which every year takes on a new life with a cover (most recently by Prince) or as the soundtrack for a television commercial. You can read more about Brian at http://www.myspace.com/brianmacleod.

*What's your kit like?*
I switched from using my vintage gear to a custom DDrum kit. They've been around for a long time making drum triggers but this is kind of a new thing from them. I still love my old Gretsch and Ludwig kits, but they made me a beautiful custom kit with a lot of pieces like different size kick drums. They made me a 20-, a 22-, and a 26-inch because they all have specific sounds. The 20-inch is punchy for R&B, the 22-inch is good for modern rock and commercial stuff, and then the 26-inch is for that John Bonham thing with both heads on.

*These are all 16 inches deep?*
The 26-inch is 14 inches deep. The other two are 16 inches deep.

This DDrum kit is all maple and really sounds warm. It has wood hoops on all the toms and is kind of modeled after the old marching kits that Levon Helm (of The Band) used to play. I've been using it a lot as my starting place, but I'll use different gear for different projects. Sometimes I won't bring everything, but I generally like to have a lot of options so I'll bring a big arsenal. And then I like to have a lot of odd toys like toy snare drums I've picked up along the way, which are great for making drum loops. I have a bunch of lo-fi trashy cymbals that I use sometimes when I don't want to go for a hi-tech sound. But I like to have a big array of available sounds to choose from that go from hi-tech to lo-tech.

I have this other drum that's really interesting called the "Trash Cat," which is like a tympani but it's made out of a trash can. I can use it like a floor tom or like a tympani. A lot of producers have really fallen in love with it.

So it's nice to have odd and different things. I interject them when the producer is looking for something special. It really takes a lot of teamwork with the producer as a session drummer. You have to go with the flow and not interrupt things but at the same time have something to bring to the table if needed.

*How many toms do you bring?*
I generally play a 12×8-inch and a 16×14-inch, but I also bring a 14×14-inch floor tom if I need another one.

*What kind of heads do you use?*
I generally use Ambassador coated heads. I'm not afraid to tape up my kit if I need to have it fit better with the song though. You have to tune your drums for the microphones. Sometimes the drum kit might not sound good in the room after you tune it, but it might sound amazing when you hear a playback. This can be very deceiving, for young drummers especially. A young drummer might have his kit tuned so they sound just wonderful live, but you tune it differently for recording. Sometimes I'll use tons of duct tape. I'm not afraid to tape up drums or pad them down to get a nice tight sound if that's what the producer is looking for.

*This is a good time to talk about this. How do you tune your drums? Do you tune to an interval?*
I'm not one of those guys who gets into interval tuning. I think that most drums have a sweet spot and that's what I try to find. It might not necessarily be an interval with another drum, although sometimes I will do that with the snare drum, especially if it's wide open for a real loud and cracking sound. Then I'll either tune it to the pitch of the song so it sits in there nicely, or just the opposite, where it's out

of pitch with the song so it clanks a bit. Sometimes that means just detuning one lug of the snare to get a nice loud crack out of it.

*When you say the sweet spot, do you mean the resonant frequency of the drum?*
Yeah, that's what it is. I learned a lot about tuning from working with the Drum Doctor (Ross Garfield) for so many years, and John Good from DW taught me a lot about the sound that each shell has. Just naturally when you're playing with the drum you'll hit a spot where it feels really good. Some of the older drums that have rounded bearing edges have kind of a deader sound so it's harder to find the sweet spot. This DDrum kit that I have doesn't have the standard 45-degree edge like most new drums. It has a 30-degree edge so it sounds more like older drums because that's the sound I really like. I'm having them build a mahogany kit for me because it's a warmer sound than maple. Some of my old Slingerland Radio King kits are mahogany and they just sound so warm. But the sweet spot you seem to instinctually find.

Like I was saying before, sometimes I'll hit a drum and it just doesn't sound good, but before I'll go and tune it I'll wait until the engineer tells me what he's hearing in the control room because the sound you hear sitting behind the kit is so different from what the mics hear. Sometimes I'll think the drum sound is amazing and the engineer or producer will go, "Man, that tom is a little ringy and high. Can you tune it down a bit?" And I'll tune it down a bit and it will sound floppy to me and might not even physically feel right hitting it, but when I go back into the control room and listen to it, it just sounds huge and wonderful.

So tuning can be a bit of a mystery. It's very instinctual. There's no real math to it, as far as I know.

*Do you use the Drum Doctor on sessions?*
When the session budget is big, I like to use him. When the budget isn't big I have to do it myself. I've learned a lot by working with Ross for so many years so I can make it sound pretty good, but it's really nice to walk into a session and know that he's tuned it up and I can just show up and play. I don't like to get bogged down in the studio tuning drums. It can really slow down the session and I like to keep the pace of the session up and moving forward.

You mentioned the fact that you bring different drums to different types of sessions. How do you determine what to bring for something like a Chris Isaac session as compared to a movie or television gig?

Generally I try to get a heads up from the producer or the producer's assistant as to what kind of song we're doing and what he wants it to sound like. For example, if he says they're doing something that's a retro '70s Led Zeppelin type of thing, then I know to bring my 26-inch kick and an old Radio King snare. If he says it's a mid-tempo R&B kind of thing, then I'll know to bring my 20-inch or 22-inch kick. So I try to get as much information from the producer before the session and find out as much about the artist, the specific band, and the direction of the music.

*It sounds like you have a big drum collection.*
Oh yeah (laughs). I've got a huge collection parked at the Drum Doctors, and my garage is completely full with just a very small isle down the middle. I'm constantly scouring eBay for new weird things like plastic snare drums and odds and ends. I like to have a lot of toys just to make sure the recording is interesting. That's something I got from Jim Keltner (another well-known session drummer). He taught me a lot about that. Sometimes if he's in a session in the studio next to mine we go hang out together and we're like little kids, comparing our new odd toys and instruments. He's always been a big help on that kind of stuff.

*How many snares do you bring to a session?*
I have two trunks that I generally bring that contain ten snare drums, plus I have an old vintage '70s Black Beauty that I hand-carry with me. That always stays at home with me and I bring it to work just like it was my brief case (laughs). I've got some old '20s chrome-over-brass drums, and some big old mahogany drums that are great for that '70s sound. They have six lugs and round bearing edges so they tune down really low, and if you tape it up it gets a really fat sound that's great for ballads. I generally don't use a piccolo, but I have one in my arsenal. You have to make sure you have everything because whatever you don't bring to the session is what the producer will ask for, so I like to be prepared and have plenty of options.

But once again, that has to fit with the budget. If it's a full record, I try to bring as much stuff as I can and almost every day that I come in I'll bring even more stuff. If I hear something for a specific song, I'll dig around and maybe find something that I think will work if I bring it. So it varies, but I generally have ten snare drums that represent a good spectrum from piccolos to big fat '70s sounds.

*What do you use for cymbals?*
I've been using Paiste Giant Beat cymbals but I have so many old vintage Zildjians from the '50s and '60s, which I collect. I like to have a pair of 13-, 14-, and 15-inch hi-hats available at a session. The 13s are really tight and the 15s are really dark and warm. I've noticed over the years that recording hi-hat can be really tricky. You might put a mic on it and never even use it because the hi-hat is so loud, so I like to have some quiet hats around. I have these 15s that are quiet and nice sounding.

Then I generally use 17-, 18-, and 20-inch crashes and a couple of 20-inch and a couple of 22-inch rides. Then I have one sizzle cymbal that I bring, although some engineers are allergic to them (laughs). The sizzle cymbal opens a whole floodgate of people who either love them or hate them, but I make sure I have some with me at all times.

*How about sticks?*
I usually play 5As because they're such an all around good stick, but sometimes I'll use different types. I'll use the Fatar Recording drumsticks that have a small bead on them, which I really like because then you can get a really good cymbal sound. It's really amazing how a different bead can make the cymbal sound completely different when you're riding on a cymbal. If you use a round head you'll get a lot of attack. If you use a plastic head you'll get more attack. If you use a larger wood you can get more of a wash from the cymbal. So I definitely have a lot of different sticks and brushes, and mallets too, because someone will always ask, "Can you do a cymbal swell?" If you look in your stick bag and you don't have them, it is embarrassing to tell them, "I can make some with some tissues and duct tape (laughs hard)." That's the part of being a session drummer where you have the most anxiety. I like to make sure that my stick bag is loaded with hot-rods, brushes, different size sticks and mallets.

*You don't do too much live work these days do you?*
No, I don't do much at all. It's so funny because since I've moved to L.A. I've played live maybe 10 times in 15 years. I don't really tour too much because I like to be available for sessions. The last big tour I did was with Tears for Fears, but I had to come back and re-establish myself with all the producers because I was gone for such a long period of time. Out of site, out of mind, as they would say. Now if Nick Mason decides he doesn't want to play with Pink Floyd anymore, then that would be something I'd have to think about (laughs).

*That begs the question: would your road kit be different than what you'd use in the studio?*
Probably. I probably wouldn't use wood hoops and it would be tuned more open and live. I'd work with the front-of-house guy to dial in the kit. Then visually, I'd probably do something a bit different too. When I did the Jay Leno Show with Seal I used my clear acrylic DW kit because it just looks so good on TV. The lighting people just love it. So yeah, I'd use a different kit live because I'd go for the fashion (laughs). It's like wearing different ties with your suit. And that's what's so funny about the studio because sometimes I'll have such a mismatched kit with like my red sparkle 14-inch Ludwig floor tom with my DW 26-inch kick and an old Gretsch 13-inch rack tom. They look like a disaster together but sound great.

*What are you looking for in the phones when you record?*
That's a great question. Generally it depends on how we're tracking. If I'm tracking with a bass player and we're doing overdubs to an existing track, I'll try to get a nice even level so it sounds like a record with the vocals and the bass player just above the music. I want to hear the bass player so I can be sure to lock my kick drum with him. Then if I'm tracking live, I want the leader of the song to be above the track. Like if the guitar player has written the song, he might be doing some important inflections that I need to hear. If it's a vocalist who has written the song and they're evoking some emotion they really want, I'll make sure that is above everything else. So I latch on to whatever the main instrument of the tracking date is, or what the biggest concern seems to be when laying down the basics.

I'll also have the click at an ungodly level, which can drive producers and engineers crazy, so I like to use closed headphones for that. I'm still looking for the perfect set of headphones because you don't want the click track leaking into the song. On Christina Aguilera's "Beautiful," you can hear a bit of the drum machine on her vocal track, but the vocal was so amazing that they just went with it. You have to be careful especially on endings of songs. I try to get the engineer to cut the click off so that the cymbal sustain doesn't have any click bleed. I'll even punch in the ending of a song if they can't catch it at the right time.

*What kind of a click sound do you like?*
In the old days I used to be very specific about it. I used to like a cowbell or some sort of side-stick sound with a shaker doing 16ths or 8ths depending on the feel of the song. I have to say that's still my favorite click track, but I'm getting used to just the Pro Tools click.

I've adjusted over the years, but my preference still is the cowbell and shaker.

*There's a defining moment for every player when they finally "get it." What was yours?*
That's an interesting moment for me. I think it was on my first trip to L.A. on my first big session. It was with Patrick Leonard (producer for Madonna, Rod Stewart, Jewel, Bon Jovi, Elton John, and Pink Floyd among others). He flew me down from San Francisco where I was teaching drums and playing live. I had toured a bit and done a few albums in England at that point. Pat was starting a band and was auditioning me to be the drummer. I played on a couple of tracks that were already finished with a click. After the second song he said, "Hey Brian, can you come in here for a minute," (to join him in the control room). I thought to myself, "That's my audition. I guess I'm outa here," so I actually grabbed my stick bag and zipped it up so I wouldn't have the embarrassment of having to walk back out into the studio to get it. I figured that the door out of the studio was in the control room and if he was firing me, I just wanted to leave as fast as I can.

So I zipped up my stick bag and walked into the control room and he looked at it with a confused look on his face like "What are you doing?" So I said, "What's up?" and he said, "I love the way you play to the song with the click track. You know how to lock into the click track and not make it sound mechanical. I love your feel and I want to hire you to do this record." Then he said, "Oh, by the way. Listen to a track I just finished," and he cranked up Madonna's "Like a Prayer" at full volume. That was the moment I felt like, "Wow, I think I get this. This guy has done all this amazing work and he's telling me that my feel with the click is nice." I realized at that moment that I really could play to a click and make it breathe at the same time. And that really is an important thing for drummers to learn. If you play to a click, don't be so focused on the click that you lose sight of the fact that you're actually playing a song.

*Do you have any other advice for a young drummer just starting out?*
Yeah, I'd say try to play to a click as much as you can so you can learn to play with it yet lose sight of it at the same time. You want the feel of the click track to become like intuition, so it doesn't make you feel shackled to it.

Also, when you work with a producer, be as flexible as you can. Don't be stubborn. Instead, trust the people you work with. If the engineer or producer has a suggestion, trust their advice. I was talking to a producer the other day about how he'll sometimes have a drummer come in who will insist on playing his own kit. If I work with a producer who wants me to play his old vintage kit, of course I'll play it because I think it's important to be flexible. Even if I show up with my gear, if he has his kit miked up and he knows what it sounds like, I'll generally do that. Then, if they're not satisfied, I'll use my drums.

Another thing: if you have any ideas, make the suggestion if the time is right because it's all about teamwork and you're on the team.

*Do you have any advice for the guy who's playing in clubs to bring up his level of playing?*
I think one thing is to realize that you are a drummer but you are also are a musician. You're not a drum machine just there to keep time; you have to play everything with a great feel. Listen to your favorite albums and check out the feel of the drummers and how they make the music breathe and how their dynamics go along with the music. It's all about being a musician to me. A lot of the best drummers I know also play another instrument besides drums, even if not well. That way you start to understand music more. Playing piano is a great thing for a drummer to learn at some point. I'm still working on it myself. But be able to be in touch with the music and the songs and really understand what's going on besides the time aspect of the music.

So work on your feel, your time, and your fills. A lot of drummers have great time except for when they do fills. I've heard from producers, "So and so has such a great feel, but his fills are always out of time." So just trying to be musical is important. Rushing the fill is a really common thing for a lot of drummers. The way to cure that is just practicing to a click track a lot.

*You mentioned before about Patrick Leonard inviting you to L.A. to record. Would you consider that your big break?*
I think so because after we finished that I record I was pretty much planning on moving back to the Bay Area. But Patrick said, "Hey Brian, if you lived in L.A. I would use you on the records I work on." Ironically the engineer/co-producer on that record was Bill Bottrell (who eventually went on to produce Sheryl Crow, Michael Jackson, and Shelby Lynn) and he said the same thing to me. So I had two top-of-the-line producers tell me that if I lived in L.A. they'd use me on their records. It became a no-brainer for me to run up to the Bay Area, pack my things in a U-Haul, and get my butt to L.A. Then it kind of expanded from there.

I had no delusions of moving to L.A. before those sessions. I was too content in the Bay Area where I had a nice life teaching drums and playing live almost every night. It was wonderful, so I really didn't want to move to L.A. unless there was a good reason because I didn't want to try to break in the way everyone seems to do it. It would have been too frustrating for me.

But this is actually some good advice for a young drummer. If you're in a band and working with a producer, really pay attention and work with him to help him make that record sound better. You're more likely to be called for another project afterwards. He might have had so much fun working with you in your band that he'll think of you for a solo artist he's working with. That's how I developed myself. I worked with Tim Palmer in London with my own band, and that's how I got the job playing with Tears for Fears. So I've developed relationships with all the producers I've worked with over the years in my own band.

*What's your favorite type of music to play?*
It's an interesting spectrum. I love retro-funk, and I love old hard rock. I think that stems from my older brothers blasting Beatles to Led Zeppelin in their bedrooms while my mom was out vacuuming the living room listening to R&B. With my mom listening to Aretha Franklin and The Supremes and my brothers teaching me about rock 'n' roll, that's really how I got started. My brothers were guitar players and they needed a drummer, so they got me a drum kit. They were trying to make me the first human drum machine at eight years old (laughs). But I just fell in love with it and became obsessed. I knew even at that age that's what I wanted to do. I used to stare at pictures of The Who and Led Zeppelin playing in the studio and go, "That's what I want to do. I want to work in studios."

*What's the best gig you've ever had?*
I would have to say being part of the band that created The Tuesday Night Music Club. As you know, we wrote and conceived what became Sheryl Crow's first album. It was awesome. We were all working in the studio and (producer) Bill Bottrell made sure that everybody participated to the point where sometimes I wasn't even playing drums. He'd make me play bass or something. It was kind of frightening but fun at the same time. It was one of the most incredible experiences in my life to participate in, not just as a drummer but as a musician and a lyricist. He really opened the door to all of us to push the envelope. That whole period of time was really wonderful, but continuing on writing songs with Sheryl Crow after that was really great too. She's always been open to my ideas.

It's great to have someone believe and trust in you like she has. I just wrote a song and played on her new record as well.

And I have to say that touring with Tears for Fears was really wonderful too because they had such great songs. Just playing those songs live was pretty awesome.

*What's the worst gig you've ever had?*
The artist name shall remain nameless, but this artist lost his drummer in the middle of a tour and desperately needed me to come out and play with him. He called me on the phone and said, "I'll make this really easy on you. Just learn these twelve songs and if you can be out here by tomorrow that would be great." So on my flight out to the East Coast I just crammed all night long learning these songs, making charts and mental notes. I got to the gig and out of those twelve songs we only played three of them. He threw all these other songs at me and kept turning to me during the show and yelling, "That's not right!" "Play faster!" "Play slower!" "You're blowin' it!" He ended up firing me after about three gigs and it was just the most miserable experience of my life (laughs). It scared me enough not to play live for a while which actually improved my studio work, so my hat's off to him in a strange way.

*Was there a particularly bad session?*
There was one session where I can't even remember the producer's name. We set up all the gear and played maybe half a song when the producer came into the studio and went, "I'm just not feeling this. There's something wrong. You guys are all getting paid, but this is just not right. I can't do this." And he walked out. We all just looked at each other like, "Okay, what just happened here?" That might be one of the worst sessions because we all left with a question mark over our heads. Did he not like our playing? Was he having a personal problem? Didn't the artist like us? We never found out, but we got paid. Everyone involved still laughs about it to this day.

*What kind of gig is the hardest for you?*
The hardest gig is when the artist or the producer doesn't know what they want and they're not open to suggestions. That can be really difficult because even though they don't know what they want, they won't accept any help to find out what they may want. I've done a couple of records like that where I pull my hair out because they just keep experimenting. "Let's try it reggae style." "No, let's try it as a waltz." They just keep going around in circles but at the same time don't want to hear your opinion or suggestion. "We

just want to keep going around chopping the legs off the chair until there's no vibe left."

*I've had the same thing with songwriters who keep re-writing the song over and over. They don't make it better; they just make it different.*
Exactly. It's like, is this getting better or is it just different? I actually avoided a session with another very famous female singer because I was given the heads up that she never knows what she wants and is always going around in circles. They asked me to do the record but I had to decline because I just wasn't prepared to be that patient, even though it was good money. I realized that mental and physical health is more important than flying out of town and working with an artist who doesn't know what they want. And I was not the only drummer. There was a line of drummers who either quit or got fired from the gig. I don't really need that in my life.

*What gigs are the most fun?*
Working on this Chris Isaac record that I just did is really fun because we tracked it live. Tracking live is so much fun when I play with musicians I really connect with. That's the most fun for me because I get a little of that live feel and edge, but it's in the studio so it sounds good. It's musical communication and connection. I like that feeling. I guess it goes back to looking at those records when I was a kid. To see the Beatles all set up in the studio with George Martin in the middle talking to them; I pine for those days (laughs).

*Is there an aspect to recording that you don't like?*
Yes, when they "drive past the money." If there's an amazing take that was done live and they say something like, "We don't like the ending to the song. Can we do another take?" When you feel like you've done something really wonderful and either the producer or the artist just drives right past it and then beats the song into the ground and sucks the life out of it. Sometimes there's magic in takes that end up never getting used. That can be really frustrating. That's happened a lot, unfortunately.

I think that it's one of those things where you almost have to be playing to know when you've really nailed it. It's really hard to be on the other side of the glass and know when you've caught the magic.

*That's the trick of being a producer.*
Exactly, and I've had to swallow my pride and play something faster or slower and it doesn't sound as good, but if they want that way, you've just got to do it. This isn't my record, after all; it's theirs.

*Is there an aspect of drumming that you don't like?*
Hauling my gear around (laughs). I think the day when I bought my convertible and could drive it to a session I felt like success. I thought, "I don't have to drive a van around any more. I can just come in my Alfa Romero to this wonderful studio with these wonderful musicians with my drums already tuned to where I just walk in and play." I know that sounds spoiled, but at some point in any musician's life, that's a reward.

# PETER THORN

Peter Thorn proves that if someone is willing to take the giant step of leaving home for the big city and work hard at his craft, a lot of really good things can happen along the way. As you'll soon read, Peter left his native Canada for Hollywood, soaked up as much information as he could, worked constantly on his chops and sound, and eventually became a much-in-demand session and touring guitarist and artist in his own right. Peter is a shining example of a professional musician—excellent chops, excellent sound (who sings great as well), yet easy-going, humble, and approachable. Below he outlines his keys to success.

*How about some of your background?*
I grew up in Edmonton, Canada and started playing guitar when I was fourteen. When I was nineteen, I moved to Los Angeles to go to Musician's Institute and attended there for a year. When I got out of school I joined a band with a couple of older musicians who were pretty well known in L.A. (Frank Simes and Jennifer Condos) who were touring with Don Henley at the time. Frank had a bunch of songs and was trying to get a record deal when he wasn't playing with Don. It was cool because they were much older than me—they were in their mid-thirties and I was like nineteen—so I learned a lot from them. I spent about five years in the band and we did a record for Japan and Southeast Asia. When that ended around 1995, I started doing a lot of sessions and touring.

Right now I'm playing with Chris Cornell but before I played with a bunch of other artists like Jewel, Daniel Powter, Alicia Keys, and Courtney Love. I was also in the group Five for Fighting for a while and toured with them.

*What's your live setup like?*
With Chris I'm using a "wet-dry-wet" rig, which uses a typical head and speaker cabinet combination, but takes a tap from the signal going to the cabinet. That's fed at line level out to some effects, which are fed into a stereo power amp that's connected to a couple of cabinets sitting on either side of the main one in the center. So the center cabinet is the dry, direct guitar sound and the outside cabs have a stereo delay or a bit of reverb in them. That allows both me and the soundman to have independent control over the dry signal and a blend of the stereo effects, so if I've got a stereo Leslie thing going on, or stereo delays bouncing back and forth on those outside cabs, he can control it if he thinks he's got too much in the house. I can mix the dry signal into the wet cabinets to get louder if I need to for a solo boost or something. It's a very flexible way to do it.

*What kind of amps?*
Right now I'm using a few different things. In the studio I'll use all types of different amps from vintage amps like Fenders and Marshalls and weird things like Supros, but on the road I use a combination of different heads. I'm using one built by a guy named John Suhr (suhrguitars.com) that's a custom-made head based on his OD-100 amp and called a PT-100 for my name. It has two channels—one that's Fender clean, and one that's a Marshall-like distortion channel. I also use a Divided by Thirteen (dividedby13.com) RSA-31 head, which is another boutique amp. At times I'll also use an amp by Comet (electrosonicamplifiers.com), so I'm sort of a boutique amp guy. I like the hand-wired, small company stuff.

*What guitars do you take with you?*
With Chris I'm using five different Les Pauls, as well as a Darco model which is like a 335, then I have a Tele and two Strat-like guitars built by John Suhr.

*What are your effects?*
Right now I've got the TC G-System which is my MIDI controller as well as a loop switcher into which I can integrate various pedals like a Trinity overdrive, a Boss Fuzz, Line6 rotary simulator and a Peterson tuner that are on the pedal board. Back in the rack for the wet-dry-wet system I use a unit called the Axe-Fx (fractalaudio.com), which is a two-rack space processor that's like a big super powerful Pod because it has amp simulators and everything in it, but I'm only using it for effects. So I have the TC and all the pedals in

front of the amp (signal-wise) and then post-amp I have the Axe-Fx for long delays and reverbs and stuff like that.

*What do you usually bring with you to the studio?*
I don't bring much any more because if I'm working at (producer/writer) Linda Perry's, she has so much stuff there that it's sort of fun to go and just pick through the stuff that's there. (Author's note: Linda's studio has the most fantastic collection of vintage gear I've ever seen in a studio, and I've been in hundreds of studios all over the world.) If I am going to do a session on my own and I need to bring something, I'll bring the TC pedal board and either a 1×12 or a 2×12 speaker cabinet with these little heads built by Suhr called Badgers; there's one that's 18 watts and another that's 30 watts. I really like them because they're versatile and sound great with pedals. For guitars, I'll try to bring a Les Paul, a Strat, a Tele, and maybe one acoustic.

*Do you have any tips as a session musician?*
I would say an important thing for me is to serve the song at all times. Try to keep an open mind and if someone has an idea in the room then always let that idea be heard. If it involves trying something different in the part that you're playing, you can't get defensive about it. You have to just let it happen because that really goes a long way toward creating a good atmosphere in the room. When everybody drops their ego and just tries to serve the song, I find that the best idea will rise to the surface and everybody will recognize it. It's human nature to want our ideas to be the best ones, but if you can be open to others' suggestions, you can learn something and maybe do something that you wouldn't have thought of doing.

Now that you've worked your way up through the ranks, what advice would you give to someone who's working in a club or cover band?

If you're in a bar band and playing covers, it really depends upon your goals and aspirations. A lot of people don't want to write songs and go any further than that because they're happy just playing on the weekends, so then it comes down to honing your songs and your chops and maybe taking singing lessons to make sure that your background vocals are really tight.

If what you're trying to do is break out to have a career as an artist, I'd be playing in the clubs on the weekends but be constantly writing songs and recording as much as possible. When I first moved to L.A. and was in that band I was telling you about, we'd play cover gigs two or three nights a week for fun and to make some money, but during the week we'd always be writing and recording. We cranked out about 50 songs over a couple-year period and that eventually got us a record deal (which is what everyone wanted back then). When you do that, you just get better and better at writing and honing the sound of your band. I've got a lot of friends who played in cover bands, particularly where I came from in Canada because there was a really strong cover band scene there, but they never were really able to bust out of that because all they did was play covers and never tried to write anything. But like I said, it all depends on your goals. Some people don't want the work that comes along with developing their own music because they only want to do it for fun.

One of the things that will really help if you're in a cover band is to work individually on your parts before you get to rehearsal because you can get so much more done. You can get through a lot of songs if everyone has done their homework because it's just fine tuning the song in rehearsal at that point.

*What was your defining moment as a guitar player, the moment when the light when on and you went, "Now I get it"?*
I had a couple. One was at GIT (Guitar Institute of Technology in Hollywood). Everyone thinks of GIT as strictly academic and thinks you can't learn about the real world there, but I had a couple of moments. They had these live-playing workshops where everyone would learn a song by AC/DC or something like that. There would be a bunch of drummers and bass players and guitar players that the teacher would randomly assign so you never knew who you were going to play with, but there was a set song for everybody to play, then the teachers would critique you afterwards. I remember that I went in and really played this song perfectly (I can't remember what it was now). A guy got up after me and played the song about 70 percent of what I did, but he had a lot of feel and attitude. A teacher pointed it out afterwards that sometimes that goes a long way, especially in rock 'n' roll. It's not all just about the notes, it's about performing and having a stage presence, so that was an important lesson for me. At the end of the day you're entertaining people and you have to be free and expressive and having fun with it.

Another defining moment is when I realized that the thing that's going to set you apart from people is your attention to detail, like really having your gear and your sounds together and knowing how it all works. It's going into a rehearsal or audition and really having your parts down and your scene together so you stand out.

I started getting a lot of gigs that I was auditioning for in the late '90s and after a while I tried to formulate why it was happening because I seemed to be pretty good at auditioning and scoring these gigs. I may not be the greatest guitar player in the world, but I seem to know how to get work (laughs). It kind of came down to the fact of knowing your stuff and being prepared. Like if you're auditioning for an artist that's about to go on tour and they just spent a year working on an album, they know it inside and out and they're passionate about it. A lot of people will just learn the chords and blow their own solo over the section and maybe plug into the rental amp that's at the audition. But if you're the guy that goes in with your amp dialed in with all the right sounds off the record and you've learned the parts really well, you're really putting your best foot forward and also stroking their ego in a way that leaves them thinking, "Wow, this guy really cares about my music. He's really put the time in." That's when I went, "Oh, I get it." Be it in a session or an audition, having your gear together and being able to play the parts is it for me. There are a lot of guitar players but you have to go one step beyond the other guy to get the work.

## BRIAN RAY

At a time of life when many professional musicians are a bit jaded or burned out, Brian Ray still has the same sense of fun and enthusiasm of a 15-year-old in his first garage band. Never mind that he may be at what many might consider a musical pinnacle by being in Paul McCartney's touring band, or that he's had a career studded with great gigs and hit writing (like a number-one song in three formats for Smokey Robinson), Brian's still the same down-to-earth guy that you'd expect to find at the local Tuesday-night jam.

As an example, a few years ago I met Brian for the first time outside of a James Gang reunion concert. I gushed about how I just saw him with McCartney on the last tour and how great I thought the show was (I wasn't patronizing. It really was an 11 on a scale of 1 to 10), and his response was, "You should hear us now. We're so much better." I walked away from the conversation thinking that it doesn't matter how big or how small your band is, it's all the same. You're always trying to get better. Brian is that kind of guy. It only takes a brief conversation to tell that he really loves what he does and has a dedication to his art that goes way beyond the norm, as you'll soon read for yourself.

Brian was kind enough to share some of the insights he's garnered from a wide range of experiences that vary from playing clubs and parties to writing a number-one song, to sharing the stage with a number of musical legends all over the world.

*Let's start from the beginning of your career. How did you get started playing?*
I started playing as a kid in Glendale, California when I was given a $5 gut-string guitar by my sister Jean. She was in a folk-rock duo called Jim and Jean at that time and they had a record out on Verve-Folkways. They were touring with acts like the Beach Boys and Blues Project and opened for a lot of famous folk stars. When she would come home from her tours she would regale us with her stories from the road, and I found that whole world fascinating. She knew that I wanted to play, so she surprised me with a guitar when I was about nine years old. I started playing by ear and the first song I learned was "Gloria" (by Van Morrison's first band Them). Of course, with those three chords from that song you could play about a thousand other rocks songs too (laughs), but I was on my way.

My first professional job where I was playing onstage and getting paid for it was later as a sideman with my sister during her solo career. During the summer between my junior and senior year of high school, we did a small tour of club dates from New York to Los Angeles, but a pivotal moment in my career came when I was playing at Six Flags over Texas with Bobby "Boris" Pickett and his Crypt Kicker Five (who had the famous Halloween hit "Monster Mash"). We were playing a party for Phil Kaufman to raise money for his legal defense. [Author's note: In one of the most bizarre incidents in rock 'n' roll, Phil stole the body of acclaimed country-rocker Gram Parsons after he had died and took it to the desert to be cremated as per his wishes, before his family could have the body returned to Texas. Phil was Gram's best friend and was eventually arrested for grand theft of the casket.]

Phil just took to me and one morning asked if I wanted to come along to an Etta James rehearsal because the guitar player couldn't make it. So I went to a house up in the Hollywood Hills, met Etta and did a little rehearsal with her. She took to me as well and I played a show that night with her in Long Beach, California. One night about a month later I got a call from her and she said, "Brian, I'm about to go onstage. Can you get up here to Ventura?" I told her I'd be there, and an hour and a half later I was onstage. That was the beginning of fourteen years with Etta James from the mid seventies to the late eighties.

*Did you record with her as well?*
I recorded a record that's out of print and impossible to find called *Etta is Betta* and another for Warner's called *Deep in the Night* that was produced by the famous Atlantic producer Jerry Wexler. I also recorded and co-produced a live record with her called *Hard to Handle* that was released in the early '90s where she was just on fire.

*What happened after Etta?*
I really wanted to pursue songwriting and tour less so I applied myself to writing as if it were a paid job five days a week. Out of that came a song I wrote for Smokey Robinson that was a hit on three formats—pop, R&B, and adult contemporary called "One Heartbeat." My partner and I just wrote and wrote, then eventually put a band together called Charm School and gigged around L.A. After a few years I got call from Rita Coolidge to be her musical director, then I did a couple of records with Willy DeVille (from the '80s new wave band Mink DeVille). I actually just did another one with him about eight months ago.

From there, I got a gig from 1996 to 2000 with Mylene Farmer, who's a French superstar and sort of like a French Madonna. While doing that, I also got to work with Johnny Hallyday, who was France's biggest artist and equivalent to Elvis over there. I toured with both of them back and forth for about five years, which brings us to 2001.

At my birthday party, my friend Abe (drummer Abe Laboriel Jr.), who toured with me with Mylene Farmer and Johnny Hallyday, told me he was now working with Paul McCartney and they were going on tour but were looking for a guitar player who could play bass. I just put my arm in the air and said, "I'd love a shot at that," which was way out of my character to do something like that. I'd always gone from gig to gig by word of mouth and I was normally too shy to stick up for myself like that. A couple weeks later I got a call from Paul's producer David Kahne to come to his office in Hollywood. We just talked music and then he handed me a bass and I played a little while we were just chatting. Then he handed me a guitar and we chatted some more when he finally said, "We're doing one song at the Super Bowl in 2002 and we're looking for someone to play bass. Are you into it?" Of course I was into it! He said that they were looking at a couple of other guys but he had a good feeling about me and would put my name forward. The next day I got a call to see if I could be on a plane to New Orleans the day after that to play a song with Paul McCartney!

I played the gig and it seemed to have worked out well. I was shaking Paul's hand at the end where I said, "Thank you. It was a real privilege and if I don't get to see you again, thank you very much," when I realized that I couldn't let go of his hand (laughs), but he invited me back to the bar for a drink with the rest of the band. At the end of the night he was saying his goodbyes to everyone when he said, "Welcome aboard, Brian. Stick with Abe and Rusty (guitar player Rusty Anderson) to show you the ropes and I'll see you in five weeks." I couldn't believe that I was in after only one song! So I ran home and started woodshedding and cramming. I set myself up like I was training for the Olympics and went through all his material from the Beatles to Wings to the solo stuff and just applied myself to it for five weeks, knowing that he may come in and change everything I had learned or even let me go. So I didn't treat it like I had the gig, I treated it like I had another audition. It just so happens that we had five days of rehearsal as a band before Paul got there so we were all prepared by the time he arrived. After the first rehearsal he said, "Hey guys, sounds great. I'll see you tomorrow." That was really the first time I allowed myself to think, "I'm going on tour with Paul McCartney."

*Did you play bass before then?*
Yeah, but just on demos, I wasn't really a live bass player. I was a guitar player my whole career, but I just applied myself. It's funny because that New Year's I had made a resolution to learn a new instrument, but I didn't think it was going to be a bass guitar (laughs)! But there I was three weeks later cramming bass at my house for the gig.

*It must be intimidating to play his parts with him being there.*
I just didn't put that in my mind. I guess I was nervous but I just didn't look up too much for the first couple of weeks. It was all I could do just to play and sing the parts right at the same time because there's a lot of counterpoint vocals where you're singing and playing in two directions. I didn't have any time or energy for the existential idea of playing bass for the Beatles' bass player (laughs).

*What are your live rigs like?*
I have two Ashdown bass rigs with the heads kept off-stage. Then I have two Divided By 13 guitar amps as well. I use two 19 watt 9/15 heads and two 2×12 cabinets onstage with a simple pedal board.

Also, I play 12-string on Band On The Run and acoustic six-string on a lot of songs, so I have to be ready to play a different instrument on every song that we do.

*What guitars and basses are you using?*
When I'm playing with Paul, I use a '61 Les Paul SG, a '65 Reissue SG and a '59 Gretsch Double Anniversary that I like to use. For bass, I use a Gibson SG bass and a Guild M85 bass from the early '80s. I also use a Taylor 12-string and a '63 Gibson Dove six-string. Sometimes I'll also use a James Trusart guitar, a Patrick James Eggle guitar, or a variety of other guitars like Les Pauls, although I think I'm going to play Les Paul Juniors on the next tour.

*You said you use a simple pedal board. What are you using?*
I'm using a Demeter Compulator, a Divided By 13 Joyride (a great overdrive pedal) and Dyna-Ranger treble boost, Line 6 delay and modulation pedals, a volume pedal, and a Divided By 13 Switchazel that has a buffer in it. Then, believe it or not, I use an Alesis Micro-Reverb for some of the Beatles stuff when I want some reverb onstage. It's the best-sounding stage reverb I've heard.

*What do you bring with you to a session?*
I have a great rack that I really love using that's built by David Freedman of Rack Systems Ltd. here in L.A. It includes some vintage pedals like an Electro-Harmonix Memory Man and Micro Synth, a Cornish pedal that's fantastic, a DigiTech Experience pedal, and a blue Boss VB2 vibrato pedal that's really rare. It also has these great Randall preamps and amps that have a convertible preamp system and a MIDI-switchable power section. They can sound like a great black-face Fender, a great Marshall Plexi, an AC-30, and then a sort of rectified Mesa, all with MIDI-switchable power sections between EL-34's (like a Marshall) and 6L6's (like a Fender) so you can have any combination of presets. There's also a Rocktron Replifex, which works great in the post-preamp position before the amps. The rack also has an auxiliary amp send that allows me to use a different head with the different preamps, so I usually bring an AC-30 or my Divided By 13 9/15 head along. Then I have baritone guitars, lots of different Les Pauls, and lots of vintage stuff that I don't bring out on the road much but I'm happy to bring to sessions in town.

*How is it different playing with Paul than all the other gigs you've had?*
He calls upon us to want to do everything we can at the highest possible level. He's really great to work for and he's not tough on

us, but the material itself is very demanding and keeps me focused. There's a lot to think about when I have to sing some of those background vocal lines while playing that intensely during an almost three-hour show. And a lot of his post-Beatles stuff has a lot of the song structures that are not as simple or predictable as you would think. We just learned a song from Wings called "Mrs. Vanderbilt" that we played in concert in Kiev recently. It only has three chords, then a release section with another three chords, and you'd think it'd be very simple but the song form is so strange and completely unpredictable that I defy anybody to play that song down faithfully the first time. So the music requires a lot of concentration. You want to do your very best when you're playing those songs along with that voice for the audience we get to play for.

*If you were able to go back and give some advice to the early bands that you played in, what would that be?*
There's no "me" in "team." You've got to really think of the band being more important than any individual in the band. There's no time or place for ego problems or for people who want to be noticed above the others, it's really about thinking about the songs and the music as being bigger than any of the individuals. That can't be done well unless you really listen to each other and play in the moment. And not just the rehearsed part, but real music that's dynamic and ever changing even though it might be the same song you've played 160 times. You've got to find new things to keep you interested.

*What advice do you have for someone just starting out playing in bands?*
I would say to listen more than you play. Pay attention to downbeats from the drums and bass and play those downbeats with total conviction. Play with good time and think of that as more important than playing with energy or technical ability. Playing with good time and with good attentive energy is the most important thing.

And keep your ears and your body pointed toward the singer. Showboating and facing the other way when somebody's carrying the song doesn't help the whole. It's really got to be about the singer when you're playing.

# GLOSSARY

**attack**—the first part of a sound or phrase.

**backline**—the row of amps at the back of the stage that the musicians play through.

**basic tracks**—recorded tracks of the band's rhythm section, which may include drums, bass, rhythm guitar, and keyboards, but could be drums only.

**basics**—see **basic tracks**.

**bottom**—bass frequencies; the lower end of the audio spectrum. See also **low end**.

**bpm**—beats per minute; the measure of tempo.

**bridge**—an interlude that connects two parts of a song and builds a harmonic connection between them.

**build**—usually a two-bar section of a song where the volume builds from soft to loud.

**capo**—a device that temporarily clamps onto the neck of a guitar and artificially moves the nut. This allows the player to change keys yet still play chords that require open strings like E and A.

**chorus**—the refrain of the song, which usually follows each verse and contains the hook.

**clip**—overload.

**clipping**—the state created when an audio-input signal level is too high and overloads the circuitry, causing distortion.

**data-compressed**—when a computer file's size is reduced for easier transmission. This usually results in a loss of audio quality.

**DAW**—digital audio workstation. A software package for multitrack recording on a computer.

**DI**—see Direct box.

**digital over**—a digital overload; the point beyond 0 on a digital processor's meter where the indicator marked "Over" lights red.

**direct box**—a device that allows a high impedance instrument like a guitar or bass to be interfaced with a low impedance input on an audio console.

**eSession**—an Internet service that allows studio musicians to remotely play on your recordings.

**feedback**—the ringing sound that occurs when sound coming out of a speaker re-enters a microphone and is re-amplified many times.

**feedback eliminator**—an electronic device that uses digital processing to track the audio and watch for feedback. When feedback is sensed, a filter is automatically inserted at the proper frequency and adjusted to the right amount to help eliminate it.

**feel**—the groove of a song and how it feels to play it.

**flatwounds**—strings that have a ribbon-like winding along the core of the string. Used to suppress finger noise.

**footballs**—whole notes that look like footballs when transcribed.

**gel**—a thin sheet of transparent, colored material used to color light from a stage-lighting fixture.

**graphic equalizer**—an audio equalizer on which each frequency band has its own control (usually a slider).

**groove**—the pulse of the song and how the instruments breathe with it.

**hook**—a catchy phrase either played or sung.

**humbucking**—a guitar pickup that uses two coils in reversed polarity to eliminate outside noise and interference (they "buck the hum"). Humbucking pickups have much higher gain than single coil pickups.

**IEM**—in-ear monitor (see **in-ear-monitor**)

**in-ear monitor**—earbuds that take the place of a stage monitor's speakers to provide a monitor mix to the musician or singer.

**lazy fill**—a drum fill that wavers behind the beat.

**LED**—Light emitting diode, which is an electronic device that is replacing incandescent light bulbs.

**Leslie**—a speaker cabinet that features rotating speakers; primarily used with organs.

**loops**—a small audio file, usually of four or eight beats (or measures) that's edited in a way to seamlessly repeat.

**low end**—the lower end of the audio spectrum, or bass frequencies usually below 100 Hz.

**merch**—short for merchandise (CDs, T-shirts, etc. sold at a gig).

**mic splitter**—a box that splits an audio signal so that the same signal appears in multiple places. Typically used to split an onstage mic feed to the house audio console, the monitor console, and possibly to recording and broadcast audio consoles.

**monitor mix**—a separate mix that's different from the mix that the audience hears and is specialized for the musicians onstage.

**moonflower**—a specialty stage lighting fixture that splits the light beam into separate smaller beams.

**null**—the point on a microphone that has the most pickup rejection.

**outro**—the section of a song after the last chorus until the end of the song.

**overdub**—to record along with previously recorded tracks.

**pad**—long sustaining note or chord.

**parametric equalizer**—a multi-band equalizer that allows control of not only the amplitude of a particular frequency, but also the center frequency and the number of frequencies as well.

**passion**—the ability to sell the lyrical content of the song to the audience or listener through performance.

**phantom power**—external power, usually supplied by the mixing board; needed to power condenser microphones.

**pitch**—a musical tone.

**pocket**—playing or singing in time and in the groove (in rhythm) with the song.

**polyphonic**—able to produce more than one note at a time.

**power chords**—long, sustaining, usually distorted guitar chords.

**power tubes**—the larger tubes found in a tube amplifier; these electronic devices power the speakers of an amplifier.

**practice**—repeating a section of a song to improve skill and proficiency.

**pre-chorus**—a section of a song between verse and chorus sections. Not found in every song.

**preamp tubes**—the smaller tubes found in a tube amplifier; these electronic devices take a weak signal from a guitar or bass and boost the level.

**producer**—the equivalent of a movie director, the producer has the ability to craft your songs technically, sonically, and musically.

**pyro**—short for pyrotechnics, or the art of working with fireworks.

**rehearsal**—a practice or trial band performance.

**release**—the end of a sound or phrase.

**root**—the note on which a chord is based.

**roundwound**—a bass or guitar string that has an outside winding. All the strings on a bass and the low E, A, D, and sometimes G strings on guitar.

**rushed fill**—a drum fill that wavers ahead of the beat.

**side fills**—full-range speakers that point across the stage and contain a full mix of the band to provide the performers with a more enveloping and well-balanced sound.

**single coil**—a guitar pickup found primarily on Fender guitars.

**spectrum analyzer**—a device that displays the amplitude of each frequency band.

**stems**—a recording mix broken into manageable parts, i.e., one or two tracks of drums instead of each one individually, all guitars on one track, all voices on one track, etc.

**swag**—see **merch**.

**tempo**—the rate of speed at which a song is played.

**throne**—the drummer's seat.

**triad**—a three-note chord consisting of the root, third, and fifth of the scale.

**turnaround**—the two- or four-bar part of a song between sections of a song, i.e., between the verse and chorus, chorus and bridge, etc.

**voicing**—the way the notes of a chord are distributed.

**wedge**—a regular speaker cabinet that's had its back cut off at an angle and is laid on the floor so that musicians can hear themselves.

# INDEX

acoustic 8, 68, 83, 98–99, 101, 111, 155, 157, 176, 183, 210, 212, 215, 219, 234, 240
Alesis 140, 240
Allman Brothers Band 16, 195
Allman, Duane 16
Altman 184
American Dad 12, 69
American DJ 184
Ampeg 9, 28–29, 213–214
amplifier, amp 4, 6–9, 15–19, 22–25, 29–30, 32–33, 54–56, 58–59, 92, 96, 132–133, 148, 155, 159–160, 170, 180, 186, 193, 198, 214, 216, 233–234, 236, 239–240, 243, 246–247
Arp 53
arrangements 20, 95–97, 101–107, 203, 212
Ashford, Jack 73
Atkins, Chet 8
AudioSkin 56
Audio-Technica 74, 162
Aviom 162–163

bands xi–xvi, 3, 5–7, 12–13, 15, 17–22, 27–30, 35, 37–39, 46, 51–52, 54, 59, 61, 63–64, 68–69, 73, 77, 81–87, 89, 90–93, 95–97, 99, 101–102, 104, 107, 109–137, 139, 141, 143–145, 149–152, 158–159, 163–165, 167–173, 175–176, 178–179, 181–183, 185–187, 189–191, 193,–199, 203–207, 209–213, 218–219, 224, 227, 229, 232, 234–239, 241, 243, 245–247
banjo 77, 100

Barkley, Gnarls 100
bass guitar 27, 239
Bass Player's Utility Kit 33
Beatles 146, 150, 172, 217, 229, 231, 239–v241
Black Crows 42
blues 36, 77, 103, 154
Boardman, Chris iii, xv, 203–209
Boss 10, 233, 240
Bozio, Terry 42
B-roll 192–193, 200
Brooks, Garth 101
Buckley, Jeff 118

cables 10, 23–26, 29, 31–34, 49–50, 56, 58, 59–60, 141, 148, 170, 198, 216
Caldwell, Bobby 37
capo 6, 64
cello 77, 220
Chauvet 184
Clapton, Eric 4, 20, 195
Coldplay 52, 53, 104, 120
Corgan, Billy 5
Craigslist 171
Cream 4, 195, 216
Crow, Sheryl xvi, 42, 221, 228–229

Danelectro 9
Davis, Miles 36
DAW 12, 21, 91, 137, 140, 178, 244
Deep Purple 54

Deicide  118
de la Rocha, Zach  5
demo  104, 110, 135, 137, 143–144, 151, 200, 239
Derek and the Dominos  20
DigiTech  240
DJs  73, 75, 77, 117, 183, 184
DJ's Utility Kit  77
Doobie Brothers  103
Dowd, Tom  195, 219
Drayton, Charlie  42
Dresel, Bernie  36, 44–46, 48
drum  4, 5, 7, 10, 21, 28, 30, 35–47, 49–50, 63, 69, 88, 111, 145, 154, 164, 177, 193, 214, 217, 221–224, 226, 228–229, 245, 247
Drum Doctor  41, 42, 223
drummers  xiv, xvi, 10, 12–13, 16, 21, 27–28, 35–38, 40–41, 43–44, 48–49, 51, 68–69, 74, 83, 88–89, 91–92, 105–107, 130, 133, 147, 151, 170, 177–178, 183, 188, 214–215, 217–218, 221–222, 224–225, 227–231, 235, 238, 248
Drummer's Utility Kit  49, 74
drums  12, 19, 21, 35, 37, 39, 40–45, 47–48, 73, 74, 87, 88, 90, 93, 97–101, 107, 121, 139–140, 143, 145–146, 160–162, 177, 186, 197, 205, 211, 218, 221–224, 227–229, 232, 241, 243, 247

Eagles  20, 96
Echoplex  10
Edirol  136, 139–140
effects  7, 17–18, 114, 130, 133, 180, 183, 186, 214, 233
Elation  184
Electro-Harmonix  9, 10, 240
Electronic Press Kit  196
Epiphone  8
Erskine, Peter  42

Faith No More  119
Feiten, Buzz  11
Fender  4, 7–10, 16, 28–29, 31, 52, 98, 213–v215, 220, 233, 240, 247
fiddle  100
Fitzpatrick, Frank  iii, xv, 63–v64, 87, 209–213
Flatts, Rascal  100
Fleetwood Mac  103
Foo Fighters  42
frequency range  101, 199
Future Sonics  162–163

Galaxy  160
Gibson  8, 9, 44, 240

gig  xiii, xvi, 5–7, 23–25, 30, 32–33, 47–49, 53, 57, 58–59, 64–66, 74, 83, 85, 91, 93, 111, 113–116, 118–120, 122–123, 127, 131–133, 135, 137, 143–144, 149, 151, 153, 155, 163, 166–167, 170–172, 180, 184–186, 189–190, 192, 196, 198–200, 206–207, 212–214, 217–219, 223, 229–231, 234–236, 238–240, 245
graphic equalizer  154–155
Green Day  152
Groom, Gerry  iii, 16
Guess Who  103
guitar  xiv, 4, 6–9, 11, 15–30, 34, 38, 51–52, 54–55, 62–64, 68–69, 73–74, 83, 87–89, 93, 95–107, 111, 114, 121, 124, 126, 132–133, 138, 140–141, 143, 148, 151, 157, 159, 160–161, 164, 170, 176–177, 179, 183, 185, 193, 199–200, 210–212, 214–215, 218, 220, 226, 229, 232–240, 243–247
Guitar Player's Utility Kit  25

Hamilton, Jeff  42
Hammond  7, 10, 52–53, 98–99, 149
harmony  68–70, 93, 98, 100, 102, 111, 164, 198
harp  77, 154
Hearback  162
Hear Technologies  163
Hernandez, Johnny "Vatos"  44
Hill, Faith  103
Hiwatt  9
Hofner  9, 31, 32, 214–215
Hohner  10
horn  10, 19, 53–54, 75–76, 78, 93, 102, 158
Horn Player's Utility Kit  76
humbuckers  8
humbucking  8, 18, 245

Ill, Paul  iii, xv, 21, 28–33, 146, 148, 166, 213–221
internal time  36
iPod  162, 178

Jackson, Michael  36, 42–43, 63, 211, 228
Jagger, Mick  5
Jane's Addiction  42
Jones, Quincy  63, 204, 206, 211

keyboard  xiv, xv, 7, 10, 51–59, 68, 77, 103, 140, 143, 147, 149, 161, 164, 170, 177, 186, 193, 204, 220, 243
Keyboard Player's Utility Kit  59, 77
Killswitch Engage  119
Kiss  69, 103, 117, 179, 208

Kravitz, Lenny   20, 42, 96, 103

*The Language of Music*   195
Lawson, Ricky   36, 43, 48
Led Zeppelin   88, 194, 224, 229
Leslie   10, 53, 58, 149, 233, 245
Les Paul   6–8, 16, 18, 234, 240
Lord, Jon   54
Ludwig   7, 10, 221, 226
Lynyrd Skynyrd   12, 20, 102, 195

MacLeod, Brian   xvi, 38, 48, 91, 167, 215, 221–232
Marilyn Manson   42
Marshall   4, 7, 9, 16, 54, 233, 240
Martin   8
M-Audio   136, 139–140, 162
Metallica   21, 42
microphones, mics   7, 26, 34, 42, 44, 47, 50, 56, 60, 67, 74–77, 135–138, 140, 142–143, 154–158, 160–161, 163, 186, 191–192, 200, 217, 222–223, 225, 244,–246
MIDI   59, 178, 216, 233, 240
Miller, Steve   53
Minimoog   10, 53
Morbid Angel   118
Morissette, Alanis   42, 99
MOTU   140
MusicMan   9
Musitronics   9
Mu-Tron   9
MXR   9, 10

Note Bandit   76

Octavia   9
Oingo Boingo   44
Olympus   136, 139

PA   22, 29, 54–55, 122, 124, 132, 136, 138–139, 153–163, 170, 178–179
pad   52–53, 98, 101
Paiste   225
Palmer, Robert   102
Peart, Neil   35
pedals   5, 7, 15–18, 26, 28, 56, 58–59, 77, 214, 216, 233–234, 239–240
pedal steel   77
percussion   19, 73, 177, 219
Percussionist's Utility Kit   74
piano   10–11, 51–53, 55, 57, 62, 98–99, 104, 160, 203, 205–206, 228

pickups   8, 18, 32, 214, 245–247
plug-ins   53, 57
the Police   88, 103
Porcaro, Jeff   42
Pro Tools   146, 178, 217, 226

Queens of the Stone Age   118, 130

Ray, Brian   iii, xvi, 236–241
recording   3, 6, 10, 13, 19, 21, 23–25, 28, 30, 32, 38, 41, 44, 46–49, 53, 56–58, 70–71, 87, 89, 91, 96, 105, 110, 113, 119, 135–140, 142–152, 166, 171, 189, 190, 195, 199, 207, 212, 215, 219, 222, 224–225, 231, 234–235, 244–245, 247
Red Hot Chili Peppers   42
rehearsals   7, 68, 92, 109–111, 113–114, 135–136, 200
Remo   42–44
reverb   17, 140, 166, 217, 233, 240
Rhodes   10, 52, 98
rhythm section   20, 21, 27–28, 54, 88–89, 97–99, 243
Rich, Buddy   35, 37
Rickenbacker   8, 9, 28, 31
ringing out the system   155
Rock-N-Roller   55
Rolling Stones, Stones   73, 104, 122, 195–196
Rolls   161–162

SDS Systems   75
Seger, Bob   98–99
Sennheiser   74, 162
Sensaphonics   162
Sevendust   119
*Shine a Light*   196
Shure   74–75, 161–162
singers   13, 62–70, 82, 113, 154, 157, 164, 194, 206, 211, 218, 220, 231, 241, 245
singing   6, 12, 61–70, 85, 89, 135, 151, 167, 169, 189, 210, 234, 239, 246
single-coil   8
sitar, Coral/Dano electric   8
Slayer   119
solos   4, 21, 53, 93, 95, 98, 100, 102–103, 107, 126, 138, 179, 185, 204, 210, 229, 233, 236–237, 239
songs   xi, xiv, xv, xvi, 3–4, 6, 12–13, 18–21, 23, 31–32, 35, 38, 42, 44–45, 47, 52, 58, 62–64, 67, 69, 73, 81–84, 86–93, 95–97, 99–104, 107, 109–115, 123, 126, 130–132, 135, 138–139, 143–144, 146–147, 149–151, 157, 166–167, 172, 175–178, 183, 185–186, 194, 196, 199–200, 209, 210–215, 216, 218–219, 221–224, 226–232, 234–241, 243–248

Soundback   76
Sound Mirror   76
Southern Culture on the Skids   118
speaker cabinet   22, 29, 56, 158, 233–234, 245, 248
Springsteen, Bruce   42
stage lighting   179
Standback   22
*Standing in the Shadows of Motown*   194
Sting   158
*Stop Making Sense*   194
Strand   184
Stratocaster   8
strings   8, 10, 20, 23–25, 27, 30–33, 53, 93, 96, 98, 111, 197–198, 213–214, 220, 237, 240, 243–244, 247
Strobotuner   10–11
studio   xiv, xvi, 9, 18–21, 23–25, 27, 30, 32–33, 47–49, 57–59, 61, 63, 70, 96, 101, 104, 137–138, 143–151, 161, 166, 200, 210–211, 214–217, 219, 223–224, 226–227, 229–234, 244
Supra-Phonic   10
sustain   4, 16, 17, 53, 59, 181, 226

Talking Heads   194
Tascam   140
TC Electronic   160
Telecaster   8
tempo   12–13, 35, 37, 83–85, 90–92, 178, 185, 206, 224–243
Thorn, Peter   iii, xvi, 110, 147, 166, 232–236
time management   110
tone controls   18, 19, 22, 29–30, 96
Townshend, Pete   8, 103
tubes   24–25, 31, 33, 58–59, 197–198, 246–247

tuner   10, –12, 26, 33–34, 93, 148, 216, 233
12-string   8, 240

Ultimate Ears   162
Uni-Vibe   10
Univox   10

Van Halen   103
Vaughn, Stevie Ray   102
vibrato   4, 17, 240
video   7, 92, 114, 119, 177, 189, 190, 192–193, 196
violin   77
vocals   6–7, 12, 20, 61–70, 73–75, 82, 89, 95, 97, 98–102, 105–107, 111, 113, 136–141, 143, 153–154, 157–164, 178, 186, 198, 219, 226, 234, 239, 241
voicings   6, 20, 96–97
Vox   9, 10, 143

Walker, Chris   116
Westone   162
White, Jack   5
the Who   103
Winehouse, Amy   5
Winter, Johnny   8, 37
Woodstock   195
Wurlitzer   10, 52

Yamaha   136, 139
Yoakum, Dwight   42

Zildjian   46
Zoom   136, 139
ZZ Top   103